The Boxcar Children Mysteries

THE BOXCAR CHILDREN
SURPRISE ISLAND
THE YELLOW HOUSE MYSTERY
MYSTERY RANCH
MIKE'S MYSTERY
BLUE BAY MYSTERY
THE WOODSHED MYSTERY
THE LIGHTHOUSE MYSTERY
MOUNTAIN TOP MYSTERY
SCHOOLHOUSE MYSTERY
CABOOSE MYSTERY
HOUSEBOAT MYSTERY
SNOWBOUND MYSTERY
TREE HOUSE MYSTERY
BICYCLE MYSTERY
MYSTERY IN THE SAND
MYSTERY BEHIND THE WALL
BUS STATION MYSTERY
BENNY UNCOVERS A MYSTERY
THE HAUNTED CABIN MYSTERY
THE DESERTED LIBRARY MYSTERY
THE ANIMAL SHELTER MYSTERY
THE OLD MOTEL MYSTERY
THE MYSTERY OF THE HIDDEN PAINTING
THE AMUSEMENT PARK MYSTERY
THE MYSTERY OF THE MIXED-UP ZOO
THE CAMP-OUT MYSTERY
THE MYSTERY GIRL
THE MYSTERY CRUISE
THE DISAPPEARING FRIEND MYSTERY
THE MYSTERY OF THE SINGING GHOST
MYSTERY IN THE SNOW
THE PIZZA MYSTERY
THE MYSTERY HORSE
THE MYSTERY AT THE DOG SHOW
THE CASTLE MYSTERY
THE MYSTERY OF THE LOST VILLAGE
THE MYSTERY ON THE ICE
THE MYSTERY OF THE PURPLE POOL
THE GHOST SHIP MYSTERY
THE MYSTERY IN WASHINGTON, DC
THE CANOE TRIP MYSTERY
THE MYSTERY OF THE HIDDEN BEACH
THE MYSTERY OF THE MISSING CAT
THE MYSTERY AT SNOWFLAKE INN
THE MYSTERY ON STAGE
THE DINOSAUR MYSTERY
THE MYSTERY OF THE STOLEN MUSIC
THE MYSTERY AT THE BALL PARK
THE CHOCOLATE SUNDAE MYSTERY
THE MYSTERY OF THE HOT AIR BALLOON
THE MYSTERY BOOKSTORE
THE PILGRIM VILLAGE MYSTERY
THE MYSTERY OF THE STOLEN BOXCAR
THE MYSTERY IN THE CAVE
THE MYSTERY ON THE TRAIN
THE MYSTERY AT THE FAIR

THE MYSTERY OF THE LOST MINE
THE GUIDE DOG MYSTERY
THE HURRICANE MYSTERY
THE PET SHOP MYSTERY
THE MYSTERY OF THE SECRET MESSAGE
THE FIREHOUSE MYSTERY
THE MYSTERY IN SAN FRANCISCO
THE NIAGARA FALLS MYSTERY
THE MYSTERY AT THE ALAMO
THE OUTER SPACE MYSTERY
THE SOCCER MYSTERY
THE MYSTERY IN THE OLD ATTIC
THE GROWLING BEAR MYSTERY
THE MYSTERY OF THE LAKE MONSTER
THE MYSTERY AT PEACOCK HALL
THE WINDY CITY MYSTERY
THE BLACK PEARL MYSTERY
THE CEREAL BOX MYSTERY
THE PANTHER MYSTERY
THE MYSTERY OF THE QUEEN'S JEWELS
THE STOLEN SWORD MYSTERY
THE BASKETBALL MYSTERY
THE MOVIE STAR MYSTERY
THE MYSTERY OF THE PIRATE'S MAP
THE GHOST TOWN MYSTERY
THE MYSTERY OF THE BLACK RAVEN
THE MYSTERY IN THE MALL
THE MYSTERY IN NEW YORK
THE GYMNASTICS MYSTERY
THE POISON FROG MYSTERY
THE MYSTERY OF THE EMPTY SAFE
THE HOME RUN MYSTERY
THE GREAT BICYCLE RACE MYSTERY
THE MYSTERY OF THE WILD PONIES
THE MYSTERY IN THE COMPUTER GAME
THE MYSTERY AT THE CROOKED HOUSE
THE HOCKEY MYSTERY
THE MYSTERY OF THE MIDNIGHT DOG
THE MYSTERY OF THE SCREECH OWL
THE SUMMER CAMP MYSTERY
THE COPYCAT MYSTERY
THE HAUNTED CLOCK TOWER MYSTERY
THE MYSTERY OF THE TIGER'S EYE
THE DISAPPEARING STAIRCASE MYSTERY
THE MYSTERY ON BLIZZARD MOUNTAIN
THE MYSTERY OF THE SPIDER'S CLUE
THE CANDY FACTORY MYSTERY
THE MYSTERY OF THE MUMMY'S CURSE
THE MYSTERY OF THE STAR RUBY
THE STUFFED BEAR MYSTERY
THE MYSTERY OF ALLIGATOR SWAMP
THE MYSTERY AT SKELETON POINT
THE TATTLETALE MYSTERY

THE TATTLETALE MYSTERY

created by

GERTRUDE CHANDLER WARNER

Illustrated by Hodges Soileau

ALBERT WHITMAN & Company
Morton Grove, Illinois

ISBN 0-8075-5526-6

Published by Scholastic Inc., 557 Broadway, New York, NY 10012, by arrangement with Albert Whitman & Company. BOXCAR CHILDREN is a registered trademark of Albert Whitman & Company.

1 3 5 7 9 10 8 6 4 2

Printed in the U.S.A.

Contents

CHAPTER 1

Who Threw That?

"I sure hope it flies!" cried six-year-old Benny as he jumped to his feet. "Do you think it will?"

"There's only one way to find out," said Henry, who was fourteen. "Toss it in the air and see what happens."

It was a warm August afternoon and the four Alden children — Henry, Jessie, Violet, and Benny — were in a little park on the edge of the town of Greenfield. They were making paper airplanes while their dog, Watch, dozed in the sun nearby.

"I guess you're right, Henry," said Benny. "There's only one way to find out." And he tossed his paper airplane into the air. "Look!" Benny began hopping up and down excitedly. "It's flying!"

"Way to go, Benny!" Ten-year-old Violet clapped her hands and cheered.

Jessie, who was twelve, gave her little brother a thumbs-up. "Great job, Benny!"

Watch, who was awake from his nap, went racing across the park. A moment later he came running back with Benny's airplane in his mouth. Wagging his tail, the dog dropped the airplane at Benny's feet.

"Thanks, Watch!" As Benny bent to pick it up, a frown crossed his round face. "Uh-oh."

"What is it, Benny?" Jessie asked.

"Watch chewed it up a bit," Benny told her. "I don't think it'll fly anymore."

"Never mind, Benny." Violet had folded a square sheet of purple paper into the shape of an airplane. Then she drew a rainbow pattern on the wings with her colored pencils. "You can have this one when I'm done," she offered. Violet was artistic and liked making beautiful things.

Sitting down again, Benny shook his head. "That's okay, Violet." He shoved the chewed-up airplane into his back pocket. "I can make another one in no time." And he reached for another sheet of paper.

"Just remember," said Jessie, who often acted like a mother to her younger brother and sister, "the important thing is to make sure the corners and the ends of the paper fit together when you make the folds."

Violet looked up and waved to Mrs. Spencer. Mrs. Spencer was a neighbor and a good friend of the Aldens. She lived across the street from the park, and today the children had helped her bring groceries home from the supermarket. Now she waved to them from her front porch.

"Why don't you come and get some lemonade before you go," she called.

"Oh, thank you, Mrs. Spencer," said Jessie, walking up the steps with her brothers and sister. "We could use something cold right now."

Mrs. Spencer poured lemonade into tall glasses. Then she sighed and smiled. "Watching you in the park cheers me up a bit. I remember my school days with my best friend, Milly Manchester. I used to pass her messages — on paper airplanes!"

"Really?" Benny stared wide-eyed. "Did you ever get caught?"

"Yes, I did," Mrs. Spencer replied as she made herself comfortable on a porch chair. "And the teacher made us stay after school. We had to write *I will not throw paper airplanes in school* a hundred times on the blackboard."

"Wow!" Benny's big eyes grew even rounder. "I bet that took a long time."

Henry, Jessie, and Violet laughed. They couldn't imagine Mrs. Spencer throwing paper airplanes. She was such a sweet lady, and it was hard to think of her getting into trouble at school.

"Have we ever told you about *our* old days, Mrs. Spencer?" Jessie asked. "When we lived in the boxcar?"

"Why, your grandfather told me. It

sounds like quite an adventure!" said Mrs. Spencer.

After their parents died, the four Alden children had run away. For a while, their home was an old abandoned boxcar in the woods. But then their grandfather, James Alden, found them, and he brought his grandchildren to live with him in his big white house in Connecticut. Even the boxcar was given a special place in the backyard. The children often used it as a clubhouse.

"Did our grandfather tell you about Watch?" Benny wanted to know. "About how we found him when we were living in the boxcar?"

Jessie smiled. "Mrs. Spencer knows, Benny," she said. "And she knows how lucky we are to have Grandfather and Mrs. McGregor now, too." Mrs. McGregor was the Aldens' housekeeper and a wonderful cook.

"Speaking of Mrs. McGregor," said Benny, "it's almost time for — "

"Lunch," Violet finished for him.

This made everyone laugh. The youngest Alden was *always* thinking about food.

"Making paper airplanes gives me an appetite," Benny said with a grin.

"*Everything* gives you an appetite, Benny!" Henry teased.

The children thanked Mrs. Spencer for the lemonade and headed home with their paper airplanes. By the time they reached their own backyard, Violet had been quiet for a long time. She seemed lost in her own thoughts. Jessie could tell something was troubling her.

"Violet?" she asked. "Is anything wrong?"

"I was just thinking about Mrs. Spencer," Violet answered. "Did you notice anything different about her today?"

Jessie thought for a moment. "Well . . . she *did* seem a bit distracted."

"I noticed that, too," said Henry.

Violet sighed. "She just wasn't her usual cheery self."

Just then, Watch flattened his ears and let out a whine. Henry looked up. "What is it, Watch?"

Their little dog tilted his head as if he were listening to something that no one else could hear. A moment later, he ran over to the back fence and began to bark.

"I wonder why Watch is acting so weird," said Benny.

Jessie pulled a dog biscuit from her back pocket. "Come here, Watch!" she shouted, waving the biscuit in the air.

At the sound of Jessie's voice, Watch came running. It wasn't long before his tail was wagging happily as he munched on his treat.

"Well, that did the trick," said Violet.

Benny nodded. "Food always does the trick for me, too."

"We get the hint, Benny." Henry laughed. "Let's have an airplane race, then you can get lunch."

On the count of three, they threw their paper airplanes into the air. Jessie's took a nosedive first, followed by Henry's, and then Violet's. Benny's airplane made it all the way to the fence, and the others let out a cheer.

"Looks like we have a champ!" said Henry.

Benny beamed. "I never thought I'd beat *you* in a race, Henry."

Henry smiled. "Size doesn't matter, Benny. Not when it comes to flying paper airplanes."

"Or finding clues," Benny reminded his brother. "Right?" The others nodded in agreement. The Aldens loved mysteries, and together they'd managed to solve quite a few.

As their dog came running over, Benny hurried off to get their airplanes. Henry knelt down and wrapped his arms around Watch's neck. "Better stay here, Watch," he said. "Airplanes won't fly if they're all chewed up."

A moment later, Benny came running back, shaking his head. He was still shaking his head when they sat cross-legged under the tree. "There's something I don't get," he said.

"What is it, Benny?" Jessie asked.

Benny looked around at them. "I thought there were *four* airplanes in the race."

"That's right," Henry replied. "Couldn't you find them all?"

"Oh, I found them all," Benny was quick to reply. Then he got a funny look on his face. "The problem is, I found too many!"

They all looked over at him in surprise. "What do you mean, Benny?" Violet asked.

Benny set the paper airplanes down, one at a time, on the grass while he counted aloud: "One . . . two . . . three . . . four . . . *five*!"

"That's weird," said Jessie. "How can there be five airplanes?"

"Well . . . " Violet thought for a minute. "Benny *did* make two. Remember?"

"But I've still got the chewed-up one in my pocket," said Benny. And he pulled it out for Violet to see.

"Then one of those airplanes isn't ours," concluded Henry.

Jessie blinked. "How can that be?"

"Maybe Watch made one when we weren't looking," said Henry. He sounded serious, but there was a teasing twinkle in his eye.

Benny looked up at his older brother. "Watch is a smart dog, but not *that* smart!"

Jessie took a closer look at one of the airplanes. Carefully, she unfolded it. As she flattened out the creases, her eyebrows suddenly shot up. "What in the world . . . ?" Her voice trailed off.

Violet moved closer to her sister. "What's wrong, Jessie?"

Jessie didn't answer right away. "It's the strangest thing," she said at last. "There's a . . . a message on this airplane!"

Confused, the other Aldens looked at one another. What kind of message would be on a paper airplane that came from out of nowhere?

CHAPTER 2

The Strange Message

Everyone stared wide-eyed at the message on the airplane. It was printed in thick black ink. "I can't believe it," Violet said in a hushed voice.

"Read it, Jessie," urged Benny.

Jessie tucked her dark hair behind her ears, then read the message out loud:

"In a bed of pansies,
A snapdragon lurks;
In the house of Spencer
A mystery perks."

"That sure is weird," remarked Henry. "I wonder who wrote it."

Jessie had an answer. "The Tattletale," she said, pointing to the paper. "At least, that's how he—or she—signed the message."

Benny looked confused. "What's a tattletale?"

"Somebody who tells secrets," explained Jessie.

"But you're not supposed to tell secrets," Benny said with a frown.

This made Jessie smile a little. Benny was famous for not keeping secrets. "Well, it's not very nice," she said, "if it's somebody else's secrets you're telling."

"But . . . who is it?" Violet wondered. "Who's the Tattletale?"

Henry answered, "That's a good question."

"One thing's for sure," said Benny. "The Tattletale knows we're detectives."

Violet looked over at her younger brother. "Why do you say that, Benny?"

"Well, why else would a message about a mystery come flying into *our* yard?"

"Good point," said Violet.

"That's not all," Jessie put in. "He — or she — knows Mrs. Spencer, too."

Henry suddenly looked around. "Maybe the Tattletale is still close by." He put a finger to his lips, signaling for his brother and sisters to be quiet. "I'll check it out."

"We'll help you," volunteered Benny.

Henry jumped to his feet. So did everyone else. Without wasting another minute, the four Aldens and Watch took a long and careful look around the house and in the neighboring yards. Henry put his hand up to shade his eyes as he glanced up and down the street out front. The only person in sight was Mrs. Turner, who was driving away after visiting with Mrs. McGregor. But the children didn't think there was anything suspicious about Mrs. Turner. She worked at Cooke's Drugstore and was good friends with the Aldens' housekeeper.

"It's almost as if . . ." Jessie stopped in midsentence.

"As if the message came from out of nowhere," finished Benny.

Violet looked around a little nervously. "It does seem that way."

But Henry wasn't having any of that. "We're just too late," he said. "Whoever threw that airplane took off."

As they sat down in the backyard again, Benny thought of something. "I bet that's why Watch was acting weird before."

"You're right," said Henry. "I bet Watch knew somebody was close by. We should've paid more attention."

After Jessie read the message aloud one more time, Violet said, "I wonder what it means about a snapdragon in a bed of pansies." It seemed very odd to her.

"There's no such thing as a dragon," stated Benny. He paused. "Is there?"

"No, there isn't," Jessie assured Benny. "But there *is* such a thing as a snapdragon."

Violet nodded. "A snapdragon's a flower with petals that look like a dragon's face, and — "

"Look at this!" Jessie broke in as something caught her eye. There was a bright pink snapdragon drawn on the other side of the airplane. She held it up for the others to see.

"Oh!" Violet put one hand over her mouth in surprise. "Whoever drew that picture is a wonderful artist," she said. Violet loved to draw and paint. And she was good at it, too.

Henry added up the clues. "The Tattletale is artistic *and* knows we're detectives. Plus, he — or she — knows Mrs. Spencer."

"It's not much to go on," Benny pointed out.

Henry scratched his head. "It's a mystery, that's for sure," he said. "And it's a mystery that landed right in our own backyard!"

CHAPTER 3

A Mystery Perks

"The Aldens!" Mrs. Spencer looked surprised. She stood at the door, wiping her hands on an apron. Her snowy white hair was pulled back into a bun. "Back again! Did you forget something?"

Jessie shook her head. "We didn't forget anything, Mrs. Spencer," she said. "We just . . . wanted to ask you about something."

"If you're not too busy," Violet quickly put in.

"Oh?" Mrs. Spencer looked around at them in surprise.

Jessie said, "This is going to sound a little weird, but — "

"A strange message landed in our backyard!" Benny blurted out before Jessie could finish her sentence.

Henry added, "On a paper airplane."

"A message on a . . . a paper airplane?" The elderly woman looked startled. "I don't believe it." She went into the kitchen and sat down at a table. The Aldens joined her.

"I know it must sound very odd," admitted Violet. "I mean, you were just telling us about your school days, and how you passed messages on paper airplanes. But . . . it really did happen."

"And we were wondering if it has anything to do with you, Mrs. Spencer." Jessie pulled the message from her pocket and passed it across the table.

"Another thing," added Benny. "Do you have any snapdragons in your garden, Mrs. Spencer?"

Mrs. Spencer caught her breath. "Any . . . *what*?"

"Snapdragons."

Benny's words seemed to frighten Mrs. Spencer, and she stared wide-eyed at him. Her eyes grew even bigger when she looked down and read the strange message.

Jessie glanced at Henry. There was no doubt about it. It *was* about Mrs. Spencer. The look in Henry's eye told her he was thinking the same thing.

"Do you have any idea who wrote that message, Mrs. Spencer?" Henry asked.

But their friend didn't answer.

"Mrs. Spencer?" Jessie asked again. "We were wondering if you knew who the Tattletale might be."

Mrs. Spencer still didn't answer. She seemed to be in a daze.

Violet rested a hand on Mrs. Spencer's arm. "If something's wrong," she said softly, "won't you let us help?" She hated to see their friend so upset.

"We're good detectives," Benny couldn't help adding.

"I have no idea who this Tattletale person is," Mrs. Spencer said at last. "How could anyone know about all the . . . the

strange things that have been happening? I haven't breathed a word of it to anyone." She shook her head in disbelief.

"Is it true, then?" Henry wanted to know. "Is there really a mystery?"

Looking pale and shaken, Mrs. Spencer nodded. "You won't be able to make any sense of it, though" she said. "After all, *I* can't make any sense of it, and I knew Milly Manchester all my life."

The children looked at one another in surprise. "Wasn't Milly your friend from school?" Jessie asked.

"Could you tell us more about her?" urged Henry.

"Oh, it happened such a long time ago," Mrs. Spencer told them, a faraway look in her eyes. "Milly and I were just young girls when we spotted that bright pink snap-dragon."

The Aldens inched their chairs closer. They wanted to catch every word.

"You see, somehow it had managed to seed itself right in the middle of my mother's purple pansies." A slow smile spread across the elderly woman's face. "We laughed so hard. We thought that snapdragon was playing a great joke on those pansies, and Milly got out her sketch pad and drew a picture of it." Mrs. Spencer paused. "That was the day she decided to become an artist."

"Because of a snapdragon?" Benny found it hard to believe.

"It made Milly realize that anything's possible," said Mrs. Spencer, smiling over at Benny. "And she never forgot the reason she became an artist. Instead of signing her paintings, she put a bright pink snapdragon somewhere in each one. She said it was the only signature she needed."

"Then Milly really *did* become an artist?" Violet asked.

"A truly gifted one," answered Mrs. Spencer, "even though she never sold a single painting."

"Why didn't she sell any?" Henry wondered.

"Milly simply wasn't interested in fame and fortune." Mrs. Spencer shrugged a little. "Believe me, I always encouraged her to enter her paintings in art shows. There's a contest sponsored every year by the Mona Lisa Gallery here in Greenfield. I told her she'd be a shoo-in to win. I figured if she'd only put her paintings on display, it wouldn't be long before art dealers and collectors were beating a path to her door.

"But Milly didn't want to spend her time like that, promoting her work," Mrs. Spencer went on. "She just wanted to spend her time painting, even if it meant never having any money. And that's exactly how she lived her life — right up until the end." Mrs. Spencer sighed deeply. "I'm afraid my dear friend passed away a few months ago."

"Oh!" Jessie cried. "How sad."

"Milly lived a long and happy life," Mrs. Spencer assured them. "Nobody can ask for more than that."

"Do you have any of Milly's paintings, Mrs. Spencer?" Violet asked. "I'd love to see them."

"I'm afraid you're out of luck, Violet," answered Mrs. Spencer. "I wish you could see her self-portrait. I was especially fond of it, and Milly left it to me in her will. After she died, I tried to find the painting. But it was never found among her possessions."

Henry raised his eyebrows. "That's strange."

"Not as strange as you might think, Henry," Mrs. Spencer told him. "Milly often painted over her finished works. You see, there were times when she was short of cash to buy new canvas. I imagine that's what happened to the self-portrait," she added. "It was always the act of creating that Milly valued, not the finished work."

Benny asked, "But what about her other paintings?"

"Milly left those to her nephew, Jem Manchester. A lot of people thought that was very odd, of course. She didn't always get along with Jem, and he'd never taken any interest in art. But he was the only family Milly had, so she left her paintings to him on one condition."

The Aldens were instantly curious. "What was the condition?"

"That her paintings never be sold," replied Mrs. Spencer. "Milly always felt her nephew was too interested in money for his own good."

"Interested enough to sell the paintings?" Violet asked in surprise.

"It's hard to say. But I guess Milly wasn't taking any chances. Jem's not a bad person, but he does place too much importance on money. I think Milly was hoping her paintings would change that. Her real gift to him was an opportunity to appreciate art. Of course, it's too late for that now."

"Too late?" Violet looked puzzled.

Mrs. Spencer nodded. "Jem took the paintings up north to his cabin. Somehow a fire started, and all of Milly's paintings were destroyed."

"Oh, no!" Violet cried, horrified.

For a few moments, no one spoke. Then Mrs. Spencer leaned closer, as if she were about to share a secret. "It was a few weeks after the fire that strange things started happening." The elderly woman pushed her chair back. "There's something I must show you." And she led the way outside.

Curious, the children followed Mrs. Spencer out to a small garden edged with flowers.

"It's really beautiful out here," Violet said admiringly.

"Thank you, Violet." Mrs. Spencer sounded pleased. "Gardening is a great hobby of mine. And my daughter, Rachel, comes over to help with the weeding now and again."

Jessie suddenly gasped. "Look!"

The other Aldens looked in the direction she was pointing. "Oh, my goodness!" cried Violet. "That's . . . that's — "

"Yes, it is," Mrs. Spencer cut in, nodding. "It's a snapdragon."

Sure enough, a bright pink snapdragon was growing in the very middle of a bed of purple pansies. The four Aldens stared at it in disbelief. Finally Henry gave a low whistle. "Wow," he said, astonished. "It happened again!"

Mrs. Spencer shivered a little. "It's the strangest thing."

Benny squatted down next to the flower bed. "It's just like before, Mrs. Spencer. Just like when you and Milly found that snapdragon in your mother's pansy bed."

"But . . . how did it get there?" Violet wanted to know.

Mrs. Spencer was shaking her head. "I have no idea. Oh, I thought it was just a coincidence at first." She took a deep breath to steady her voice. "But then . . . something else happened."

"What?" asked Benny, his eyes huge.

"Last week I was reading in the park," she told them. "I got up for a moment to feed bread crumbs to the birds and left my book on the bench. When I sat down again, I found something stuck between the pages."

The children waited breathlessly while Mrs. Spencer fished around in the pocket of her apron. Benny couldn't stand the suspense. "What did you find?"

Mrs. Spencer held up a bookmark with a bright pink snapdragon painted on it.

"Ohhhh," Violet breathed.

They all moved closer for a better look. "I don't understand," Henry said, puzzled. "How could a bookmark suddenly appear like that inside your book?"

Jessie added, "Did you notice anyone nearby?"

"I looked around, but I didn't see anyone."

"Are you sure?" Henry looked uncertain.

Mrs. Spencer nodded. "Quite sure, Henry."

"I bet it came from out of nowhere," offered Benny. "Just like the paper airplane."

"There must be an explanation for it," insisted Henry. "We just have to figure out what it is." Then he noticed something half hidden in the long grass. "Look at this," he said. He bent down and picked up a shiny gold hair clip.

"What sharp eyes!" exclaimed Mrs. Spencer. "No wonder you children are such good detectives."

"Is it yours, Mrs. Spencer?" Henry wondered, holding it out to her.

"No, it isn't, Henry." She examined it

closely, then handed it back to him. "I've never seen it before."

"Could it belong to your daughter?" suggested Jessie.

Mrs. Spencer shook her head. "Rachel keeps her hair very short. She'd have no use for hair clips."

Henry slipped it into his pocket. He wasn't sure, but he thought it might be a clue.

As the Aldens followed Mrs. Spencer back to the house, Jessie noted, "That makes two strange things that have happened: the snapdragon growing in the garden, and the bookmark appearing inside the book."

Mrs. Spencer glanced back at them. "*Three* strange things," she corrected. "There's something I haven't shown you yet."

The Aldens looked at one another. Everything was becoming more and more mysterious.

CHAPTER 4

The Key to a Rhyme

As the Aldens settled around the table again, Mrs. Spencer opened a kitchen drawer. She pulled out a white envelope. "I found this in my mailbox this morning," she told them in a quiet voice.

"What is it, Mrs. Spencer?" Violet couldn't help asking. She was almost afraid to hear the answer.

Mrs. Spencer sat down. "Maybe you should see for yourself." She pushed the envelope across the table.

Violet hesitated. Then, with a slow nod,

she opened the envelope and unfolded a sheet of white paper. Her eyes widened. "Oh!" she gasped.

"Is anything wrong, Violet?" inquired Henry.

"What is it?" asked Jessie at the same time.

Violet's eyebrows drew together in a frown. "I don't know what it is," she told them. "It's impossible to read."

Violet passed the note to Henry. Henry passed it to Benny. Then Benny passed it to Jessie. But nobody could make any sense of it.

"Violet's right," Jessie said, after turning the note upside down. "It's impossible to read."

Henry said, "It must be written in some kind of code."

"Look on the other side, Jessie," suggested Mrs. Spencer. "There's a message on the back that isn't in code."

Jessie flipped the paper over. It was a note from the Tattletale:

She is guarded in Greenfield
By night and by day
And the smile on her lips
Never does go away
The smile is more famous
Than any in history
And behind it there lurks
A snapdragon mystery

"To solve this code
Go back in time;
Leonardo da Vinci
Holds the key to a rhyme."

Benny made a face as Jessie read it aloud. "Who's Leonardo da . . . da — "

"Da Vinci," finished Mrs. Spencer. "He was an artist who lived a long time ago."

The Aldens looked at one another but didn't say anything. They didn't have to. They were all thinking the same thing. How could an artist who lived a long time ago help them break the code?

"He was one of Milly's favorite artists," said Mrs. Spencer. Then she lowered her voice to a whisper. "Sometimes I get the feeling it's Milly herself doing all these strange things."

"What do you mean, Mrs. Spencer?" Benny's eyes were huge.

Mrs. Spencer shrugged a little. "I can't help wondering if she's trying to tell me something."

Violet felt an icy chill go through her.

Was Benny right about the paper airplane coming from out of nowhere? Was the ghost of Milly Manchester responsible for everything that had happened?

Jessie spoke up. "You don't really believe that, do you, Mrs. Spencer?" she asked.

"I don't know what to believe," Mrs. Spencer answered. Then she gave her head a shake and laughed. "I'm sure I'm getting all worked up about nothing. This is probably just somebody's idea of a joke. Nothing more than that."

"Well, if it's a joke, it's not a very funny one." Henry frowned. "But I don't think we should jump to any conclusions until we do some investigating."

Mrs. Spencer nodded. "That's a good suggestion, Henry."

"Mrs. Spencer, do you mind if we take this message with us?" Jessie asked. "We might be able to break the code."

Mrs. Spencer thought this was a good idea. As Jessie tucked the coded message into her pocket, Henry and Violet looked at each other and smiled. They could always count on Jessie to think of everything.

On the way home, Benny asked the other Aldens a question. "Do you think it's true?"

"What do you mean, Benny?" Jessie asked, as they stopped to wait for a light to change.

"Do you think Milly's doing everything?"

"No." Henry shook his head firmly. "The Tattletale is *not* the ghost of Milly Manchester, Benny." But the youngest Alden didn't look convinced.

That evening at dinner, the children told their grandfather everything that had happened. Jessie finished by saying, "The problem is, we don't have any idea how we're going to solve this mystery."

James Alden finished helping himself to some of Mrs. McGregor's delicious meat loaf. Then he passed the platter to Henry. He looked at his eldest granddaughter. "Unless I miss my guess," he said with a chuckle, "it won't be long until you think of something."

Benny scooped mashed potatoes onto his plate. "Leonardo holds the key."

Grandfather looked over at his youngest grandson. "Leonardo?"

"Leonardo da Vinci," replied Benny. "He was an artist."

"A brilliant artist." Grandfather nodded. "But that's not all. He was also an inventor. In fact, Leonardo da Vinci was probably the greatest genius who ever lived."

The children looked at their grandfather in surprise. "What kind of things did he invent?" Benny wanted to know.

Taking a bite of his meat loaf, Grandfather chewed thoughtfully. "As I recall, he drew designs for diving equipment and a submarine. Even a helicopter and a parachute."

Violet looked puzzled. "But . . . I thought Leonardo da Vinci lived a long time ago."

"He did," Grandfather told her. "Long before the days of flying machines. That's why his ideas are so amazing."

"But I don't get it," said Benny, putting his fork down. "How can he give us the key to a rhyme if he lived in the olden days?"

Henry said, "I think we should find out more about Leonardo da Vinci."

"How will we find out?" asked Benny.

Jessie thought about this. "We can go to the library. We should be able to find lots of information about a genius." And the others agreed.

Right after breakfast the next morning, the Aldens set off on their bikes for the Greenfield Public Library.

"Do you think this is somebody's idea of a joke?" Jessie asked.

Violet looked at her sister. "Oh, Jessie!" she gasped. "Do you really think it's possible?"

"I don't want to think anyone would do something like that, Violet," said Jessie. "But we have to consider everything."

"I have a hunch there's more to it than that," Henry insisted. "After all, the Tattletale went to a lot of trouble making up codes and clues."

"I hope we can figure out why he — or

she — went to so much trouble," Violet said as they slowed to a stop outside the library. She propped her bike against a tree. So did the others.

Inside the library, Henry said, "Let's start by checking the computer catalog." He led the way to a long table with a row of computers on it.

The others gathered around while Henry sat down in front of a computer. His fingers tapped against the keyboard as he searched for any books about Leonardo da Vinci. Before long, a list of titles appeared on the screen. Jessie wrote the Dewey decimal numbers on a piece of paper, then they all hurried off to search the shelves.

When their arms were full, the children headed for an empty table by the window. They sat down with their books piled high in front of them.

"How nice to see the Aldens again!" said a voice behind them, and the children turned around in surprise. An attractive young woman with reddish brown hair smiled at them.

"Hi, Janice!" said Jessie, returning the young woman's friendly smile. The children were regular visitors to the library and often ran into Janice Allen.

"I'm impressed," said Janice, noticing all the books in front of them. "What's all this about?" She took a closer look at the titles. "Oh, you're reading about Leonardo da Vinci! We were just studying about him in school." Working at the library was Janice's part-time job while she went to college.

"Do you know a lot about art, Janice?" Violet wondered.

"I know a little about art history," said Janice. Then her smile faded and she sighed. "But when it comes to drawing, I have no talent whatsoever." She noticed someone waiting by the information desk and hurried away.

The Aldens wasted no time getting started. Jessie helped Benny with the harder words. Before long, Henry came across a drawing in red chalk. He turned the book around so the others could see.

"It's a self-portrait of Leonardo da Vinci,"

he said, as they all stared in fascination at the drawing of an elderly man with long hair and a long beard.

"What's a self-portrait?" Benny wanted to know.

"That just means Leonardo drew a picture of himself," explained Jessie.

Violet had found something interesting, too. "This is the *Mona Lisa*." She showed them a painting of a dark-haired woman with a gentle smile. "It's the most famous painting in the world. But Leonardo da Vinci didn't even sign it."

"Just like Milly Manchester," whispered Benny. "She never signed her paintings, either."

After a moment's thought, Jessie said, "That's interesting, but . . . it doesn't help us decode the message."

"That's true," admitted Henry. "I guess we'll just have to look harder." And the others nodded.

A few hours later, Benny finally slumped in his chair, his hands on his cheeks. "We're getting nowhere," he groaned, looking defeated.

Henry glanced up from his book. “Don’t be so sure! Listen to this: ‘Leonardo da Vinci was afraid his ideas would be stolen, so he wrote his notes in codes and in mirror writing.’ ”

Benny straightened up. “Wow, Leonardo da Vinci liked mysteries, too! But . . . what’s mirror writing?”

“It’s writing that’s backward,” explained Henry. “But if you hold it in front of a mirror, you can read it.”

“Do you think the code is mirror writing?” asked Violet.

Jessie fished the message from her pocket. After studying it carefully, she had to admit it was possible. “It just might be.”

“There’s only one way to find out,” said Benny excitedly. “Right, Henry?”

“Right!” Henry sounded just as excited as Benny. “We can use the rearview mirror on my bike.”

After returning their library books to be reshelved, the Aldens hurried outside. Benny hopped up and down impatiently as

Jessie held the message up to Henry's rear-view mirror.

"Can you read it, Jessie?" He wanted to know. "Is it mirror writing?"

With a nod, Jessie read the message aloud.

"She is guarded in Greenfield
By night and by day
And the smile on her lips
Never does go away
The smile is more famous
Than any in history
And behind it there lurks
A snapdragon mystery."

"All right!" cried Benny. "Now we're getting somewhere!"

Violet didn't look so sure. "But . . . what does it mean?"

"Beats me," said Henry.

Benny grinned. "We're good detectives," he reminded them. "We'll figure it out."

"I hope so, Benny," said Henry. "I hope so."

CHAPTER 5

A Warning

"Solving mysteries is hard work," Benny said as they wheeled their bikes back onto the road. "But it's fun, too," he quickly added.

"That's for sure!" Jessie said. And the others agreed. The Aldens were never happier than when they were figuring out clues.

Henry looked at his wristwatch. "It's almost lunchtime. Why don't we get something to eat at Cooke's Drugstore."

Benny was grinning from ear to ear. "That's a great idea!"

It wasn't long before they were sitting at the long lunch counter of the drugstore, studying the menus.

"Aaah, my favorite customers!" Mrs. Turner greeted the children with a big smile. Her gray hair was pinned back from her round face. "What'll it be today?"

Henry ordered a ham sandwich, coleslaw, and a cola. Jessie had a bacon and tomato sandwich and milk, and Violet ordered a grilled cheese sandwich and a strawberry milk shake. Benny decided on a hamburger, french fries, a chocolate sundae with extra sprinkles, and milk.

"Benny, you eat like a bird," Mrs. Turner teased good-naturedly. "And I don't mean that kind of bird!"

The children looked at Mrs. Turner, then in the direction she was pointing. Through the big plate-glass window, they could see a small pigeon on the top of the minuteman statue. They couldn't help laughing at Josiah Wade. The Revolutionary War hero was standing in the middle of Town Square with his musket at his side — and a pigeon on his head!

"No, you don't eat like a pigeon, Benny," Mrs. Turner went on. "I was thinking more of those big prehistoric birds."

Benny grinned. "I wonder if they liked extra sprinkles, too," he said, making them all laugh.

While they waited for their food, the Aldens turned their attention to the mystery. "I wish we knew more about the Tattletale," said Jessie. "I can't stop wondering who it is."

"At least we have another clue," put in Henry.

The others looked surprised to hear this. "We do?"

"Sure." Henry nodded. "The Tattletale must be somebody who knows a lot about art history."

Nodding, Violet said, "That's true. How else would he — or she — know that Leonardo da Vinci wrote his notes in codes and mirror writing?"

Benny took a spin on his red-leather stool. "Leonardo really *did* have the key to a rhyme! I can't wait to tell Mrs. Spencer all about it."

"We'll do that right after lunch," Henry said. "And then we can try to figure out what the message means."

As soon as they finished eating, the Aldens biked over to Mrs. Spencer's. Just as they were turning into the driveway, Jessie looked up and saw the elderly woman waving to them from an upstairs window. She was motioning for the children to come in.

After parking their bikes, the Aldens hurried up the front walk. Benny raced ahead of the others. When he stepped inside, his eyebrows shot up in surprise. A woman with short sandy-colored hair was sitting in the living room, flipping through a photograph album.

When the screen door clicked shut, the woman suddenly jumped. She closed the photograph album with a sudden bang, then tossed it quickly onto the coffee table. It was almost as though she'd been caught doing something she shouldn't.

Just as the other Aldens came inside, the woman spotted Benny standing in the doorway. Leaping to her feet, she snapped, "How dare you come in without knocking!"

Benny's face turned bright red. "I'm sorry," he said in a small voice, taking a step back.

Henry was quickly at his brother's side. "We thought Mrs. Spencer wanted us to — " he began.

The woman cut in, "Whatever you're selling, my mother isn't interested."

"You must be Rachel," said Jessie, smiling a little. "We're the Aldens. I'm Jessie. And this is my sister, Violet, and my brothers, Henry and Benny."

"And we're not here to sell anything," Henry assured her.

Violet put in, "Mrs. Spencer's a good friend of ours."

"Well, isn't it just wonderful to meet the Aldens!" Rachel responded, though it was clear from her voice that she didn't think it was wonderful at all. "My mother told me what's been going on, you know," she said, coming out into the hallway. "And I don't like it. Not one little bit!" She gave the children a hard look.

Henry and Jessie turned to each other in disbelief. Why was Rachel so angry?

"You'd better stop this little game of yours. I'm warning you, you'll be sorry if you don't!" And with that, Mrs. Spencer's daughter hurried out the door.

When she was gone, Henry shook his head in astonishment. "What was that all about?"

"I thought we were supposed to come right in." Benny took a deep breath.

Jessie put an arm around her little brother. "Don't worry, Benny," she said, trying to comfort him. "You didn't do anything wrong."

"Did I just hear Rachel leave?" Mrs. Spencer asked as she came down the stairs. When the children nodded, she said, "Oh, dear. I was hoping we could all have a nice visit together."

"I don't think Rachel likes us very much." Benny still felt upset.

"I'm sure she likes you just fine, Benny," Mrs. Spencer assured him. "Rachel has a good heart, but sometimes she gets a bit grumpy. You mustn't let it bother you. She's been a bit worried about money lately. She's a real estate agent, and things are slow for her at work right now. I keep telling her to go into nursing. Rachel always wanted to become a nurse, you know. But she says she can't afford to go back to school. The truth is, she *could* afford it if she'd move back home with me for a while. But she insists she doesn't want to get in the way. And she thinks she's too old to go back to school."

"That's a shame," said Jessie, softening a little toward Rachel.

Mrs. Spencer suddenly changed the subject. "I'm glad you stopped by," she said. "I have something to show you." Then she led the way into the living room.

"You mentioned you wanted to see one of Milly's paintings, Violet." Mrs. Spencer made herself comfortable on the sofa. "I remembered a picture I'd taken in Milly's backyard." She reached for the photograph album. Everyone gathered around as she turned the pages one by one.

"Here it is." Mrs. Spencer put her finger under a snapshot of an elderly woman sitting at an easel, her hair hanging down her back in one long silver braid. There was a young woman standing nearby. "You can see what Milly's painting. It's the self-portrait I was telling you about."

Violet looked closely at the photograph. "Oh, she really *was* a wonderful artist!" she said, admiringly.

Benny pointed to the young woman in the photograph. "Who's that?" he asked.

The other Aldens had been wondering about her, too. The young woman was wearing jeans and a white T-shirt, and her blond hair was pulled back into a ponytail.

"Oh, that's Peg," Mrs. Spencer answered. "She was a promising young artist Milly'd taken under her wing. Milly was always encouraging her to develop a style of her own. But Peg was too eager to make a name for herself in the art world. She liked to imi-

tate the latest up-and-coming artists. Milly, on the other hand, was one of a kind." Mrs. Spencer suddenly sighed. "Oh, I do miss her!"

None of the Aldens liked to hear the sadness in Mrs. Spencer's voice. Violet was trying to find something cheery to say when Jessie spoke up.

"You won't believe this, but we figured out the coded message!"

Mrs. Spencer looked surprised — and pleased.

After telling Mrs. Spencer about their visit to the library, Jessie read the rhyme they'd decoded out loud.

"It doesn't make any sense to us," finished Violet.

Mrs. Spencer threw up her hands. "I'm afraid it doesn't make any sense to me, either."

The Aldens looked at one another. They were each thinking the same thing: How were they going to solve such a strange mystery?

CHAPTER 6

Keep Smiling!

It rained in Greenfield for the next few days, and the children spent their time inside, puzzling over the strange rhyme. They thought and thought, but they still couldn't come up with any answers.

"I have an idea," Violet said when the sun finally came out. "Let's pack a picnic lunch and eat in the park."

The others agreed. "We could use a break," said Henry.

"I love picnics!" Benny got out the peanut butter and jelly.

"Maybe we should stop at Mrs. Spencer's on the way," Jessie suggested. She got out the bread, cold cuts, lettuce, and mustard.

But Violet wasn't so sure this was a good idea. "We're not having much luck with the mystery. Mrs. Spencer will be so disappointed."

"You're right, Violet," Jessie said after a moment's thought. "Let's wait until we have good news."

Benny looked relieved. "I didn't want to go over there, anyway. Rachel wasn't very nice to us."

"I wonder why she was acting so weird," Henry said.

"Things are slow for her at work right now," Jessie reminded them.

Benny filled a thermos with water for Watch. "She said we'd be sorry if we keep playing games," he said in a worried tone of voice. "I wonder what she meant."

"I don't know," Jessie said. "But I think we should concentrate on one mystery at a time."

After cleaning up the kitchen, the children loaded their picnic lunch into Jessie's backpack and set off for the park. Henry held Watch's leash as they pedaled along. They were careful not to go too fast so that Watch could keep up with them.

At the park, Jessie spread the old blanket on the grass, and the children sat cross-legged on it. Watch curled up close to Benny, keeping an eye on the sandwiches. Watch loved peanut butter.

"I don't get it," said Benny. He held out his special cup as Violet poured the lemonade. It was the cracked pink cup he had found when they were living in the boxcar.

"What don't you get, Benny?" Jessie looked over at her little brother as she unwrapped a ham sandwich.

Benny looked puzzled. "How can anyone smile *all* the time? My face would get sore from all that smiling."

"Maybe it's a snapshot of someone smiling," Henry said thoughtfully as Jessie handed him a sandwich.

"Or a painting," Violet was quick to add.

Jessie recited the first few lines of the rhyme. " 'She is guarded in Greenfield/ By night and by day,/ And the smile on her lips/ Never does go away.' "

"Don't forget the rest of it," put in Benny. " 'The smile is more famous/ Than any in history,/ And behind it there lurks/ A snapdragon mystery.' " The Aldens had read the rhyme so many times, they knew it by heart.

No one said anything for a while. They were all completely baffled by the strange rhyme. After lunch, they put all thoughts of the mystery aside as they played a friendly game of touch football, with Watch running all around them in circles. When they sat down to catch their breath, Watch slurped up his water noisily.

"An ice-cream cone would sure hit the spot right now," Benny hinted.

Henry took out his money and counted the change. "You're in luck, Benny. Looks like I have enough for ice cream."

After cleaning up and making sure they

hadn't left any litter, they wheeled their bikes back onto the road and headed for Cooke's Drugstore.

"This was a good idea, Benny," Jessie said, as she leaned against the minuteman statue in the middle of Town Square. She licked a drop of strawberry ice cream from the back of her hand.

Benny grinned. "I told you it would hit the spot! Right, Watch?"

Watch looked up and barked as if in agreement. Then he went back to chewing on his special doggy treat.

Violet put a hand up to shade her eyes. "Isn't that Janice from the library?" Everyone turned to look at the young woman coming toward them across the brick-paved square.

"Hi, kids!" Janice greeted them with a warm smile. She was wearing a pale green skirt and matching blouse. "Enjoying the sunshine?" she asked them.

"We sure are," said Jessie. She smiled back at Janice.

"I just wish I could enjoy it, too." Janice

sighed as she gazed up at the clear blue sky. "But I'm scheduled to work at the library all afternoon and then tonight at my other job."

"You have *two* jobs?" Violet asked in surprise.

Then Henry added, "That must be hard."

"It's the only way I can afford to go to college," said Janice. "But I like my jobs," she added. "Especially the one at the Mona Lisa Gallery." The children followed her gaze to the gallery, tucked between stores on one side of Town Square. A sign hung out front with a picture of the *Mona Lisa* on it.

"The art critics had a sneak preview of the latest exhibit," she went on, "and they gave Peg's — I mean Margaret's — paintings rave reviews. Of course, that means it'll be crowded at the gallery this evening. But I don't mind. It's always so exciting when there's a new exhibit."

Violet looked puzzled. "Who's Margaret?"

"Margaret Longford," answered Janice.

"Peg's her nickname. I know her from school, but . . . I had no idea she was such a brilliant artist. She won the contest this year. The one sponsored by the gallery."

"Milly Manchester could have won that contest," put in Benny. "She could've won just like that!" He snapped his fingers.

Janice looked over at the Aldens in surprise. "It's funny, I just heard that name recently. Did you know Milly Manchester?"

"No." Henry shook his head. "But a good friend of ours did."

"And so did the Tattletale," added Benny, not noticing Jessie's warning look.

"Who?"

Jessie quickly changed the subject. "Benny, I think you have more chocolate ice cream on your face than in your mouth," she said, handing him a napkin.

Janice looked down at her wristwatch. "I'm going to be late if I don't hurry. See you later," she said, dashing away. She turned and waved back to them. " 'Bye, kids! 'Bye, Watch!"

Jessie stared after her, puzzled. Nobody

had mentioned Watch's name. How did Janice know it? Jessie couldn't shake the feeling that something wasn't quite right. She was trying to sort out her thoughts when Benny suddenly spoke up.

"I bet Josiah Wade's happier today," he observed. The youngest Alden was gazing up at the statue of the Revolutionary War hero.

"What do you mean, Benny?" Henry wanted to know.

"I don't think he liked it before," said Benny. "When he was standing guard with a pigeon on his head, I mean."

Violet giggled. "He *did* look funny. Didn't he, Benny?"

Benny didn't answer. His mouth had suddenly dropped open.

"Benny, are you okay?" asked Violet.

"It's . . . it's Josiah!" Benny was pointing up at the minuteman.

The others looked from Benny to the statue and back again. "What about him?" Henry asked.

Benny was so excited, he was hopping on

one foot. "Remember how the rhyme begins? 'She is guarded in Greenfield/ By night and by day.' "

Jessie's eyes widened as she caught Benny's meaning. "Josiah Wade is standing *guard*!"

"And that means—" began Henry.

"That the lady with the famous smile must be close by!" finished Violet.

The Aldens let out a cheer.

"That was good detective work, Benny," praised Violet.

Benny beamed. "Thanks."

The Aldens let their eyes wander around Town Square. Their gaze took in the parking lot on one side of the square, the shops and businesses that lined two sides, and the Town Hall that occupied the fourth side.

"Let's check out the stores," Henry suggested.

Jessie nodded. "Good idea."

The children finished up the last of their cones, then headed across the brick pavement. Henry looped Watch's leash around his wrist so he couldn't pull away. He didn't want him to get lost in the crowd of shoppers.

Taking turns waiting outside with Watch, they went into every store along one side of the square. Then they went into every store along the other side of the square. When they were finished, though, they were still no closer to solving the mystery.

The children turned to one another in dismay. They had been so sure they were on the right track.

As they headed toward the lot where their bikes were parked, Benny said, "Maybe Mrs. Turner's the lady with the smile."

"Mrs. Turner *is* famous for her friendly smile, Benny," admitted Jessie. "But I don't think she has the most famous smile in history."

Violet drew in her breath as a sudden thought came to her. She stopped so quickly that Henry almost ran right into her. "Of course!" she cried. She gave her forehead a smack with the palm of her hand. "Why didn't I think of that before?"

"What's the matter, Violet?" Jessie asked her in alarm.

"It's the *Mona Lisa*!" Violet's eyes were shining as she turned to her sister and brothers. "She's the one with the most famous smile in history!"

Jessie raised her eyebrows in surprise. "You mean that painting by Leonardo da Vinci?"

"Yes!" cried Violet, her voice excited.

Jessie looked puzzled. So did Benny and Henry.

"What makes you so sure, Violet?" Henry wanted to know.

"Remember how her lips curl up just a little? Nobody knows why she's smiling like that. That's what makes her smile so mysterious."

"But that painting's in a museum far away, Violet," Benny pointed out. "Josiah Wade isn't guarding it."

Henry suddenly snapped his fingers. "Wait a minute!"

They all turned to look at Henry.

"Josiah Wade *is* guarding the Mona Lisa

Gallery," he said. "And there's even a picture of the *Mona Lisa* on the sign out front."

"That's right!" Jessie cried in surprise. "We didn't go inside because it was — "

"Closed," finished Benny, suddenly remembering.

"Then that's where the Tattletale's clues are leading us," Jessie concluded, looking back over her shoulder toward the Mona Lisa Gallery.

"But why?" Benny wanted to know.

It was a good question. But none of them had the answer.

CHAPTER 7

The Invitation

"It was the *Mona Lisa*," Henry told Grandfather that evening at dinner. "She's the lady with the famous smile."

"And thanks to Violet," added Jessie, helping herself to the roasted potatoes, "we finally figured it out."

Benny, who was pouring gravy onto his roast beef, suddenly looked up. "I helped, too," he reminded them.

"You sure did." Henry nodded. "You figured out that Josiah Wade was the one standing guard."

Violet lifted green beans onto her plate. “We stopped in to tell Mrs. Spencer about it. But she wasn’t home.”

“What I can’t understand,” put in Henry, “is what the Mona Lisa Gallery has to do with a snapdragon mystery.”

“Milly Manchester’s the key,” said Benny. “I just know it.”

The others had to admit Benny was right. All the clues had something to do with Milly.

Jessie started adding everything up on her fingers. “There’s the message on the paper airplane. Didn’t Milly and Mrs. Spencer pass messages like that in school? And how about the snapdragon in Mrs. Spencer’s pansy bed? Milly became an artist because of a snapdragon.”

“She even put them in her paintings,” Benny reminded them.

“Don’t forget about Leonardo da Vinci,” put in Violet. “He was Milly’s favorite artist.”

“Even the Mona Lisa Gallery has a connection,” Henry pointed out. “Mrs. Spencer always wanted Milly to enter their contest."

Jessie nodded. "I bet that's where we'll find the missing piece of this puzzle."

"Speaking of the gallery," said Grandfather, as he reached into his pocket, "I have something you might find interesting." He pulled out a square white envelope and handed it to Violet.

Curious, Violet put down her fork and opened the flap of the envelope. Pulling out a white card, she read aloud the words in fancy gold script: " 'To James Alden and Guests, You are invited to the opening-night exhibit of works by Margaret Longford, winner of the annual art contest sponsored by the gallery. Mona Lisa Gallery. Greenfield Town Square.' "

"I'm on the gallery's mailing list," explained Grandfather.

"Oh, Grandfather!" cried Violet. "That's tonight! Are you going?"

"Well, I just might," said Grandfather, his eyes twinkling. "If I have some company, that is."

Violet clasped her hands together. "It

would be wonderful to go to an art show."

"And we can look for clues while we're there!" Benny was so excited, he was bouncing in his seat.

James Alden smiled at the children's eager faces. "I'm not sure you'll get a chance to do much detective work," he warned them. "I have a hunch the gallery will be packed to the rafters tonight. From what Edmund tells me, Margaret Longford's paintings have caused quite a sensation."

Henry lifted an eyebrow. "Edmund?"

"Edmund Rondale's the owner of the Mona Lisa Gallery," Grandfather told Henry. "He takes great pride in discovering new artists."

"Oh, I can't wait to go!" cried Violet. She sounded very excited.

Soon enough, the children were coming down the stairs, ready for their night out. Jessie was wearing a pale pink skirt and a white blouse. Violet had a lavender ribbon in her hair that matched her frilly lavender dress. Benny had changed into a gray blazer and navy trousers. And Henry was wearing a maroon blazer and gray trousers.

"My, what a fine-looking group!" said Mrs. McGregor, smiling fondly at the children.

"We wanted to look especially nice for the art show." Benny gave his neatly combed hair a little pat.

James Alden was adjusting his tie in the hall mirror. "No one will ever guess you're on the trail of a mystery, Benny." He smiled over at his youngest grandson.

"No one except the Tattletale!" Benny said.

"I wonder if the Tattletale will be there tonight," Violet said, climbing into Grandfather's station wagon.

"It's hard to say." Henry, who was sitting up front beside Grandfather, looked over his shoulder. "But we'll keep an eye out for anything suspicious."

As they pulled into the busy parking lot, Jessie said, "You were right, Grandfather. I think everyone in Greenfield is headed for the art show."

Violet looked around uneasily at all the smartly dressed people making a beeline for the Mona Lisa Gallery. She was shy, and meeting new people often made her nervous. As they crossed the square, she slowed her step.

Grandfather put a comforting arm around his youngest granddaughter. "It'll be worth braving the crowds," he assured her. "Edmund says Margaret Longford's paintings are the finest work by a new artist that he's ever seen."

Violet smiled up at her grandfather and quickened her pace. She *was* eager to see Margaret's paintings.

As they entered the gallery, a tall man in a tuxedo rushed over. "James! I was hoping you could make it." He put out his hand.

"I always enjoy coming to your gallery, Edmund," said Grandfather, shaking hands. He introduced the children to the owner of the Mona Lisa Gallery.

"It's nice to meet you, Mr. Rondale," Henry said politely, speaking for them all.

"Please call me Edmund. Everyone around here does."

Benny glanced over at all the guests crowded around the paintings. He saw one familiar face. It was Mrs. Turner. When the waitress spotted Benny, she smiled and waved her hand. Benny waved, too.

Violet followed Benny's gaze. "I didn't know Mrs. Turner liked art," she said in surprise.

"I didn't, either," said Jessie. "But I guess everybody wants to see Margaret Longford's work."

"Will all those people buy paintings?" Benny wanted to know.

Edmund laughed. "I wouldn't be surprised, Benny. Everybody's very impressed with this year's contest winner." He lowered his voice, leaning closer. "The art world's just buzzing. It won't be long before Margaret Longford makes quite a name for herself."

"If the paintings are half as good as you say, Edmund," responded Grandfather, "I just might buy one myself."

"The paintings in this room will be on exhibit all week," Edmund told Grandfather. "But if anything strikes your fancy, I'll tag it and you can pick it up when the show's over. Of course, we have a number of Margaret's canvasses in the back room that haven't been framed yet. If you decide to purchase one of those, you can take it away with you tonight. Then you can get it framed later."

Grandfather nodded. "I'll keep that in mind."

"We have our usual assortment of sandwiches and pastries, of course," Edmund went on. He gestured to a long table where Janice Allen was busy pouring coffee for the guests. "Please help yourselves." With that, the gallery owner hurried away.

"I can't wait to get a close look at the paintings," Violet said, feeling less shy now.

Jessie nodded. "I'm curious to see them, too." Then she noticed Benny eyeing the refreshment table. She guessed what was coming next. "You want something to eat. Right, Benny?"

"I am getting kind of hungry," Benny

said, to no one's surprise. He looked at his grandfather expectantly. "Is it all right, Grandfather?"

James Alden chuckled. "Edmund said to help yourselves."

Henry knew there was no stopping his little brother. "Come on, Benny," he said, and led the way over to the table in the corner.

While Grandfather mingled with the other guests, Violet and Jessie threaded their way through the crowds to see the paintings. Violet caught her breath as she gazed at a canvas splashed with color. "Oh, how beautiful!" she breathed.

Jessie nodded. "No wonder everyone's so impressed."

As they moved from painting to painting, Jessie and Violet kept a sharp eye out for any clues. Although they didn't mean to eavesdrop, they couldn't help overhearing what people were saying about Margaret Longford's work.

"Just look at the bold swirls of the brushstroke!"

"Magnificent!"

"This artist is one of a kind."

Jessie smiled over at her sister. "One day your paintings will be hanging here, Violet."

"Do you really think so?" Violet asked her, hopefully.

Before Jessie had a chance to answer, Henry and Benny came rushing up. "Did you find anything suspicious?" Benny wanted to know. He swallowed a bite of his egg sandwich.

"Not a thing." Jessie shook her head. "Grandfather was right. It's hard to look for clues when it's so crowded."

Violet looked over at Henry and Benny. "Did you strike out, too?"

"Not exactly. We came across something kind of . . . weird," Henry said, and Benny nodded in agreement.

Full of curiosity, Jessie and Violet quickly followed Henry and Benny, weaving their way around the guests. On the far side of the room, Henry pointed to the wall, where a sheet of paper had been pinned.

"Everybody who entered the contest is on that list," he said. "And guess who got an honorable mention?"

"Oh!" exclaimed Violet, her eyes widening when Henry placed his finger under Janice Allen's name. "But . . . Janice told us she couldn't draw. Remember?"

Benny nodded. "I wonder why she lied to us."

"That's what I'd like to know," said Henry. "It seems kind of strange. Don't you think, Jessie?"

Jessie didn't answer. She was thinking hard. Suddenly she said, "There's something else that's strange. When Janice said good-bye to Watch today, she called him by name. What I can't figure out is how she even *knew* Watch's name. I'm sure we never told her."

Henry, Violet, and Benny had thought nothing of it. But now they wondered about it, too.

"We always leave Watch at home when we go to the library," Henry commented.

Benny nodded. "Dogs aren't allowed in the Greenfield Public Library."

"Maybe somebody else told her about Watch," Violet offered.

Benny thought this was possible. "Watch *is* a very nice dog. Everybody in Greenfield likes him. I bet they talk about him all the time."

"Or . . ." said Jessie, "maybe Janice was there the day the paper airplane flew into our yard. Maybe she heard us calling Watch."

Slowly, the others understood Jessie's meaning.

"You think Janice might be the Tattletale?" Violet asked in surprise.

Still glancing at the list, Jessie nodded. "It's possible. She *has* been studying art history in school," she pointed out.

"If Janice lied when she said she couldn't draw," Henry reasoned, "maybe she was trying to throw us off the track. So we wouldn't suspect her of being the Tattletale, I mean."

Violet looked confused. "But why would Janice leave a trail of clues for us to follow?"

"One thing's for sure," said Benny. "Now we have *two* Tattletale suspects." When he saw their puzzled looks, he added, "Janice Allen and the ghost of Milly Manchester."

Henry looked as if he wanted to argue with Benny, but there was no time. Grandfather was waving them over. James Alden was deep in conversation with Edmund and an attractive young woman with straight blond hair. The woman, wearing a pale yellow dress, looked vaguely familiar to Jessie.

"Your paintings are wonderful," Violet said shyly, as Grandfather introduced the children to Margaret Longford.

"Thank you." Margaret reached out to shake hands with Violet. "I hear painting is a hobby of yours."

"And she's good at it, too!" put in Benny. He sounded proud.

A flush of crimson crept over Violet's face. "I still have a lot to learn," she said modestly. "But I do love to draw and paint."

"That's what really matters," said Edmund. "When you look at Margaret's paintings, you just know she loves to paint more than anything in the world. You can see it in the brushstrokes and the vibrant colors. That's what makes her paintings so special."

"Just like Milly Manchester!" Benny chimed in. "Milly liked painting more than anything, too."

Margaret's smile suddenly faded. "I'm afraid I'm not familiar with that name." She seemed annoyed by Benny's remark. "I've never met Milly Manchester."

Edmund thought for a moment. "I believe she was a local painter." He looked over to where a middle-aged man was talking to a small group of people. "Isn't that her nephew, Jem Manchester?"

They followed Edmund's gaze to a man dressed in a checkered sports jacket and charcoal trousers. His dark hair was slicked back, and he was gesturing to the paintings with a sweep of his arm.

Just then, a voice said, "Yes, that's Jem." As Mrs. Turner joined their group, she told them, "He runs a car dealership in town."

Jessie caught Henry's eye. What was Jem Manchester doing at a gallery? According to Mrs. Spencer, Milly's nephew had no interest in art.

"I'm not surprised he's in sales," remarked Edmund. "He's quite the smooth talker. I overheard him praising Margaret's paintings, saying they'll be worth a fortune in a few years. Comments like that can't hurt business."

Margaret didn't look at all pleased. "My paintings will sell without anyone's help," she snapped. Then she turned on her heel and walked away.

Henry, Jessie, Violet, and Benny exchanged looks of amazement. Why was Margaret Longford so upset?

"I certainly didn't mean to insult anyone," Edmund remarked, puzzled.

"Margaret's from a wealthy family," put in Mrs. Turner. "She probably doesn't understand what it takes to run a business."

Edmund changed the subject. "I'll duck into the back room, James, and wrap that painting of yours." Then he hurried away.

Seeing the questioning look on the children's faces, Grandfather smiled over at them. "I bought one of the unframed canvasses," he told them. "I just couldn't resist. Margaret really is a brilliant artist."

"Mrs. Turner!" Jem Manchester suddenly came toward them, holding his hand out. "I had no idea you were a patron of the arts."

"I could say the same thing about you, Jem," she responded, shaking hands. Then she introduced the Aldens to Milly's nephew.

"The truth is, I've never spent much time in art galleries," Jem confessed, after saying hello to everyone. "But I wanted to find out what all the fuss was about. The whole town's doing cartwheels over Margaret Longford." He paused to glance around the room at the colorful canvasses. Slapping a hand over his heart, he said, "Her paintings have absolutely taken my breath away! Superb! No other word for it." Jem strode off, leaving everyone to stare after him.

Mrs. Turner laughed a little. "That's

quite a sales pitch he's giving. You'd almost think there was something in it for him, wouldn't you?"

When Edmund returned with Grandfather's painting, the Aldens thanked the gallery owner and said good-bye. As they were leaving, Jessie turned around for one last look at Margaret Longford. She still had the oddest feeling she'd seen her somewhere before. But she couldn't quite put her finger on where it was.

CHAPTER 8

A Snapdragon Lurks

When they got back from the gallery, Grandfather wasted no time in tearing the wrapping away from the painting he'd bought. He held up a landscape of clover fields edged with autumn trees that seemed to glow with light and color. In a bottom corner was Margaret Longford's signature.

Violet let out the breath she had been holding. "Oh, it's beautiful!" she said in an awed voice. And the others were quick to agree.

"I was hoping you'd like it, Violet." Grandfather smiled over at his youngest granddaughter. "I thought your bedroom would be the perfect place for it."

Violet gasped. "You bought this for . . . for me?" She looked as if she didn't quite believe it.

Nodding, Grandfather said, "I can't think of anyone who appreciates art more than you do."

"How can I ever thank you, Grandfather?" Violet gave him a warm hug.

James Alden chuckled. "The look on your face is all the thanks I need." Then he added, "I'll get Edmund to frame it for you after the exhibit."

"Your bedroom really is the perfect place for it, Violet," Jessie said, smiling happily at her sister.

"It sure is!" Henry was smiling, too.

"And don't forget," put in Benny, "it'll be worth a fortune in a few years. That's what Jem Manchester says."

Later, as the children sat in Violet's room,

Henry brought up something he had been thinking about.

"There's somebody else we might want to include on our list of Tattletale suspects," he said.

"Who is it?" they all asked at the same time.

"Mrs. Spencer."

"What . . . ?" The others were so surprised, all they could do was stare at their older brother.

"You don't really mean that, do you, Henry?" asked Jessie, who was sitting on the edge of Violet's bed. "You can't suspect Mrs. Spencer."

"We have to consider everybody."

"But why would she want to play a trick on us, Henry?" Violet couldn't believe Mrs. Spencer would do something so awful. "She's always been so nice to us."

"We all like her," said Henry, "but still . . . she could've planted all those clues herself. She wants her daughter to move in with her, remember? Maybe Rachel *will* move in if she thinks her mother's frightened by all the strange things that are happening."

They had to admit that it was possible. Didn't Mrs. Spencer want her daughter to go back to school and become a nurse? Wasn't moving in with her mother the only way Rachel could afford to do that?

"I still think our best suspect is Janice Allen," Violet insisted. "She even works at the gallery."

"*And* at the library," added Benny. "Don't forget, Mrs. Spencer likes to read. So Janice probably knows her." He thought for a minute. "I bet Janice knows everybody in Greenfield. She even knows Margaret Longford from school. Only . . . she calls her Peg."

Jessie clapped her hands. "Benny, you're brilliant!"

The youngest Alden was perched on the window seat, his arms wrapped around his knees. "Thank you," he said, grinning.

The others looked at Jessie, puzzled.

"I couldn't figure out where I'd seen her before," Jessie explained. "Margaret, I mean. Just now, when Benny mentioned the name Peg, it suddenly hit me. Margaret's the woman with the blond ponytail! She was in that snapshot with Milly."

"Mrs. Spencer *did* say her name was Peg," Henry realized. "I guess it could be the same person."

Benny looked doubtful. "Margaret said she'd never met Milly."

"We only got a quick look at that snapshot," said Violet, who was sitting right next to Jessie. "You can't be sure it was Margaret." Violet admired the young artist's work and didn't like to think she was dishonest.

"True," admitted Jessie. "There's no way of knowing for sure until we see the photograph again."

Henry got up from his chair. "If it *was* Margaret in the photo," he said in the middle of a yawn, "what do you think it means?"

"I don't know," replied Jessie, yawning, too. "I wish I did. Right now I'm too tired to think about it anymore."

It had been a long day, and the Aldens decided to get a good night's sleep.

Just before climbing into bed, Violet took one more admiring glance at Margaret's painting. But as she looked a little closer, she couldn't help noticing that the background was a different color around the edges of the canvas—almost as though the landscape had been painted over a finished work. It seemed odd to Violet. If Margaret was from a wealthy family, wouldn't she have enough money to buy new canvas? Why would she paint over another one of her paintings?

Violet was still wondering about it when she climbed into bed. But soon enough, she put it out of her mind as she closed her eyes and drifted off to sleep.

Leaving Watch with Mrs. McGregor, the Aldens rode their bikes over to Mrs. Spencer's the next morning. It wasn't long before their good friend was flipping through the pages of her photograph album.

"It's . . . it's gone!" cried Benny, as they all stared down at the empty space where the snapshot used to be. "The photograph has disappeared."

To their surprise, Mrs. Spencer did not seem at all shocked. "I'm sure it's around the house somewhere," she said matter-of-factly. "I must've taken it out for some reason." Brushing back wisps of her snowy white hair, she frowned a little. "I do hope I didn't misplace it. With everything that's been happening, I haven't been thinking clearly these days."

When the Aldens walked outside again, Violet said, "Poor Mrs. Spencer! I hope she finds her photograph."

"She won't find it, because Rachel stole it."

"Benny!" Jessie exclaimed. "You shouldn't say things like that!"

"But it's true," insisted Benny. "That day we met Rachel, I caught her looking through her mother's album. And I could tell by the look on her face that she was up to no good."

This made Henry smile a little. "Why would Rachel steal her mother's photo, Benny?"

"I don't know. But I'm pretty sure she did."

"I know Rachel wasn't very nice to us, Benny," said Violet, "but that doesn't make her a thief."

After a moment's thought, Jessie said, "It does seem odd, though, that the photograph suddenly disappeared."

Henry grinned over at his sister. "Remember what you said, Jessie? One mystery at a time."

At that, they voted to take another look around the gallery for clues. Hopping on their bikes, they headed for Town Square. When they arrived, they were surprised to find the gallery doing a brisk business even early in the day.

"Hi, kids!" Edmund called out as Henry, Jessie, Violet, and Benny came into the gallery. "What brings you here again to-day?"

"We were hoping to take another look at Margaret's paintings," Henry told the gallery owner. "If that's okay."

"Take all the time you want." As Edmund hurried away to greet a customer, he called back, "Hope you find what you're looking for."

Jessie and Henry exchanged glances. Did Edmund know they were looking for clues? Or was it just a coincidence he'd said that?

The Aldens kept their eyes peeled for anything unusual as they walked around the gallery . . . once . . . twice . . . three times. Sharp-eyed Benny was the first to notice something, and he was soon dashing from painting to painting.

Benny looked around to make sure no one would overhear him. Then he whispered to his brother and sisters what he'd discovered. "Margaret Longford put a snapdragon in all of her paintings, just like Milly!"

Henry looked puzzled. So did Jessie and Violet.

"What do you mean, Benny?" asked Henry.

It wasn't long before they were staring wide-eyed as their little brother led them from painting to painting. Sure enough, there was a bright pink snapdragon in every one!

Benny swallowed a bite of his toasted tomato sandwich. "So Margaret knew Milly after all."

The Aldens were sitting on cushions on the floor of the boxcar. They were talking about the mystery while they ate their lunch, with Watch curled up on his rug nearby.

"No doubt about it," said Henry. He wiped some mayonnaise from the corner of his mouth with a napkin. "It's not just a coincidence Margaret put snapdragons in her paintings."

"That means she copied Milly," Benny said indignantly.

Henry nodded. "That's exactly what it means."

But Jessie wasn't so sure that's what it meant. Her mind was racing. "Unless . . . " A sudden thought came to her.

"Unless what, Jessie?" Violet questioned.

"Unless Milly's paintings weren't really destroyed in a fire."

The others looked at Jessie in surprise. "What do you mean?" Benny asked.

Jessie answered, "What if Jem just wanted everyone to think they were destroyed?"

This got Henry thinking. "Now that you mention it, Milly never signed her paintings. Margaret could've added her own signature to them easily."

"And then Milly's paintings could be sold," finished Jessie.

"Do you really think the paintings are Milly's?" Violet's eyes were huge.

Jessie nodded. "That would explain why Margaret lied about knowing her."

"I suppose so," Violet admitted reluctantly. She didn't want to believe Margaret would take credit for someone else's work.

But deep inside, she knew Jessie could be right.

Henry said, "It would also explain Jem's sudden interest in art." He crunched into an apple.

"And it proves someone stole the photograph," Benny added. "I bet Rachel is working with Jem and Margaret. They'll probably split the money they make from the paintings."

Henry couldn't argue. "You might be right, Benny. That photograph was the only evidence linking Margaret with Milly Manchester." He paused for a moment. "And Mrs. Spencer did say things are slow for Rachel at work. Maybe she saw Milly's paintings as a way to make some quick money."

"Mrs. Spencer will be so upset if her daughter really is involved in this," Jessie said, sighing.

"They would've gotten away with it, too, if it wasn't for a tattletale." Benny reached for one of Mrs. McGregor's homemade potato chips. "A tattletale by the name of Janice Allen, that is."

Henry had to admit it ruled out any possibility that Mrs. Spencer had planted the clues. It still seemed likely that Janice was the Tattletale. But if she knew Margaret had done something underhanded to win the contest, why wouldn't she just tell Edmund about it? After all, Janice had entered the contest, too, hadn't she? Something didn't add up.

"The problem is," Jessie put in, "how can we prove Milly's the real artist of the snapdragon paintings?"

Violet, who had been thinking quietly, spoke up. "I have an idea how we can prove it, but . . . it will depend on Grandfather."

The others stared at her, puzzled.

"What's your idea, Violet?" Benny asked, unable to keep the excitement out of his voice.

"I'd rather not say anything yet," Violet answered. "Just in case I'm on the wrong track."

The children quickly finished lunch, then

raced into the house to find Grandfather. As James Alden listened to his grandchildren, he looked more and more shocked.

"Even *this* painting might be one of Milly's," Violet was saying. She held up the landscape her grandfather had given her and pointed to a bright pink flower in the corner. "A snapdragon was Milly's only signature."

Grandfather got up from his desk and began to pace all around the den. "I can't believe this," he said. "If it's true, Margaret Longford has done a terrible thing."

Henry agreed. "She put her name on someone else's work."

Benny had something to add. "What about Jem Manchester? He's up to no good, too. His aunt didn't want him to sell her paintings."

Grandfather stopped pacing. "Are you sure you want to remove the top layer of paint, Violet?" He gave the landscape another admiring glance.

Violet nodded firmly. "I'm certain there's another painting underneath, Grandfather.

See how the background's a different color around the edges?" She ran her finger along the sides of the canvas. "If my hunch is right, there's something underneath that'll prove the paintings are Milly's."

Jessie added, "If we don't get proof soon, Milly's paintings will be gone."

"I've learned that my grandchildren's hunches are usually right. But it'll take an expert to remove that top layer of paint without damaging whatever's underneath." Grandfather gave the matter some thought. "I think Edmund Rondale is the man for the job."

Henry wasn't too sure about this. "But he's so busy with the art show this week. Do you think he'll have time to work on it?"

"Unless I miss my guess, Edmund will *make* time for it. After all, his gallery sponsored the art contest. And Edmund's an honest man. He'd want to put a stop to an artist passing off someone else's work as her own." With a sudden thought, Grandfather added, "I have an appointment downtown.

Why don't I drop the painting off at the gallery on my way."

"What do you think is under that landscape, Violet?" Benny asked after Grandfather had hurried away, the painting tucked under his arm.

"The real artist, Benny," Violet said, smiling mysteriously. "The real artist of the snapdragon paintings."

CHAPTER 9

Uncovering the Truth

It was almost dinnertime when Grandfather phoned, asking the children to meet him at the gallery right away. He sounded very mysterious.

The four Aldens got on their bicycles and pedaled as fast as they could to Town Square. When they arrived, they spotted Mrs. Spencer coming out of the bookstore.

Benny ran forward. “You’ll never guess what, Mrs. Spencer,” he cried, bursting with news. “We’re on our way to the Mona Lisa Gallery—to solve the mystery!”

Mrs. Spencer gasped. "Really?"

"We can't be certain we'll solve it," Henry added honestly. "But we're keeping our fingers crossed."

"I can hardly believe this!" Mrs. Spencer's face broke into a big smile.

Jessie had a thought. "Why don't you come with us, Mrs. Spencer."

"Oh, yes!" urged Violet. "It would be so nice if you were there. Just in case we really do solve the mystery, I mean."

Mrs. Spencer was quick to agree. "I'm meeting Rachel for dinner. Just let me run and tell her what's happening," she said, pointing to the Greenfield Real Estate office. "Then I'll be right there." With a cheerful wave, she hurried off.

As soon as they were out of earshot, Violet said, "I hope Mrs. Spencer won't be disappointed."

Outside the gallery, Benny's shoulders suddenly slumped. "Uh-oh," he said. He took a step back and pointed to a sign in the window: CLOSED FOR DINNER. WILL OPEN AGAIN AT 7:00. "Looks like we're too late."

"Don't worry, Benny," Jessie assured him. "Grandfather said he'd be here."

No sooner had Jessie spoken than the door of the gallery swung open. "Hi, kids!" Janice Allen greeted them with a smile. "Your grandfather asked me to keep an eye out for you. He's in the back with Edmund," she said, ushering them inside.

Sure enough, the children found their grandfather in the back room, having a cup of coffee with the gallery owner.

"I knew you wouldn't waste any time," Grandfather said, smiling as they came into the room. "We were hoping you'd get here before the others." He looked relieved. So did Edmund.

"Others?" Henry looked surprised.

"Your grandfather suggested getting Margaret Longford and Jem Manchester over here on the double," explained Edmund. He was sipping his coffee, his shirtsleeves rolled up above his elbows. "I don't know what this is all about," he added, "but if something dishonest is going on around here, I want to get to the bottom of it."

The gallery owner gestured toward a large worktable covered with rags and bottles of solution. "I removed the top layer of paint from the landscape. Would you like to take a look at what I uncovered?"

When the Aldens nodded eagerly, Edmund went over to the worktable. He held up a portrait of an elderly woman with soft gray eyes and silver hair.

"Oh, wow!" Benny cried excitedly. "Milly Manchester!"

"Isn't that the self-portrait Milly was painting in Mrs. Spencer's snapshot?" Henry wondered, finding it hard to believe.

Jessie nodded. "I'm sure of it!" she said, astonished.

"That's the real artist of the snapdragon paintings." Violet didn't seem a bit surprised by what Edmund had uncovered.

"Self-portrait?" Edmund looked puzzled. "Milly Manchester painted this?" When the children nodded, he added, "But . . . why would Margaret paint over someone else's work?"

Henry spoke up. "We don't think it was Margaret who painted over it."

"Mrs. Spencer told us that Milly sometimes painted over her own finished work," explained Jessie. "If she was short of cash to buy new canvas, I mean."

Edmund put the portrait down. As he turned around, he raised a hand. "Wait a minute," he said. "Margaret Longford's signature was on the landscape." He looked at each of the Aldens in turn. "Surely you're not hinting that . . . that Margaret signed her name to someone else's work."

"We don't want to believe it," said Violet. "But it looks that way."

"And not just the landscape," put in Benny. "All the paintings in the gallery are Milly Manchester's."

"At least, that's what we think," added Jessie.

Edmund looked stunned. "I . . . I can't believe Margaret would do such a thing." He shook his head. "You must be mistaken."

"My grandchildren are seldom wrong

when it comes to solving mysteries," Grandfather said firmly.

As muffled sounds of conversation came from the gallery, Edmund rolled down his shirtsleeves. "I guess it's time to ask a few questions," he said, sighing deeply. Then, with a worried look on his face, he led the way out to the gallery, the portrait under his arm.

"What's this all about, Edmund?" Jem Manchester, who was standing with Margaret and Janice, was quick to confront the gallery owner. "You expect me to drop everything and come running down here on a moment's notice? I've got a business to run, too, you know!" He seemed a little rushed and out of breath.

"The next showing isn't until seven o'clock." Margaret sounded every bit as annoyed as Jem Manchester. "What's going on, Edmund?"

Benny put his hands on his hips. "Those paintings aren't supposed to be sold!" he blurted out.

Jem Manchester laughed, throwing back his head. "Now, that's a good one!"

"It's true," Benny said stubbornly. "Those are Milly Manchester's paintings."

A startled look crossed Margaret's face. But only for an instant. With an angry toss of her head, she turned to Edmund. "I certainly hope you didn't ask me down here to listen to this nonsense."

Jessie said, "Those *are* Milly's paintings. And we can prove it."

"Did you say . . . those are Milly's paintings?"

A voice behind them made everyone turn in surprise. It was Mrs. Spencer. She had just come into the gallery with her daughter. Jessie noticed Jem's eyes shift nervously when he caught sight of the elderly woman.

"It's true," said Henry, answering Mrs. Spencer's question. "Milly's the real artist."

Jem smiled over at the Alden children. "It's nice to see young people taking an interest in art," he said, although he didn't sound as if he meant it. "But you kids ought to get your facts straight before you go spouting off."

Henry squared his shoulders. "The fact is, Grandfather bought a landscape last night," he said, looking Jem straight in the eye. "Violet was sure there was another painting hidden under it, and — "

"There was!" finished Benny.

Nodding, Violet said in a quiet voice, "Edmund removed the top layer of paint, and he uncovered something that belongs to you, Mrs. Spencer."

As the gallery owner held up the portrait, Mrs. Spencer cried out in surprise.

Stepping forward, Rachel said, "Milly Manchester left that self-portrait to my mother in her will."

"If that's true, why was a landscape painted over it, Margaret?" Edmund demanded. "A landscape with your signature on it."

Margaret didn't answer right away. She took a deep breath and tried to collect her thoughts. Finally she blurted out, "It's not a self-portrait at all. I was the one who painted that picture of Milly. But I never *did* care much for it." She shrugged a little. "That's why I painted over it. What's wrong with that?" she added rather sharply.

"Why would you paint a picture of somebody you didn't know?" Benny asked, accusingly.

It was a good question. Margaret had made it clear she'd never met Milly Manchester. Why would she paint her portrait? Everyone waited expectantly for an answer.

Margaret struggled to find something to say. "I . . . I meant I didn't know Milly very well. She gave me a few tips on painting, that's all."

The Aldens looked at one another in surprise. They had been certain Margaret would confess when she saw Milly's self-portrait. They hadn't counted on her trying to bluff her way out of it.

But Henry wasn't giving up so easily. "What about the snapdragons?"

Margaret blinked. "What . . . ?"

"There's a snapdragon in every one of those paintings," stated Henry, watching Margaret closely.

Mrs. Spencer glanced around at the gallery walls. "Then they really *are* Milly's paintings," she said in an awed voice. "That was Milly's signature, you know—a bright pink snapdragon."

Edmund looked grim. "There seem to be some strange things going on around here."

"I'll tell you what's strange." Jem seemed amused. "It's strange anybody would think those are my aunt's paintings." Then he shook his head sadly. "Her canvasses were destroyed in a fire, you know. Every last one of them. Such a terrible loss!"

"Maybe that's just what you want everyone to believe," Henry suggested.

Jem pretended to look hurt. "How can you accuse me of such a thing? I'm a respectable businessman. Why, that would be . . ."

"Dishonest?" finished Grandfather.

"Unless you can *prove* what you're saying," Jem responded in an icy voice, "we have nothing more to discuss."

Edmund glanced over at Jem a little suspiciously, but did not say anything. Then Jessie caught a knowing look pass between Janice and Rachel.

Janice suddenly spoke up. "I believe I can prove it," she said. "I have something in my purse I think you should see, Edmund." With that, Janice disappeared into the back room. She returned a moment later, waving a photograph in the air.

Edmund's face grew grim as he studied the snapshot. After a lengthy silence, he looked up. "How would you explain this, Margaret?" he demanded, passing the photograph to her. "As you can see, it clearly shows Milly Manchester painting her own portrait—with you watching nearby."

Margaret's face turned very red as she looked down at the snapshot.

"That sounds like your photograph, Mrs. Spencer," observed Benny. "The one that was missing from your album."

"But how in the world did — " Mrs. Spencer began.

Rachel interrupted. "I'll explain everything to you later," she whispered. And she gave her mother a reassuring pat on the back.

Jem inched his way closer to Margaret and looked over her shoulder. As he got a glimpse of the photograph, his mouth dropped open.

"Well, Margaret," Edmund said sternly. "What do you have to say for yourself?"

Margaret didn't answer. Instead, she wheeled around to face Jem. "This is all your fault!" she cried, almost shouting. "I told you not to come to the gallery. Didn't I warn you it would look too suspicious? But oh, no, you had to come anyway, didn't you? You just couldn't resist giving one of your big sales pitches." Margaret shook her finger at him. "You're a fool, Jem Manchester! Your aunt was a brilliant artist. Her paintings would've sold without any help from you."

Jem's eyes darted from side to side. He

opened his mouth several times as if about to speak, then closed it again. Finally he let out a sigh and said, "All right, it's true. My aunt painted every last one of them. But she had no business putting a condition in her will!" He sounded upset. "There's nothing wrong with a guy wanting to make a few bucks. I should've been able to do whatever I wanted with her paintings!"

He stopped talking for a moment. Then he gave a little shrug. "Anyway, no harm done," he said, suddenly trying to make light of everything. "Why don't I just gather up my paintings and get out of your way." Then, with a few quick strides, he went over and took a painting down from the wall.

But Mrs. Spencer wasn't having any of that. "Not so fast, Jem Manchester! Aren't you forgetting something? As I recall, Milly's will makes it clear that if you try to sell her art, her paintings become the property of the Greenfield Public Library."

Replacing the painting, Jem headed for the door, muttering to himself. As he left, he called out, "You won't be seeing me in here again!"

"I'll count on it," replied Edmund.

When the door slammed shut, the gallery owner turned to Margaret. "I can't believe you'd take credit for someone else's work," he said. "How could you do something like that?" Edmund sounded more disappointed than angry.

Rachel had an opinion about this. "For the money, no doubt." She shook her head in disappoval. "Just like Jem Manchester."

Margaret's dark eyes suddenly flashed. "That's not true! Every dime from those paintings was going to Jem," she shot back. "It was always about the money with him. It never was for me."

Edmund lifted his hands in bewilderment. "Then . . . why?"

Violet thought she knew the answer. "You wanted to make a name for yourself in the art world, didn't you?"

Margaret looked down shamefully. "Yes, I did want to make a name for myself," she acknowledged. "My family always told me I was wasting my time painting. They wanted me to follow in my father's footsteps and become a lawyer." She swallowed hard. "I figured if I could win the art contest and get some good reviews from the art critics, my career would take off, and my family would finally accept my decision to become an artist."

"So you went along with Jem's plan to sell his aunt's paintings," concluded Jessie.

Margaret didn't deny it. "I was shocked when Jem first mentioned it. Milly had taught me so much, and she'd always been so kind to me." Her voice wavered. "I just couldn't imagine betraying her like that—passing her work off as my own. I told Jem I wouldn't do it. And I meant it, too."

"But then you changed your mind," put in Henry, urging her on.

"I really didn't want to do it." Margaret looked close to tears. "But my father refused to pay for my art studies at the college anymore. I was desperate to prove to him I could make it as an artist."

Margaret told the rest of the story

quickly. Jem had concocted a scheme to make everyone believe his aunt's works of art had been destroyed in a fire. Then Margaret signed her name to the paintings and entered them in the art contest sponsored by the Mona Lisa Gallery. It seemed simple enough. After all, Milly had never put her paintings on display anywhere, so very few people had ever seen them.

"Jem's plan seemed foolproof," finished Margaret. "So I agreed."

"Nothing's ever foolproof, Margaret," said Edmund. "Now you'll have to suffer the consequences of your actions." His voice was stern. "It'll be a long time before the art world will trust you again."

Margaret didn't have a reply to that. She just hung her head and stared at the floor.

Janice spoke up. "If you really want to stay in the art program, Margaret, you could put yourself through school. Lots of people do. Of course, it's not easy working *and* going to school," she added. "But it's worth it."

"I . . . I never thought of doing it on my

own," Margaret said, a faint note of hope in her voice.

Mrs. Spencer had something to add. "Milly thought you were a fine painter, Margaret. She always hoped you'd develop your own style one day."

"Milly was always a good friend to me," said Margaret. She stood twisting her hands. "I'm so ashamed of what I've done." Looking truly regretful, she turned and walked slowly from the gallery.

CHAPTER 10

Gotcha!

"I can't believe it!" said Mrs. Spencer, shaking her head in wonder. "Thanks to the Aldens, I can finally hang Milly's portrait on my wall."

After leaving the gallery, Edmund had invited everyone to join him at Cooke's Drugstore for a quick bite to eat. Now Mrs. Spencer, Rachel, Janice, Edmund, Grandfather, and the children were sitting together at the long counter, feasting on huge bowls of Mrs. Turner's chili.

"Uncovering that portrait was a surprise

to everyone," Jessie admitted. Then she gave her sister an affectionate nudge. "Everyone except Violet, that is."

"It was just a hunch," Violet said modestly as Mrs. Turner filled her water glass. "I was fairly sure there was another painting under that landscape. And I remembered that Milly might have painted over her self-portrait. At least that's what Mrs. Spencer thought."

"That was great thinking," Henry praised his sister.

Swallowing a bite of his roll, Benny said, "But now you don't have a painting for your room, Violet."

"The important thing," said Violet, smiling over at her little brother, "is that now Mrs. Spencer has Milly's portrait to hang on her wall."

"What wonderful grandchildren you have, James!" Mrs. Spencer remarked.

Grandfather smiled proudly. "You won't get any argument from me!"

"I'll have that portrait framed for you right away, Mrs. Spencer," Edmund promised. He reached out and patted the elderly woman's hand. "It's the least I can do after all that's happened. And, of course, you'll get your money back for that landscape, James." Edmund sighed. "I can't help but feel partly responsible for what Jem and Margaret tried to do. After all, it was *my* gallery that sponsored the contest."

"Nobody blames you, Edmund," Grandfather assured him. "Everyone in town knows you're an honest man."

Edmund held out his cup as Mrs. Turner poured the coffee. "Jem's plan *was* almost foolproof," he remarked. "Of course, he didn't count on the Aldens coming along and figuring everything out."

"They're first-class detectives, that's for sure!" said Grandfather.

"We like solving mysteries," said Benny. The other Aldens agreed.

But they knew the mystery was still not fully explained. They still weren't sure who the Tattletale was.

Henry spoke up. "There's something I don't understand. You entered the art contest, right, Janice?" When she nodded in reply, he questioned, "Then why did you tell us you couldn't draw?"

"I did say that, didn't I?" Janice smiled a little. "I guess I was feeling a bit discouraged at the time. You see, I had my hopes pinned on winning that contest. When it didn't happen, I began to wonder if I was just kidding myself about making it as an artist."

"Your paintings show real talent, Janice," Edmund assured her. "There's no reason to doubt yourself."

Benny had a question for Janice, too. "How did you know Watch's name?"

Janice looked puzzled.

"In the Town Square," Benny explained, "you called Watch by his name. But you'd never met him before."

Janice laughed. "You're the clue to that one, Benny. You got a book from the library about dogs a while ago. Remember? When you were checking it out, you told me all about Watch."

Benny grinned sheepishly. "I forgot about that."

Henry and Jessie looked at each other. If Janice wasn't the Tattletale, who was? Could Benny have been right all along? Was the ghost of Milly Manchester behind everything?

"Something baffles me, too," put in Mrs. Spencer. "How did you ever get hold of that snapshot of mine, Janice?"

Benny thought he knew the answer. "Rachel probably gave it to her."

"Right," said Rachel, looking surprised that Benny knew that. "Milly's portrait meant so much to you, Mother, I decided to do something about it. When I heard Janice was in the art program at the college, I asked her if she'd paint another portrait for you."

"But I had no idea what Milly looked like," put in Janice. "I'd never even met her."

Rachel nodded. "She needed a snapshot. So I took one from your album when you weren't looking, Mother. I wanted the portrait to be a surprise."

"But now you have the original portrait,

Mrs. Spencer," Janice pointed out. "Nothing can be better than that."

"I'm sorry for being so unfriendly the other day," Rachel said, smiling over at the children. She was a changed person now that the mystery was solved. "I was upset about the strange things that were happening to my mother. I'm afraid I thought it was just a game to you."

"It was never just a game to us," said Jessie, shaking her head firmly. "We wanted to help."

Still smiling, Rachel said, "I know that now. Because of you, my mother can hang Milly's portrait on her wall."

"And don't forget," added Janice, "the library has a beautiful new art collection. Now everyone in Greenfield can enjoy Milly's paintings."

Grandfather nodded. "Jem's loss is the town's gain."

"That man sees nothing but dollar signs!" Mrs. Turner suddenly blurted out as she refilled the saltshaker. "I'm not surprised he planned to keep all the money for himself.

Can you imagine? Not a penny to go into Margaret's pockets."

When he heard this, Henry was suddenly alert. "How did you know that, Mrs. Turner?" he asked suspiciously. The other Alden children were wondering the same thing.

The question seemed to catch the waitress off guard. "What . . . ?"

Henry said, "How did you know they weren't planning to split the money?"

The saltshaker suddenly slipped from Mrs. Turner's hand, spilling salt onto the counter.

"Oh, dear, now what have I done?" The waitress looked flustered. "I'll just go get a cloth. I'll have this wiped up in a jiffy." She turned and quickly walked away.

"That was a bit strange, don't you think?" Henry looked at Jessie, then over at Violet and Benny.

Jessie nodded. "I'll say."

"Something just doesn't seem right," Henry told them, keeping his voice low. He took another spoonful of chili and chewed thoughtfully. It was almost as if Mrs. Turner knew, somehow, about Jem and Margaret's plans. Was she hiding something?

Henry suddenly had a thought that hadn't occurred to him before. Reaching into his pocket, he pulled out the gold hair clip, the one he had found in Mrs. Spencer's garden. On a hunch that it just might come in handy, he had thought to bring it along.

"Is this yours, Mrs. Turner?" he asked, holding it up when Mrs. Turner returned.

The waitress smiled broadly. "I've been looking everywhere for that!" Taking the hair clip, she slipped it into her apron pocket. "Thank you, Henry. Where in the world did you find it?"

"In Mrs. Spencer's backyard," Henry answered, watching her closely.

A funny look came over Mrs. Turner's face. "Oh . . . that's quite impossible. Why, I've never been anywhere near — "

Henry cut in, "Maybe you lost it when you were planting that snapdragon in Mrs. Spencer's pansy bed."

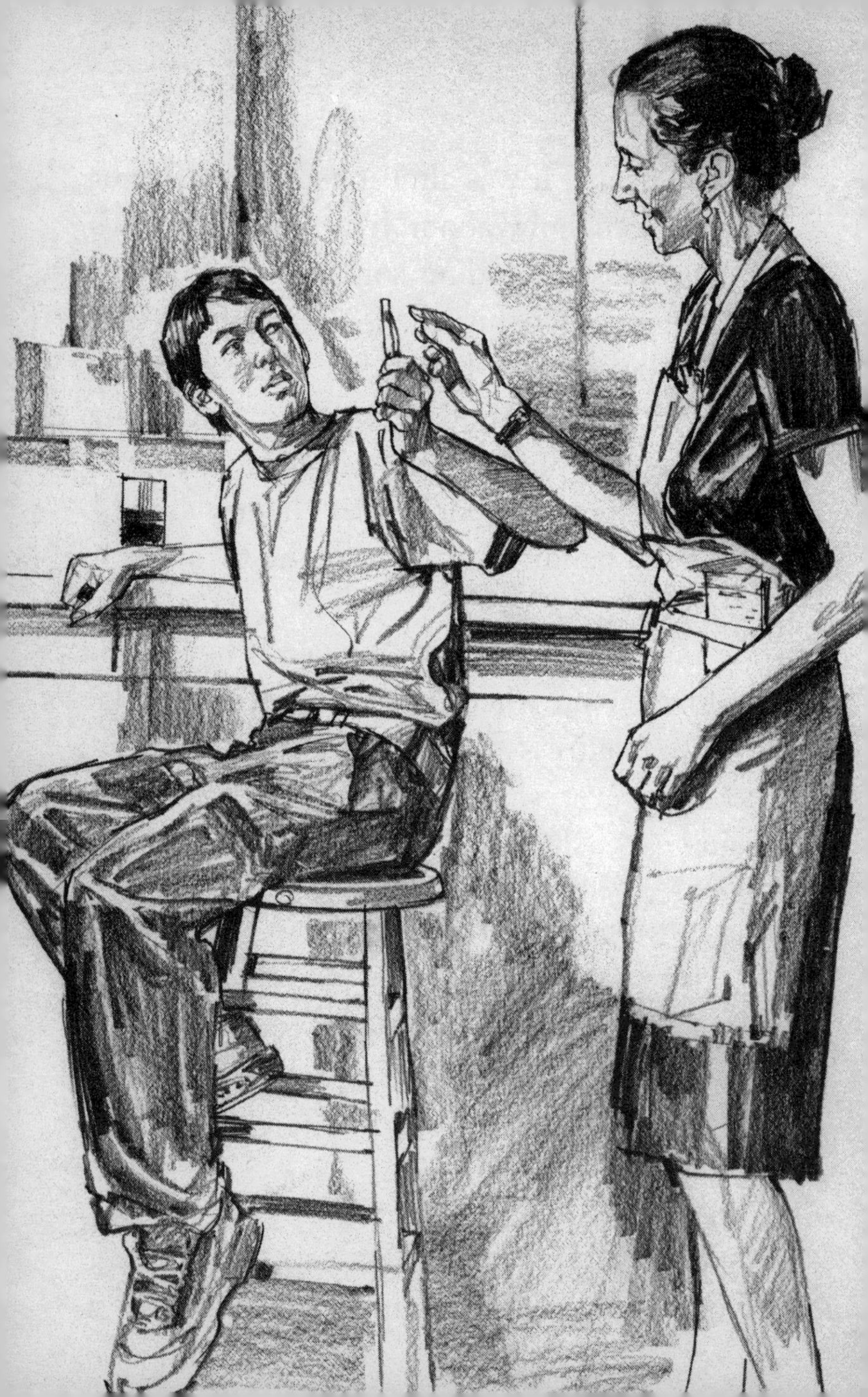

Without saying a word, Mrs. Turner busied herself wiping away the spilled salt. It was as if she hadn't even heard Henry's remark. A moment later, though, her cheeks turned bright pink as she became aware of everyone watching her.

"It all adds up," Henry went on. "You were at our house the day the paper airplane flew into our yard."

"And you were at the art show, too," Benny realized.

Jessie was thinking hard. "You even made a comment about Jem. You said he was acting as if there were something in it for him. You were trying to give us a hint, weren't you, Mrs. Turner?"

The waitress still said nothing.

"You gave us another hint, too," recalled Violet, "when you pointed to the pigeon on Josiah Wade's head. You were trying to draw our attention to the minuteman statue, weren't you?"

After a long silence, Mrs. Turner finally spoke. "I knew you kids were real pros, but I wasn't counting on this," she said with a sigh. "I had no idea you'd figure out I was the Tattletale."

"Oh!" Mrs. Spencer cried out in surprise, putting her hands to her mouth. And the others looked just as astonished.

Mrs. Turner began speaking quietly. "Milly used to stop by the drugstore for a cup of coffee. We'd always have such nice chats. She knew everything there was to know about the history of art. She especially loved talking about Leonardo da Vinci. It was fascinating just to listen to her." Mrs. Turner stopped to tighten the lid on the saltshaker. "Milly told me how a snap-dragon in a pansy bed made her realize that anything's possible in life. She even drew a sketch of a snapdragon for me. I kept it just to remind me of what Milly had said — that anything's possible."

"But then you wrote a message on the back of the sketch," guessed Violet, "and you folded it into a paper airplane. Right?"

"Right." Mrs. Turner nodded. "I was planning to leave the message somewhere in the house that day. But you kids were flying paper airplanes in the backyard. On a whim, I sent the message to you like that."

The waitress looked over at Mrs. Spencer. "I'm afraid it's true. I planted the snapdragon in your garden when you were out one day. I sent the coded message in the mail. And I tucked that bookmark inside your book one afternoon in the park." She sighed deeply. "The bookmark was one Milly made for me on my birthday."

"Then you wanted it to look like Milly was doing all these things?" Mrs. Spencer asked, disbelieving.

Nodding, Mrs. Turner lowered her eyes. "I didn't want anyone to suspect I was the Tattletale. And yet . . . I had to let somebody know about Jem and Margaret. So what else could I do?" She didn't look as if she expected an answer.

"How did you know what they were up to?" asked Rachel.

"They were in here planning the whole thing over lunch. I heard every word. But I really didn't think they'd go through with it. Later, I found out Margaret had won the art contest and I knew they'd carried out their plan."

After a moment's stunned silence, Edmund said, "Why didn't you just tell someone about it? Why all the elaborate clues?"

"When you're a waitress, you overhear things," Mrs. Turner confided. "You really can't help it, you know. I think my customers forget I have ears." She paused for a moment. "When I first started working here, I didn't know how to hold my tongue. I'm afraid I had a reputation for being a gossip."

The children looked surprised to hear this.

Mrs. Turner went on, "It wasn't long before my customers were calling me Turner the Tattletale. Oh, it took me years to live that down! After that, I promised myself that never again would I repeat something I overheard."

The Aldens nodded as they began to understand. Nobody liked being called names.

Benny looked puzzled. "But, Mrs. Turner, why did you use that name when you signed the messages? If you didn't like being called a tattletale, I mean."

"I was telling secrets about people again, Benny." A sad smile crossed Mrs. Turner's face. "The name just seemed to fit."

"But you couldn't just stand by and let Milly's paintings be sold," insisted Janice.

"Sometimes being a tattletale isn't such a bad thing," Violet added softly. "Not if you know somebody's doing something wrong."

Mrs. Turner nodded, but she looked troubled. "Still . . . I hope you won't mention my role in all of this," she said. "You see, I don't want to hear that name Turner the Tattletale again. Not ever!"

"You did everyone a great service, Mrs. Turner," Grandfather said, speaking for them all. "Your secret's safe with us."

Mrs. Turner looked relieved.

"And I'll return that bookmark," Mrs. Spencer told her. "After all, it was a gift from Milly."

Edmund took a napkin from the dispenser. "I wish I'd known Milly Manchester," he said. "She must've been a remarkable person to make such an impression on so many people."

Mrs. Spencer nodded. "She was one of a kind."

"Milly followed her dream, and she never let anything stand in her way," Rachel commented thoughtfully. Then suddenly she turned to her mother. Taking a deep breath, she said, "If that offer's still open, I just might take you up on it and move back home for a while."

"Oh, you'll make a wonderful nurse, Rachel!" Mrs. Spencer looked close to tears. She reached out and gave her daughter's hand a gentle squeeze. "It's never too late to follow your dreams."

For a moment, nobody said a word. Then Edmund spoke up. "I think this calls for a celebration. How about dessert all around?" he suggested. "Any takers?"

"It just so happens I make a great chocolate sundae," put in Mrs. Turner.

Benny grinned. "With extra sprinkles?"

"You'd better believe it!" answered Mrs. Turner.

"I bet that's why Mona Lisa was smiling," said Benny. "I bet she was thinking about a chocolate sundae with — "

"Extra sprinkles!" everyone finished in unison.

GERTRUDE CHANDLER WARNER discovered when she was teaching that many readers who like an exciting story could find no books that were both easy and fun to read. She decided to try to meet this need, and her first book, *The Boxcar Children*, quickly proved she had succeeded.

Miss Warner drew on her own experiences to write the mystery. As a child she spent hours watching trains go by on the tracks opposite her family home. She often dreamed about what it would be like to set up housekeeping in a caboose or freight car — the situation the Alden children find themselves in.

When Miss Warner received requests for more adventures involving Henry, Jessie, Violet, and Benny Alden, she began additional stories. In each, she chose a special setting and introduced unusual or eccentric characters who liked the unpredictable.

While the mystery element is central to each of Miss Warner's books, she never thought of them as strictly juvenile mysteries. She liked to stress the Aldens' independence and resourcefulness and their solid New England devotion to using up and making do. The Aldens go about most of their adventures with as little adult supervision as possible — something else that delights young readers.

Miss Warner lived in Putnam, Connecticut, until her death in 1979. During her lifetime, she received hundreds of letters from girls and boys telling her how much they liked her books.

P9-EGM-842

Practical PORTRAIT Photography

FOR HOME AND STUDIO

By

Edwin A. Falk, Sr.
Falk School of Professional Photography, Maryville, Mo.

and

Charles Abel, F.R.P.S., Hon.M.Photog. A.P.S.A.
Editor and Publisher: *The Professional Photographer.*

AMPHOTO
American Photographic Book Publishing Co., Inc.
NEW YORK

DEDICATION

Much of the credit for the appearance of illustrations in this book is due to the careful retouching of the negatives by my wife. Her assistance in helping with the posing, and in honestly appraising my writing has been most helpful. I therefore wish to dedicate this book to my wife, Evelyn H. Falk.

Published in New York by American Photographic Book Publishing Company, Inc., and simultaneously in Toronto, Canada, by Ambassador Books, Ltd.

Second edition, 1967
Third Printing November 1972

Library of Congress Catalog No. 67-17794

MANUFACTURED IN THE UNITED STATES OF AMERICA

Preface

This is a practical, down to earth book written specifically for the individual, man or woman, who wants to make portraits that will please the subjects. To the professional this means portraits that his customers will be glad to buy because of their easily appreciated, tangible values: true likeness, competent characterization, attractive posing, crisp lighting, good technical quality. These are the five simple attributes which, if followed by all professional photographers, would so greatly increase the current demand for portraiture that no one engaged in it would ever be at a loss for business. That may sound like a very broad statement but we, who between us have spent close to a hundred years in this profession, and during that time have seen and studied literally millions of portrait photographs, have no hesitation in making it.

Admittedly this book deals with what is generally thought of as "conservative" and at times called "formal" portraiture. Two other methods of portraying the human individual have gained considerable vogue during the past ten or fifteen years: "glamour" and "candid" portraiture. Both have earned a place in the field and for one—glamour—a sufficient permanent demand has arisen to warrant our devoting specific space to it, largely because it requires a technique of its own. Candids are something else again. A true candid is necessarily the capturing of a spur of the moment reaction on the part of a subject. It is not at all a matter of carefully thought out lighting or posing, or it defies its name. It does require adequate competence in the operation of a camera, although the smaller and less conspicuous the latter the better. Glamour, on the other hand, is often more difficult to attain than conservative portraiture and, because the professional must be prepared to provide it when desired, warrants our careful consideration.

The point to bear in mind is that, whatever may be your major interest or your ultimate goal, you cannot succeed in producing good likenesses and interesting characterizations (every bit as important to the glamour or candid worker as to the conservative portraitist) unless you first understand the fundamentals of standard portraiture, on which all other forms are based. You don't become a major league ball player without first learning the rudiments in the minors and you don't become even an advanced amateur photographer until you have undergone the miseries that beset all beginners. Putting it plainly, you have to know the rules before you can break them intelligently, and the chief charm that underlies both candid and glamour portraiture is that such photographs deliberately toss aside nearly all the accepted basic elements of posing and lighting.

Portraits are made, ninety nine times out of every hundred, to please someone other than the maker. Almost invariably the intent is to please the subject or the subject's nearest and dearest. So far as the professional photographer is concerned, if he does not please his subjects, he does not eat. If the amateur fails to please his subjects he will not be accorded the praise—"My! A professional couldn't have done any better!"—which is as satisfying to him as the cash register's ring is to the professional. Should the cameraman happen to be an industrial photographer, suddenly faced with the chore of portraying some member of his firm's "big brass," unless the subject is pleased the photographer's reputation will suffer and his later request for a raise will fall on deaf ears. And even in the odd case out of a hundred where a portrait is purposely made for exhibit or salon purposes, if the jury is not pleased no *kudos* will result.

It is our belief—and hope—that a careful study of this book will enable you to make more pleasing (or more saleable) portraits. Good luck.

Edwin A. Falk, Sr.
Charles Abel

Introduction

Dozens of general textbooks on photography are available, all of them helpful, and some of them excellent. Therefore, because it is our purpose to fill an existing void in photographic literature and not duplicate what is already in print, this is not a book for the beginner in photography. We shall not waste space on such customary preliminaries as suggesting what equipment you should buy, explaining how to operate a camera, or the like. We shall not delve into the "mysteries" of exposure, of processing and printing. Books have been written on each of these subjects, and if they are to be covered intelligently and comprehensively they cannot be glossed over in a chapter or two. We commence, accordingly, with the premise that you have adequate equipment and a reasonable understanding of how to use it to good advantage.

The basic equipment for making photographic portraits consists of a camera and lens, a tripod or stand and, because our subject is portraiture in the studio and at home, artificial lights of one type or another. What particular camera and lens, and just what kind of lighting you may own or prefer, is comparatively unimportant. How you make use of the equipment is what counts. Because we are writing for the average individual our subject must be still further limited to what we shall describe as "practical" portraiture, by which we mean portraits that will appeal to about ninety five per cent of the public and which, because they have that appeal, can be profitably sold without the use of high pressure salesmanship, special offers or sales "gimmicks" of whatever variety. We are not dealing here with the "salon" portraitist whose aim is the production of "character studies," nor with what is often called "modern" photography: exaggerated blowups that emphasize every facial blemish and pore in the skin, nor the compositional distortions that stare at us from so many printed pages. We have no quarrel with either of these because in this world there is a place for everything, but pictures of this nature do not sell to or please the great mass of the public, and it is that great mass with which the average photographer, no matter what his reason for making portraits, must deal.

Because ninety per cent of the actual making of a portrait consists of what goes on in the camera room or wherever the sitting is being made, the greater portion of this book will be devoted to the primary principles of portraiture: posing and lighting of the human figure, singly and in groups. Also, because in his every day work the portrait photographer does not deal with professional models, the individuals who have been good enough to act as subjects for our illustrations are exactly the same kind of people whom you may expect to find before your own camera.

In conjunction with each illustration, and where such information will be useful, we have included a lighting diagram, not because we expect you to follow exactly the placement of the lights but as a general guide. To be honest, lighting diagrams are very much over rated. Used as a starting point they can be very helpful but what must be constantly borne in mind is that because the intensity of light varies in direct proportion to the square of its distance from the subject, a variation of a fraction of an inch in distance, height, or angle in relation to the subject makes it almost a physical impossibility to duplicate any given lighting perfectly.

Lighting in itself can be an extremely complex subject or a comparatively simple one. Because we want to make it as easy as possible for you to produce not merely good, but better than average, portraits we are confining ourselves to reasonably simple placements of lighting equipment. There is a difference, which perhaps we should emphasize here, between what is known as a "lighting" and the "placement" of lighting equipment. Placement involves the arrangement of lights with respect to the subject and each other and it will depend on the strength (the wattage) of the respective lights and also on the size and type of subject (as well as the surroundings in the case of home portraiture). Whether you are working with nothing more than a 100-watt bulb in a simple metal reflector and balance it with a white sheet hung over a pole, or whether you are experimenting with several flood lights and half a dozen spots, the placement of the lights is all important. A lighting, on the other hand, is the completed effect on your subject and, depending on just what you are seeking, may be quick and simple or slow and complicated. Nevertheless even the more difficult lighting may be secured with a minimum of lighting equipment.

In the diagrams to follow, the line indicating the background, the circle representing the subject, and the camera itself are so obvious that they speak for themselves. In our accompanying *Figure 1* we show the symbols we use for different pieces of lighting equipment or controls: floods, spots, boom spots, background lights, flat reflectors, head screens. The same symbols apply regardless of the type of light you are using: incandescent, fluorescent, flash or speedlight. Light is light, regardless of its type. A flood is a flood, whether it be a 300-watt reflector flood lamp (reflector and lamp being all one unit) or a 1,000-watt or even a 2,000-watt bulb in an expensive and elaborately mounted reflector half the size of a bathtub. Spots are spots, no matter what the wattage, size or make. A boom spot, in spite of its Hollywoodish sounding name, is to all events and purposes a spot on the end of a metal rod, long or short. A background light is usually a small bulb, 75- or 100-watt, in a small metal reflector. A flat reflector is just that: a white card, a piece of white fabric stretched over a frame, a sheet of heavy cardboard or wallboard covered with aluminum foil, perhaps even a mirror. A head screen is a small frame covered with a dark mesh fabric, on a small stand which ends in a gooseneck so the frame may be readily manipulated. So much for the items you will see in the diagrams.

Now for the respective purposes of each of these items. In making a portrait you must first have a good general illumination of the entire subject, which of course includes the background, surroundings and any props that may be necessary. Ordinarily that general illumination is provided by a flood, at times by more than one, and occasionally by spots, but as a general practice your first step in preparing a lighting once your subject is seated or standing at the place you have in mind, is to

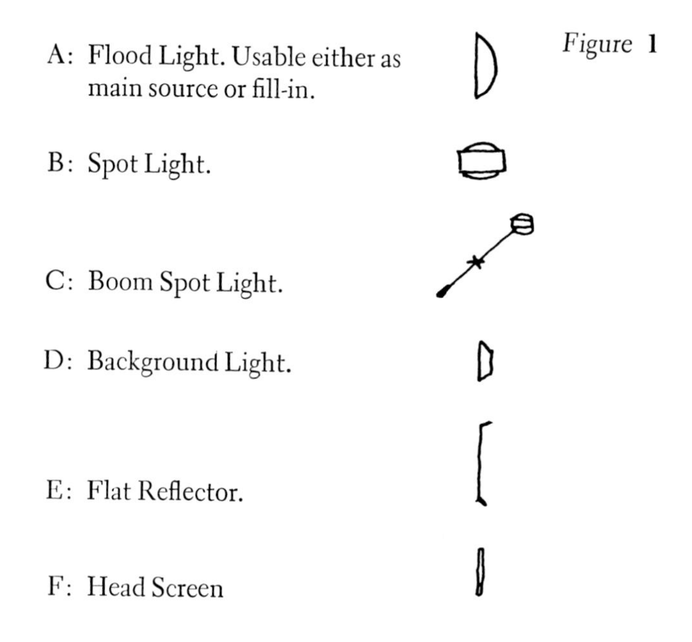

Figure 1

move a flood into position and turn it on. After a quick appraisal you may move it closer to the subject or pull it away, you may raise or lower it, you may angle it away from the subject. In any event there is your general illumination and that flood (or whatever you may be using in place of it) is your *main source* light. Bear that in mind because it is the basic element of every portrait.

The sole purpose of a spot, except in the comparatively rare cases where one or more are being used as the main source, is to direct a specific quantity of light upon a very small, or perhaps larger, area in order to illuminate more precisely or more emphatically a carefully delimited part of the subject. Spots can be, and often are, used to illuminate the background behind or to one side of a subject and may also be used, on occasion, to provide the "fill-in" light which we shall mention in a moment. A boom spot is a very advantageous affair when it is desired to place a light directly above a subject's head or high and slightly to one side in cases where, otherwise, the stand holding the spot would come into view of the lens. A background light, the purpose of which is to illuminate the background and thus provide separation and give depth to the resulting portrait (we shall discuss this in more detail later) is usually placed directly behind the subject and is thus concealed from the lens.

A flat reflector, and this will not appear in many of our diagrams because it is largely a relic of the days when daylight was the only available illumination, is used to reflect against the shadow side of the subject—and thus balance the illumination—a portion of the light coming from the main source. Without such a reflector, or some other source of light on the shadow side, the shadows cast by the main source would be so dark and heavy that the resulting lighting would be "out of balance." An old time term for such a lighting is "soot and whitewash," a hard contrasty effect with one side of the subject (let's say the face) strongly lit and the other side in almost cavernous darkness. In other words that reflector "fills in" the shadow side and that term has over the years come to be descriptive of any light used to illuminate the shadow side of the subject. Today normally a light is used instead of a flat reflector and that light is called the "*fill-in*," another term you must remember because it is of almost equal importance to the main source. Customarily, returning to the moment when you turned on your main source light, your second step would be to move another light into place on the other side and turn it on for your fill-in light. That, like the main source, must then be moved around until the general effect you seek appears.

Our last item, the head screen, is a very valuable accessory which unfortunately has fallen into disuse, largely through lack of appreciation and understanding on the part of many modern photographers whose chief goal seems to be how quickly they can snap a few poses and make room for another sitter. It is placed between the subject and any particular light—the main source, the fill-in, a spot or what have you—that is over illuminating something which had better be subdued even though it must be included: a prominent ear, a bald head, a glittering ornament, or the like.

We urge the reader to study this Introduction carefully because it has a definite bearing on the chapters to follow and their many lighting diagrams. Doing so will obviate the later necessity of leafing back and forth to refresh your memory concerning the meaning or purpose of the symbols used in the diagrams and the terms which refer to them.

Contents

CHAPTER 1

Making Full Use of Your Camera

Before we embark on our principal subject of posing and lighting, there are certain matters of importance to which we must devote a few chapters. First of these are certain adjustments on your camera which are known as the "swings" and "tilts." If you happen to be working with a 35mm or other type of small camera with a fixed back or a lens board that cannot be moved from its normal vertical position, this chapter is not for you at the moment, although you will certainly want to refer to it once you graduate to a more professional outfit. If you are seriously engaging in portraiture, your camera will almost certainly be one of three types: a standard "studio" camera with a fixed or immovable front lens board but a back which can be swung in the horizontal plane from one side to the other and tilted in the vertical plane from top to bottom; a "view" camera on which both the front lens board and the camera back can be swung and tilted as described; a "press type" camera—often selected for home portraiture—with a fixed back but a swinging, tilting lens board.

These adjustments, the horizontal swing (to one side or the other) and the vertical tilt (from top to bottom and vice versa), are recognized as tremendously important by commercial photographers, who have very frequent occasion to use one or another, and sometimes all four at once. These same adjustments can be very helpful indeed to the portraitist, but for one reason or another many just do not understand their purposes, whereas the truth is that to a really good worker a camera without them would not be worth having. No matter what type of camera you are using, the principle of these adjustments is the same. The lens board or the camera back (or both) is set on concealed pivots which makes the motions—horizontal swing or vertical tilt—possible, and the extent of that motion, which of course varies with different types and makes of cameras, is controlled by fairly large knobs on the larger studio cameras or by knurled wheels on view or press type cameras. It may seem strange, but many professional portraitists seldom if ever touch these adjustments, and too many of them do not even know why they are on the camera.

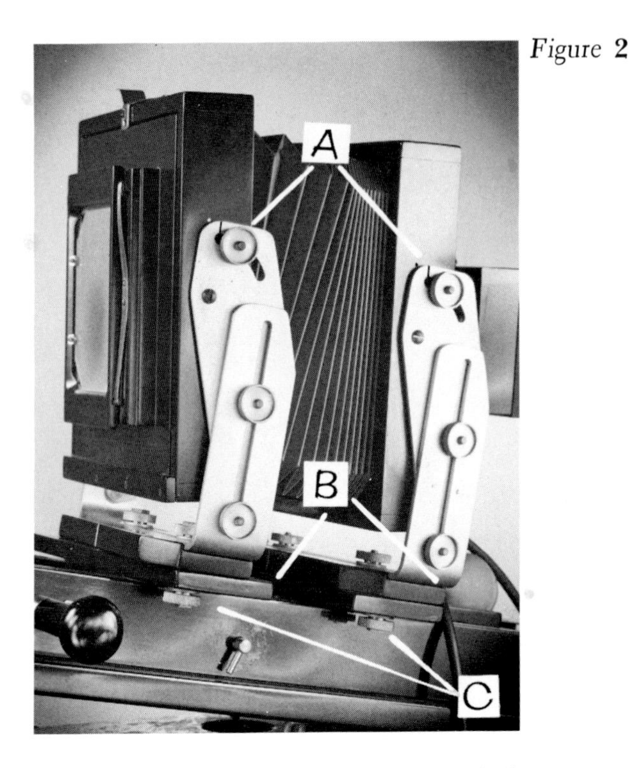

Figure 2

To clarify this we have photographed the rear or "working" end of a typical studio camera, and by means of letters and numbers on the resulting print have indicated the various points to which we shall refer. This camera is the NOBA, and while it has adjustments on front standard, we will only consider those on the rear, or ground glass end. Notice, on *Figure* 2, the letter "A" near the top of the camera; two white lines from this lead to two knobs which control the vertical swing of the ground glass. When the dots on the camera frame are in line with the black lines back of each knob, the focal plane of your film is parallel to your lens board.

Now, notice the letter "C", and the lines leading to the knobs under the camera carriage. These are for adjusting the horizontal swing of your ground glass. The lines starting at the letter "B" show a means of determining when your film is or is not parallel with your lens board in the horizontal plane. When the camera frame is lined as shown by the front line, you are in a normal or parallel position. The back line shows that the ground glass has been swung out of parallel to the extent indicated by the misalignment of the two sections of the camera frame. What has been said here will apply to studio cameras almost without variation. On a view or press type camera the lens board will move in a similar manner (and very probably can also be moved up and down in a vertical plane by means of still another adjustment, although we are not concerned with that at this time). And, on a view camera, both front and back will swing and tilt as described. Your own camera may or may not have any white lines or other marks to help you, but unless it is a 35mm or other type of small camera with fixed front and back, it certainly has these adjustments in the front, or the back, or both. Suppose that you, right now, and with no film in your camera, look for these adjustments. Experiment with them and see what happens, being careful to return the front, or the back, or both to their original positions when you have finished. That done, let us point out that if yours is a studio camera you are all set; if it is a view camera, forget about the front and use the back swing and tilt only; if it is a press type camera with a fixed back, use the front swing and tilt, and you will get practically the same results.

So, what will these adjustments do for you? Take the vertical tilt first, controlled on a studio camera by Knob "A". Let us suppose that, overlooking or not understanding the purpose of this adjustment, you are trying to make a full length standing pose of a bride. Having focused on the eyes, you find that the fullness of the gown at the bottom, or perhaps the train, is out of focus (blurred) on your ground glass. Almost certainly your first reaction will be to stop the lens down until all is in focus, which is all very well except that it immediately requires a longer exposure. This adds the danger (always present with a standing figure) that your subject may move and you will have wasted a film. By turning Knob "A" (or its equivalent on your camera), which tilts the ground glass vertically in relation to the stationary frame of the camera, you will find that the entire figure can be brought into sharp focus, and your exposure need not be longer than you had originally intended. Take a look at *Figures* 3 and 4 and you will immediately appreciate how helpful this vertical tilt can be.

Another important use for this adjustment is when you happen to be working with a large group, the kind where you have to arrange several rows of people, perhaps one row on the floor, another seated, and the third standing. Without

Figure 3

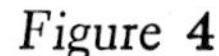

Figure 4

Figure 5 *Figure* 6

considerable stopping down it is almost impossible to get all three rows in sharp focus, but if you will use this vertical tilt wisely you will find there is no problem at all. The shorter exposure you can use with a group, the better off you are, because there is almost the certainty that one individual will move and make one or more retakes necessary. The wider the opening at which you can work your lens, the shorter you can make your exposure, and thus you can understand why experienced professionals consider these adjustments imperative.

A simple explanation of all this is to consider what happens when you focus on a distant object. The more distant the object, the closer the lens must be to your film. Conversely, when you are photographing something close up, the lens must be farther from the film. Think of the tilts and swings in that manner: if a portion of your subject is closer to the film, that portion of the film should be farther away from the lens, and vice versa. Using the tilt or swing adjustments enables you to compensate for those differences. In other words, you can adjust the position of the film in a manner that will more or less equalize this difference in the focal planes of the portions you wish to have rendered equally sharp.

Next, consider Knob "C" on *Figure 2*, which changes the horizontal position of your film in relation to the fixed position of the lens (or, again, the wheel or knob on your own camera which controls this adjustment). This is the horizontal swing, and while ordinarily in portraiture there is less use for this adjustment than for the vertical tilt, there are times when the swing is very helpful, or when a combination of both swing and tilt will make possible very much more acceptable portraits. For example, it is often desirable to bring the near shoulder (out of focus in many portraits) into sharp focus in order to display military insignia properly. These are seen more and more on uniforms that are far from military in nature, and a subject wearing anything of the sort will think vastly more of your photographic ability if such insignia are readily recognized in the resulting portrait. We have seen all sorts of awkward poses tried in attempts to accomplish this, when as a mattter of fact, more pleasing poses could have been used and the whole image brought into acceptable sharpness by using the horizontal swing in the right way. *Figures* 5 and 6 illustrate exactly what we mean. Granted, *Figures* 3 and 5 have been deliberately exaggerated, but only to make our points perfectly clear. And, before we leave the subject, one warning. Never force wheels and knobs on your camera down too tightly in an attempt to lock the adjustments too securely. Tighten them just enough to hold; excessive pressure will eventually strip the threads and you will be faced with an expensive camera repair job.

CHAPTER 2

The Background and Its Purposes

An intimate and important factor in every portrait is the background, if for no other reason than that the human eye does not recognize—willingly—disembodied objects. Human vision being three dimensional, we see simultaneously the subject at which we are looking and, although we may not at the moment actually recognize this, whatever is behind it. What is behind the subject is the background and because we do expect to see something behind every subject, even if that something be no more than a flat tone different in value from the subject, a background of some kind or other is essential.

A background may be, and in studio portraiture usually is, a flat or comparatively flat surface. In studio portraiture, where the emphasis is normally on the subject being portrayed, the less obtrusive the background the better. In home portraiture, where it is often desirable to surround the subject with familiar objects, a background is rarely flat and may embrace a wide assortment of furnishings and home decorations. When it becomes desirable or necessary to include such extras in a studio portrait, they are thought of as "props," and in later chapters we shall discuss both props and the background problem as it peculiarly relates to home portraiture.

One purpose of the background in every day portraiture is to concentrate interest on the subject by isolating it so far as possible from any surrounding or extraneous objects. Particularly is this true in the case of the head and shoulder portrait which comprises seventy five per cent or more of all portraiture. If any furniture is called for it will be only, in the case of a seated subject, a posing chair or bench and seldom will any part of it appear in the finished picture. If the portrait is to have any atmospheric effect at all, if it is to appear natural and lifelike to the viewer, and not as if the head and shoulders had been cut out with a pair of scissors and pasted on a sheet of white paper, some effect of a background is necessary. True, many portraits, especially those of babies and children and frequently those of brides, are taken against what are called "white" backgrounds. Seldom, however, are such backgrounds pure white; invariably they have a certain tonal value, and the only true exception to this is the socalled "vignetted" portrait which is the subject of a later chapter.

There is literally no limit to the number and variety of materials and surfaces that may be used as backgrounds. Normally, for monochrome portraiture with which we are dealing, they will range from white through various shades of gray to black, although some workers prefer various photogenic shades of sepias and browns. A background may be fixed, such as a wall; a fabric or even wide seamless paper pulled down from a wall or ceiling roller; it may be stretched over a frame which is on casters so it may be moved around the camera room; it may hang from a stand which can be picked up and carried from one spot to another. A background may consist entirely or partially of drapery or even lighter material hanging in softly draped folds. Plastered walls of interesting textures make fine backgrounds and, upon occasion, wallpapers with patterns that are not too obvious can be used very successfully. The one rule to be remembered is that no matter what you may decide to use as a background, your emphasis must always be on your subject. The moment your background becomes sufficiently noticeable that it draws attention away from your subject, your portrait—as a portrait—is a failure.

Many competent portraitists need no more than one background—white or light gray. By proper control of the amount of light being used in making a sitting, they can secure on that one background any tonal effect desired, from white through black. The more illumination that reaches the background, the lighter it will be; to secure a black background it is only necessary to move the subject farther away, concentrate all light on the subject and let none reach the background. It's as simple as that. That same background can be made to seem even blacker, and a spectacular effect can be secured, by throwing a circular spot on the area behind the subject's head. The possible variations are endless, all with that one background.

Another purpose of the background, and one which is too often overlooked, is to give "atmosphere" to the portrait. Giving the portrait "depth" is another way to put it, and here we return to our initial remark about vision being three dimensional. Because we are accustomed to seeing things in three dimensions we automatically seek the same effect even when we are looking at a portrait or other pictorial representation which is actually on a flat or two dimensional surface. Other terms for this are "roundness" or "projection" or "separation from the background." A photographer may say that a portrait has a nice effect of roundness, meaning that the subject truly looks three dimensional, that the viewer can seem to put his hand around it. Projection and separation similarly imply that the subject does appear to project from or be separated from the background. Too many portraits being made today lack this important effect—the subjects literally "sink into" the backgrounds with the result that the photographs are flat and uninteresting. To prevent all this is an extremely simple matter.

It may be helpful first, however, to go back in photography a few decades and see just what has happened. Years ago, when all photographers depended upon skylights for their illumination, there was an almost automatic feeling of separation between the subject and the background, an effect principally due to the skylight. The illumination resulting from that big expanse of glass was a broad light which flooded the camera room. Because it did not "fall off" (lose its intensity) very rapidly, screens were used to control its strength on the faces and clothing of the subjects,

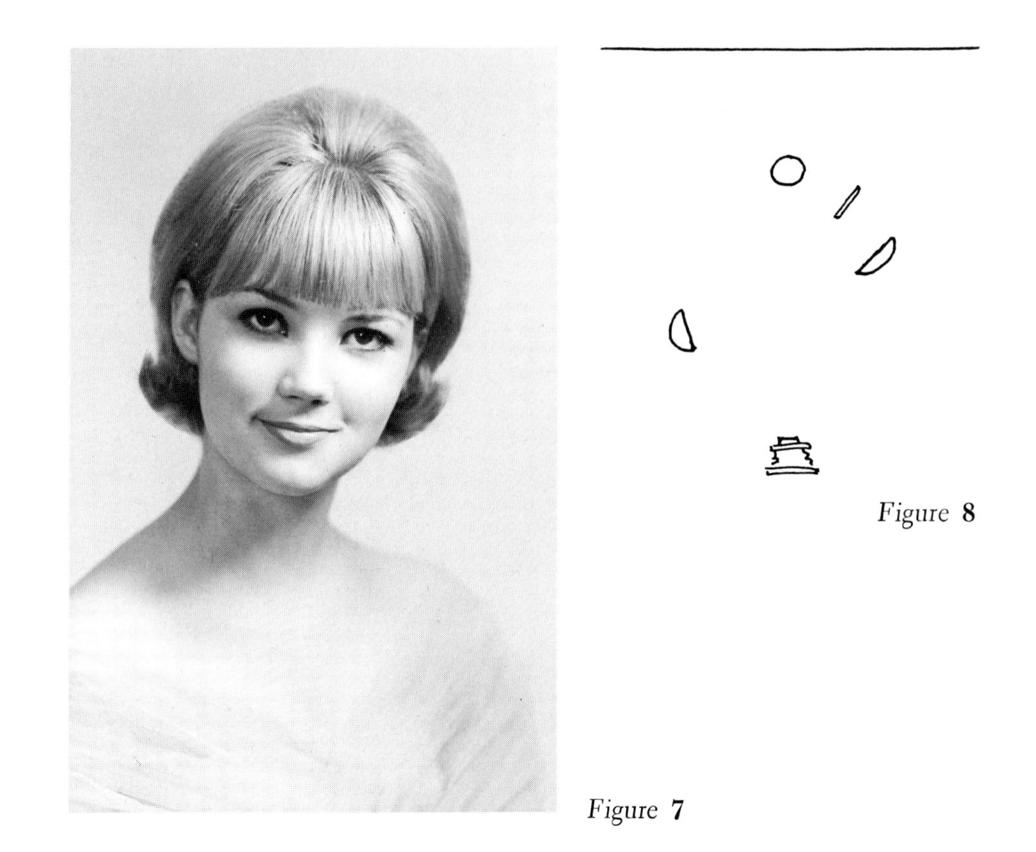

Figure 8

Figure 7

but these screens still did not prevent a considerable amount of light from falling between the subject and the background, unless they were intentionally so placed by the cameraman for some express purpose. It is that light behind the subject which we miss today, due to the fact that any source of artificial light is necessarily small and concentrated when compared to the sun's rays streaming through a skylight usually sixty square feet or more in area.

One solution would be to use as large a volume of general illumination in the camera room as possible, thus making sure that an adequate amount of light reaches the background, and then to control the actual illumination on the subject by means of that useful accessory the head screen. Because few photographers—and for no good reason—use the head screen today a tremendous percentage of the portraits that are made lack proper depth, proper separation from their backgrounds. Contributing to the problem is another evolution in photographic practice: the gradual change away from the old time large camera room to extremely small quarters. The professional today seeks a location where there is the greatest possible concentration of pedestrian traffic. Such locations command higher rents and thus too frequently photographers find themselves working in very small rooms, with their subjects too close to the backgrounds and the cameramen themselves too close to both. That this applies with equal force to the amateur working in his home, or the home portraitist who has to make do with whatever space is available in the homes of others, speaks for itself.

To bring a subject forth from the background—to avoid and eliminate this tendency to sink the subject into the ground—all we need do is introduce a light between the subject and the background, concealed behind the subject of course so it is not visible to the lens. This can be a relatively weak light and a 100-watt bulb or even one of only seventy five watts is ample for the purpose. It can be in a small spot, any small reflector, or any of the special background lighting fixtures made by all the manufacturers of lighting equipment. The main requirement is that it be of small physical size, that you have some means of raising and lowering it, and that the reflector itself may be tilted up, down or sideways. For anyone engaging in portraiture to claim that he lacks such a piece of equipment verges on the ridiculous because even the most inexpensive flexible neck desk lamp can easily be adapted for the purpose.

The two illustrations we have chosen for this Chapter speak for themselves. Both are of the same subject, a college girl, but in *Figure* 7 (as shown by its accompanying lighting diagram—*Figure* 8) no background light was used. Notice that the far shoulder merges into the background while even the subject's back above the near shoulder is almost lost. The whole result is flat and, in order to give the face any effect of relief at all, it has been necessary to over illuminate it to the point where much of the value of the flesh tones has been lost. Certainly it isn't too bad as a portrait but there is nothing distinctive about it whatever to set it off from hundreds of thousands that are turned out every day in the week. Compare this with *Figure* 9 where a background light, as shown in *Figure 10,* was added. Not only does the subject definitely stand out in relief from the background but, thanks to the added

Figure **10**

Figure **9**

background light, it was not necessary to over illuminate the face which in this case has the desirable soft tonal quality and nice feeling of roundness we mentioned earlier.

Common sense must be used at all times and the proper placement and direction of the background light must depend on the subject with whom you are dealing. Take for example a man with unduly prominent ears—women's ears are usually concealed by the hair and almost certainly will be if a woman realizes her ears are too prominent or ill shaped—and while you still want separation from the background, you surely do not want to throw those ears into startling relief. First of all you will do your best to reduce emphasis on the ears while lighting the subject—and this is one case where the use of a head screen or two can be a real blessing—but you can still ruin everything by placing the background light too high. Keep it low, so that it breaks just above the shoulders. Watch also not to over emphasize a bad jaw line. Even though such a line can be softened later by etching or retouching, proper lighting and posing in the camera room will do much to reduce if not eliminate the necessity for corrective work of that nature, always expensive because it is time consuming and, in some cases, can only be done by experts.

Portrait lighting, so far as the average subject is concerned, must always be a matter of compromise. In addition to likeness and characterization you should always aim for roundness, depth and separation, but most importantly you must please your subject. You don't want your subject to sink into the background but at the same time you must be careful not to emphasize any bad points. Just the same, if you will keep working for this extra depth in your portraits, you will find it will appeal favorably to your subjects and they will appreciate, though they may not realize just why, that your portraits are different—and better.

Looking at the more practical side of the matter, let us assume that you are unfortunate enough to be working in extremely cramped quarters and have to place your subject very close to the background, perhaps only three feet away or even less. By using a background light in the manner we have described you will be surprised how much greater you can make this distance appear. Understand one thing: we are not suggesting the use of a background light—particularly in head and shoulder portraiture—merely to eliminate the subject's shadow on the background. If you are troubled in that way then you are not placing your main source and fill-in lights properly and whatever you do to the background will not correct the errors you will have already made in lighting your subject's face.

CHAPTER 3

The Younger Woman

The majority of younger women to come before your camera will fall in the teen age classification and because it is pretty much of an axiom that all women, at least until graying hair and the lines of age make concealment no longer possible, prefer to consider themselves as young, and the younger the better, what we say here will apply quite generally to every age bracket from seventeen to forty. Beyond the teen ages women as a group do not too willingly sit for portraits with two exceptions: the event of marriage and the occasional needed publicity photograph. Bridal portraits are a thing apart and will be discussed in a later chapter while publicity portraits require only that general understanding of conservative lighting which the reader will automatically absorb as he studies this and forthcoming chapters, plus the realization that any woman beyond her teens hopes to the point of anticipation for two surprises in her portrait: that she will look younger (and probably slimmer) than she actually is and that any facial lines or blemishes will at least be softened if not entirely eliminated. Necessarily there are occasional exceptions and every professional will remember the rare woman who has told him bluntly that she wants not a single line removed. Rest assured, however, that if your practice is to err toward the side of flattery you will seldom if ever offend a sitter.

Rather than write this chapter around an assortment of portraits of different subjects, we have decided to limit ourselves to one young lady, not a professional model but a college freshman in her late teens and, so the reader may have the feeling of being actually engaged in making a normal portrait sitting, to progress step by step from a reasonably acceptable head and shoulder pose to a genuinely appealing three quarter length of the same subject. It is our intention to show how this can be done with the type of subject encountered almost any day in the week, with little if any complications in lighting and virtually nothing in the way of studio props or accessories. Anyone blessed with a reasonably fair degree of photographic competence can seat a subject before a camera and produce a head and shoulder portrait.

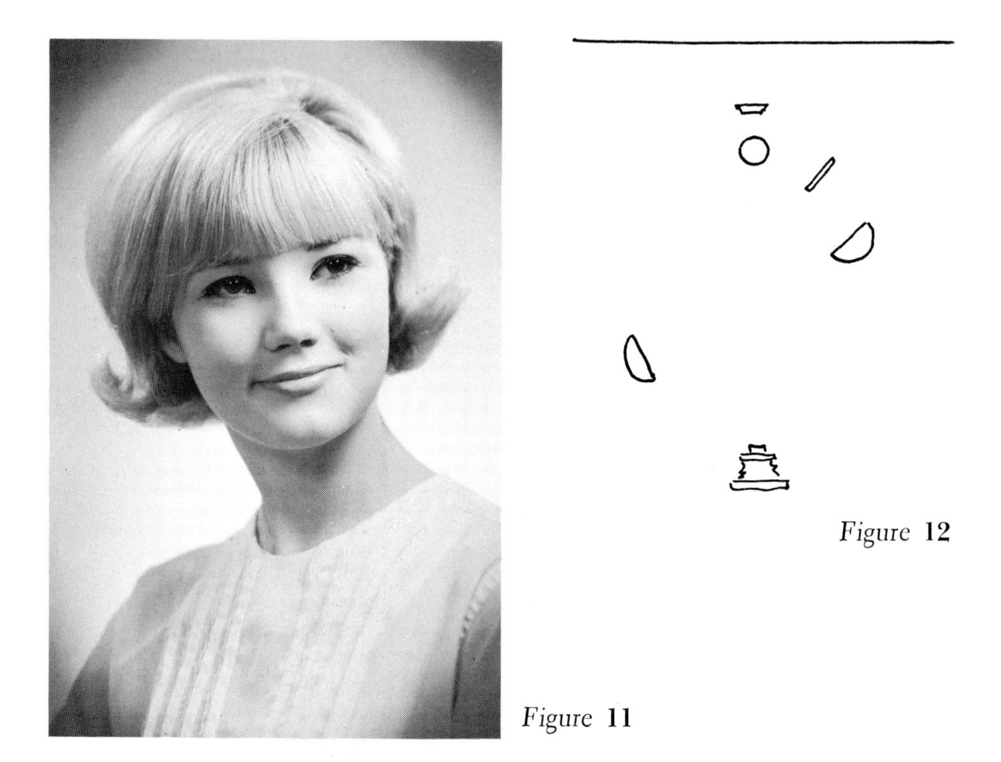

Figure 12

Figure 11

That, unfortunately, is exactly what is wrong with most portraiture—and especially professional portraiture—today. Too many photographers are satisfied to ask a subject to be seated while they turn on their lights, so seldom moved from their standard placement that the stands have left permanent dents in the floor covering, and then after a few adjustments in the pose to say: "Turn this way, please," next "Turn that way, please," after which they swing the chair in the other direction, repeat the performance and the sitting is over. That may be photography, but it isn't portraiture or at least certainly not the type of portraiture that causes people to *want* portraits. Let's see if we can explain.

Figure 11, as its accompanying diagram shows, is a first class example of a plain lighting, what the average professional thinks of as "bread and butter" work. Three lights are used, the main source at about a 45° angle to the right of the sitter, the fill-in to the left front and farther away and a background light in its normal position behind the subject. Assuming the fill-in to be a light of the same strength (wattage) as the main source and with no intention of embarking on what can become a highly controversial subject, the beginner can play reasonably safe if he adopts a three to one "ratio" between his main source and fill-in lights. That is to say that the fill-in is about three times as far from the subject as the main source.

To experiment, look at the diagram (*Figure 12*) and having placed your main source at about the distance shown, move the fill-in to the same distance from the sitter on the other side. You will find that while the main source alone illuminates one side of the face strongly and leaves the other side in harsh shadow, moving in the fill-in and turning it on wipes out the shadows, destroying the modeling of the face completely or "burning it out" as a professional would say. Now pull the fill-in light away from the subject, toward the camera, and on a line that is about a 15°

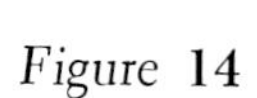

Figure **14**

Figure **13**

angle from the lens to subject line. This latter, as should be obvious, is an imaginary line running from the center of the lens to the center of the subject. As you move the fill-in farther away from the subject you will notice that the shadow area be-

Figure **15**

Figure **16**

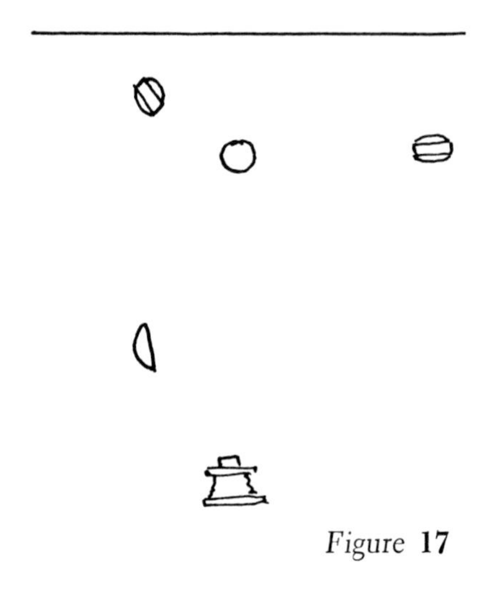

Figure **17**

comes progressively darker. You must establish a point at which your shadow detail will be such as to please your subjects and that point will be your "ratio"—the point of balance between your main source and fill-in lights. Once you arrive at this ratio with any given set of lights, film and development procedure, you can expect to produce consistently good negatives as regards shadow detail. Later, as your own appreciation and understanding of good portraiture improves, you may wish to change that ratio but at least for the present it will serve you well and, for ourselves, we shall say no more about ratios.

Usually it is advisable to "feather" the fill-in light because by so doing ears, cheek bones, and other features can be controlled as to brightness in relation to the other—the highlight—side of the face. "Feathering," we should explain here, is a professional term for the turning of a light and its reflector more or less away from the subject. In other words, while the direction from which the light comes remains unchanged, the volume of light that strikes the subject is reduced and its effect thus softened.

Returning, however, to *Figure 11* you will note that there are no deep shadows, the flesh tones are good and the face is well modeled. The pose is nothing to write home about but we do have a good likeness and a pleasing expression, and millions of portraits are sold annually with nothing more to recommend them. It's acceptable, even saleable from a professional standpoint but as we study it we realize there is a lot that can be done to make it more appealing.

Let us move on to *Figure 13* for which our basic lighting remains identical but which looks surprisingly different due to our adding two small spots and making a slight change in the pose. While the original lighting on the face has not been changed we have illuminated the edges of the hair with the spots and in addition have allowed the light from one of these to strike the subject's left cheek. The shoulders remain the same but we have tilted the subject's head slightly to her right. One important result is that the neck seems shorter than in *Figure 11* and another is to slenderize the face and make it appear more oval.

To produce *Figure 15* it is only necessary to reverse the subject's position. No lighting diagram appears with *Figure 15* because, nothing having been moved—not even the spots, it would be a complete duplication of the previous one, *Figure 14.* All we did here was to ask our young subject to lift the shoulder nearer the camera. Again the neck appears shorter while the whole portrait has a more desirable feeling of action. So far we have vastly improved upon our first attempt and yet, from the standpoint of producing something more truly appealing or saleable than what is to be seen in studio show windows from one end of the country to the other, we have accomplished very little. What else can we do that will better please this young lady and—more importantly—cause her friends who see her photographs to want portraits (made by us, naturally) of themselves?

One thing a smart photographer will not overlook when portraying any younger woman whose features warrant it at all is a profile shot. While this particular subject's profile may not be outstandingly beautiful it is certainly attractive and we should always remember that while our profiles are not so familiar to ourselves they are one aspect of our faces with which our friends are well acquainted. Profiles, furthermore, are not difficult and do not require too much rearrangement of our lights. For this one, *Figure 16,* we eliminate the main source, using only the fill-in and two small spots, as shown in *Figure 17.* Because it is the profile we are featuring, we must be careful not to over illuminate the back of the head. Therefore, with one spot used as an edge light we bring out the profile and with the other, some distance away, we throw enough light on the hair to bring out the necessary detail —after all we are still making a portrait and must retain a likeness instead of some kind of weird salon effect—and so with our fill-in brought a bit closer we give life to the face rather than leave it completely in shadow.

Because we must keep the level of this shadow illumination within a range that will be pleasing, we are careful to feather the fill-in light. In this case it is necessary to keep the fill-in light fairly high up in order not to lose the line of the jaw. Note also that the spot which provides the edge light has been brought forward sufficiently so that in addition it strikes the cheek bone and provides an interesting small V of light there. This helps to lighten an effect which otherwise might be a bit dull if we limited ourselves to the edge light on the profile only.

Finally, before we leave *Figure 16,* the cameraman should always be observant of such seemingly small things as wedding or engagement rings and especially the latter. If the subject who wears such a ring can display it in her portrait without the fact seeming too obvious, she will be well pleased and in this pose of the hands the ring, while not over emphasized, can hardly be ignored. Profiles offer one more advantage, although perhaps of not such great importance, in that, because only half of the face is shown, the necessity for retouching is reduced to that extent.

So far, commencing with what might be thought of as not much more than a standard portrait for a high school or college year book, we have step by step brought to the fore our subject's good points and thus made each successive picture not only more desirable but have departed a bit from the stereotyped head and shoulders

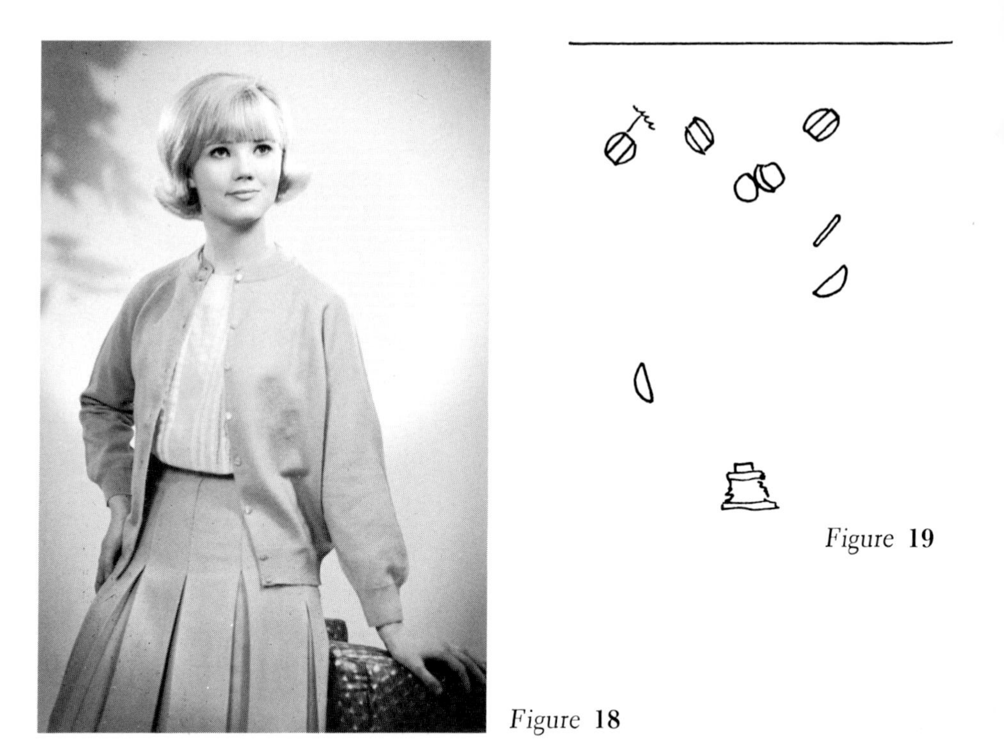

Figure 18

Figure 19

with which the public as a whole has become all too familiar. But even now, have we done full justice to our subject? Have we, as yet, achieved a portrait that presents her as she would really like to look, a portrait she will show with pride and one that will cause her to sing our praises? And if not, what then?

We face no insurmountable problem, in fact all we need is another spot and a low backed chair, plus some method of supporting before the spot a leafy branch or sprig of foliage. With these, and assuming our subject is suitably clothed, we can quite easily make a couple of three quarter lengths and still remain within a reasonable limit of six exposures for this particular sitting. A room full of props is not necessary; really for what we have in mind the fewer props the better because we do not want them to detract from our subject.

Substituting the low backed chair already mentioned for our original posing chair or bench, but placing it at an angle with the back instead of the seat toward our camera, we ask our subject to stand before the chair back, lean toward it slightly and rest her hands on the back, a type of pose to which any younger woman would be quite accustomed and which would involve no strain or effort. Our main source and fill-in lights return to approximately normal position and we use our former two spots to back light the hair and shoulders on each side although on the one side we direct that spot down a bit for a touch of light on the cheek and down the arm to outline it slightly against the background. The light striking the shoulders should be just a touch, for accent. We then adjust our third spot to provide a circular pattern of light on the background behind the subject with, at one side, a shadow from our branch or sprig of foliage to liven up the background and balance our composition. Thus we arrive at *Figure 18,* fully explained by its accompanying lighting diagram, *Figure 19.*

By now we have, although in a comparatively short time and with very little effort, come a long way from the first portrait we made of this young lady but, before we leave her, suppose we try one more pose with the deliberate intention of doing everything we possibly can for her without going to the extent of glamour lighting and posing. She happened to be wearing a sweater when she came to the studio—an accessory or prop which would be available almost anywhere at any time. We have her stand with her side toward the camera, holding the sweater draped over one shoulder and to give her skirt a touch of "flair" we pull it out a little at the back. We ask her to tilt her head a little, look over her shoulder toward the camera and raise her head just a bit, and we suggest a smile. Main source and fill-in remain where they were, but we remove one spot, retaining the other for a touch of back light on the hair. The spot we used for *Figure 18* to throw a circle of light on the background as well as some interesting shadows remains in place but is directed downward slightly more to bring that circle below the waistline. The result is *Figure 20*, the kind of portrait that will charm our subject and intrigue her friends.

Let us emphasize before we close this chapter that there has been no attempt to glamourize the subject, that nothing has been done which cannot be accomplished with the simplest of equipment and we have made only minor changes from the most basic type of lighting. Six similar poses could be made of any average female sitter and we would be willing to wager that orders would be placed from not less than three of the six. The technique is simple; what is more important is being able to appraise the subject's good points and learning from experience (it can be done in no other way) what poses to select to emphasize those features. Only such extra trouble will make you a better than average portraitist.

Figure **21**

Figure **20**

CHAPTER 4

Women Over Thirty

We might as well recognize that women beyond the age of forty, and perhaps even thirty five, do not appear before the camera very frequently, and seldom of their own volition. So true is this that many professional photographers have arrived at the fallacious conclusion that "women of that age just don't have portraits made." Understandable though the statement may be, is it not equally true that photographers themselves are to blame for this unhappy situation? From our standpoint we see no good reason why such a tremendous percentage of the population should be so casually disregarded, especially because, from a financial standpoint, such women are in most cases well able to buy whatever they want.

There is an enormous field here for portraiture and all it needs is a little intelligent cultivation. It is only necessary to convince the older women of your community of two things: that they will receive just as much courtesy and attention from you as the prettiest young girl in town, and that you can (and will) produce portraits of them that they will like. The old *cliché*—"Oh! I never take a good picture"—with which they are accustomed to pass off any suggestion that they have photographs taken has far too much basis in fact. Since she was married, or since she was a teen ager, chances are excellent that the lady really never has had a decent photograph! On the rare occasions when she has been persuaded into a sitting the photographer, instead of recognizing his subject as a challenge, has resigned himself to her as a chore. With such an approach little can be expected and one more mature individual is thereafter permanently eliminated as a prospective sitter.

A decade or two ago one could see, in studio windows and displays and in photographic exhibits, many excellent portraits of women in this age bracket. Usually the subjects were well dressed and the poses were handsome three quarter and full lengths, doing justice to the costumes. The average cameraman of today, seeking the easy way out and therefore only too ready to concentrate on head and shoulder poses, fails to realize that older women are every bit as attractive personally as they ever were, in fact more so because they have finer clothes and in far greater variety than ever before, are style conscious thanks to the many fashion magazines and, being also cosmetic conscious, have little reason to be ashamed of their looks. They represent far too important—and profitable—a market to ignore and because many of them are well aware that thanks to their financial standing and social position they can give cards and spades to their younger competitors when it comes to poise and costuming, the "I never take a good picture" attitude is in reality a defense mechanism they themselves would be only too happy to have overthrown.

While there may not be the same motive behind the older woman's need or desire for a portrait that exists in the case of a girl in her late teens or early twenties, two points should not be overlooked. The older woman is generally in a much better position to place a substantial order if you are willing—and know how—to please her. What's more, when the desire or need for a portrait does arise she is going to be far more discriminating in her choice of a photographer or a studio and will go out of her way to select an establishment that can and does produce quality work. What she may be willing to accept for her daughter, or may approve of for a younger sister or a friend, will not necessarily be what she wants for herself.

It goes without saying that many of these older subjects will require a fine job of retouching. If you are not yourself a competent retoucher, it is imperative that you at least know what a good retoucher can (and should) do so that you can explain intelligently to such subjects exactly what you intend to do to make their portraits more desirable. If you yourself cannot retouch you can learn, from any of several good books which are on the market, enough about this important adjunct to portraiture so you will not suggest or propose the impossible. Above all, if you make promises with respect to retouching, don't fail to fulfill them. Remember, too, that a mother of grown children does not ordinarily want her portrait retouched so she looks like a teen age school girl.

You may have read elsewhere, or been told, that older women should be photographed almost exclusively with soft focus lenses. Soft focus is not new; it is currently a revival of a fad which was all the vogue some thirty years ago. Soft focus lenses have their place and there are many occasions when their use is desirable, perhaps essential, but we cannot accept the theory that older women cannot be satisfactorily portrayed except with soft focus lenses. In fact we have on frequent occasions made both sharp and diffused negatives during the same sitting and have found upon showing the proofs that the majority of subjects prefer the sharper image. It is also stated that soft focus lenses materially reduce the need for retouching, and although this is true they cannot eliminate retouching entirely. What still remains to be done requires far more skill than working on a normally sharp negative because retouching required for a soft focus negative is the type known as "modeling" and very few retouchers are good at that today.

Older women will appreciate everything you can do to help them get satisfactory portraits and will cooperate with you in this effort far more than your younger sitters. You should always aim for a natural and at the same time flattering pose and by all means do not limit yourself to the head and shoulders. At the same time, when you do make three quarter lengths do not fall into the error of posing all your sitters alike, sitting at a table or in a chair reading or holding a book. It is variety that will create a demand for portraits by you rather than someone else.

Pay especial attention to the hair line when working with older women. It is

Figure 22

Figure 23

much easier, and far less expensive, to check for stray locks or wisps of hair before making an exposure than to correct errors or omissions of this nature later by retouching. Remember to watch the clothing so that unnecessary wrinkles are smoothed out before the shutter is tripped. Watch the head position carefully. In many instances a slight tilt of the head will add the dignity so necessary when an older woman is the subject and will at the same time iron out a lot of wrinkles and neck lines. If your sitter is of the buxom type it may be well to photograph her in a standing position, even if your eventual picture is to be only the head and shoulders, because a standing pose nearly always has a slenderizing effect. Those double chins which are a menace to so many of us as we grow older will often largely or completely disappear merely as a result of asking the subject to raise her chin or tilt her head. Simple tricks, all of these, and for that matter equally adaptable when photographing older men.

Because, no matter how much we sermonize, we realize this one book is not going to reverse the drift to head and shoulder portraits, we are including several of these among the illustrations for this Chapter. In the case of *Figure* 22 our subject had specific use for a head and shoulder portrait for publication purposes. That being what she wanted, that was what we made and as a result it called for an almost standard lighting of main source, fill-in and background light, (see *Figure* 23) except that because she has very beautiful gray hair we took care to outline and gently highlight it with two spots. Notice, though, that we were equally careful not to over light the hair. It would have been all too easy to "burn it up" with the spots and produce a "halo" or "cotton top" effect and while either might have been just the thing to make a young girl happy, dignity was what had to be maintained here. Notice also that this negative has been very carefully retouched, by which we particularly mean that the lines in the forehead, under the eyes and around the mouth have been softened but not eliminated. A completely smooth job of retouching—often called the "billiard ball" type—is entirely out of place and uncalled for on a portrait of an older woman. With respect to the eyes, it is a great mistake to do too much retouching below them because, with older people, the likeness is almost certain to be lost. A slight upward look helps to give this portrait a feeling of animation and keeping the shoulders rather straight adds dignity. A portrait like this will please a woman of this age, and her family and friends as well.

All head and shoulder portraits need not look alike, as is shown by *Figure 24*. In this case, too, the subject wanted a portrait for reproduction and specified head and shoulders so, complying with her wishes, we first made several poses in the suit that she was wearing. She was not only nice looking but had a pleasing personality and was amenable to suggestions, whereupon we proposed trying a drape arrangement which we felt would produce a generally softer effect. To improve still further on this we used a gray camera vignette (these will be explained in detail in a later chapter) to lift the whole result out of the ordinary head and shoulder class. While the main source and fill-in remained in much the same position (*Figure 25*) we turned one spot around to illuminate the background and substituted a boom spot for the other in order to provide a back lighting on the hair but from a higher position than before. The drape (and these also will be explained in

Figure **25**

Figure **24**

Figure 26

detail in a later chapter) is quite simply done in the camera room and, with the help of a couple of inexpensive costume jewelry pins, one on each shoulder, gives the effect of an expensive formal gown. Draping, as this indicates, is far from being a service which appeals only to younger sitters.

The reader will have noticed by now that we are very partial to the use of the head screen, which has already appeared in many of the diagrams. This does not imply that its use is essential because, as we remarked earlier, most professionals today have discarded this accessory. In our considered opinion the head screen can be one of the most useful objects in a camera room. It is quickly put in place and even more quickly adjusted thanks to its flexible neck. To accomplish the same result with the large main source light requires much moving of the light back and forth, to one side or the other, or feathering on and off the face and, all too frequently, while moving the light to effect a desired correction the overall lighting you are trying to secure on that side of the face is lost and you have to start all over again.

Before we leave the head and shoulder pose let us show you why so many older women hesitate to have formal portraits taken. *Figure 26* is a case in point, and of a very typical subject. This middle aged lady has had an interesting life, has acquired a reasonable amount of worldly assets and has achieved the poise that comes with maturity. She is not interested in a "flapperish" pose or a school girl's smile; rather

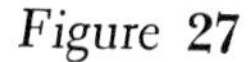
Figure 27

she wants a portrait that will reflect the composure and dignity which are naturally hers. In *Figure 26* we have deliberately included several of the "little things" which too many photographers overlook or ignore, seemingly minor matters which are easily missed on the groundglass or even (because most photographers are prone to appraise their own work too highly) unnoticed in preparing a set of proofs. Yet these same "little things" are the real reason why women in this age bracket fight shy of the camera.

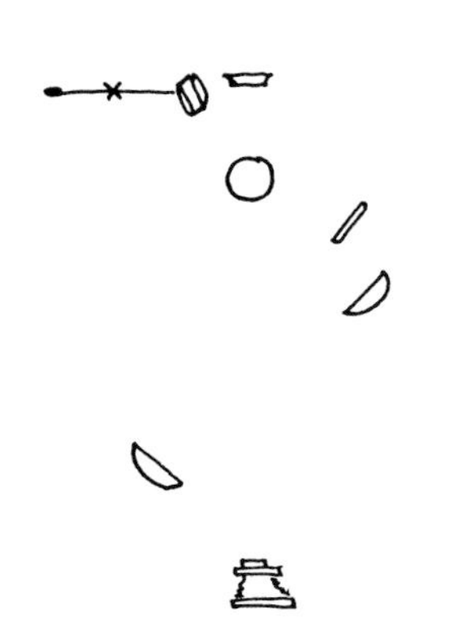

Figure 28

Figure 29

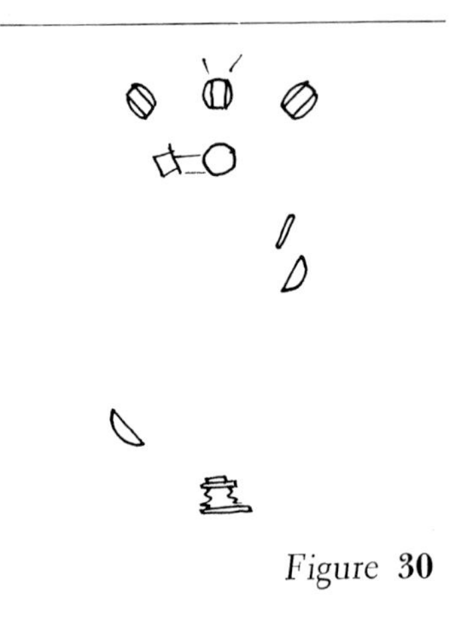

Figure 30

No lighting diagram is necessary for this, taken with an almost standard placement of main source, fill-in and two spots, practically the same as *Figure 23* and a fine example of why the cameraman who is too lackadaisical to move his lights soon finds his business disappearing. While the main source and fill-in take care of the essentials the light from the spots is much too strong. What is really a beautiful head of hair has been over illuminated so that the detail is lost and it looks like a fluffy mass of cotton. The spots are too much to the side and in addition to burning out the hair throw far too much light on each side of the forehead. Each spot should be moved back toward the background until the light no longer strikes the forehead. The pose is incorrect for a person of this age because a backward tilt of the head, which may give a younger woman a saucy "come hither" look, is clearly undignified for an older person. Such a backward tilt is also likely to accent any undue fullness under the chin, any irregularities of the jaw line caused by full or heavy cheeks, and will even add wrinkles instead of dispelling them.

How may we correct this? We need not ask our subject to move her body at all, but we do ask her to tilt her head forward and turn her face slightly toward the camera as in *Figure 27*. Thus we eliminate the emphasis on the one ear, too much of which appears in *Figure 26*, and at the same time bring a little of the other ear into our composition, giving the whole face better balance. In addition, while the backward tilt of the head in *Figure 26* tended to make the face appear wider and more angular, the forward tilt of *Figure 27* lengthens it and makes it seem narrower across the jaw line. Our next step is to substitute for the two spots one boom spot (See *Figure 28*) which just sufficiently outlines the hair against the background while retaining all its soft detail and, because none of this extraneous light strikes the forehead, our lighting is in balance and the whole face is properly modeled. To emphasize the difference between these two poses even more, *Figure 26* is from an unretouched negative while *Figure 27* has been most carefully retouched. Note, however, that none of the subject's essential lines have been destroyed and that while needless wrinkles have been removed and hard lines subdued, the all important likeness remains.

Shown proofs from these two negatives the subject, as well as her family and friends, will no doubt concede that both portraits are true to life but will discard *Figure 26* and be pleased with *Figure 27* even though unable to explain the reason for the preference. To the experienced professional the answer will be obvious: one is a portrait and the other is nothing more than a record shot or a likeness. For that matter an experienced professional, with one glance at the subject, would not attempt a pose and lighting like that in *Figure 26*, realizing it to mean nothing more than a wasted film. Rather he would commence with *Figure 27* and, if a confirmed head and shoulders worker, would make only slight changes from that as an initial pose.

Fortunately not all older women insist on a head and shoulder pose and nothing more or, at least, when a portrait is desired for some special purpose, will listen to suggestions. One occasion that does cause such subjects to give serious consideration to greater variety in photographs is when sons and daughters are going away to school and want "mother's picture" to take with them. The more attractive mother can be made to look the more proudly the resulting portrait will be displayed, and so we present *Figure 29*. Here is a photograph which will stand out in any display of pictures and which at the same time has all the dignity and forcefulness that the most respected club officer, career woman or even lady politico could ask for in a publicity portrait. Again we return to a three quarter length for the simple reason that if you want your portraits to be outstanding you must get away from the limitations of the head and shoulder pose.

To produce results like this, first explain to your subject what you have in mind and ask her to bring several changes of costume. For one thing she will immediately be flattered to think you are going to so much trouble and for another—and from your own standpoint—you will have the advantage of selecting a costume which will be most advantageous photogenically. For a pose like this a ladder back chair is a helpful accessory but beyond that little comment is necessary. Even though this looks so different from our other illustrations the lighting remains almost standard except that for our normal background light we have substituted an additional spot, concealed by the subject, but directed on the background at an angle as in *Figure 30*. The pose of the body automatically helps to slim the figure and give the result a feeling of movement; the light touch of the fingers of one hand on the chair makes it appear that the subject was caught in the action of turning toward the camera. This pose, like all other illustrations, is only a suggestion, a starting point. Learn to make one pose and lighting like this well, and you can ring your own changes on it indefinitely thereafter.

CHAPTER 5

Budding Manhood

Don't let anyone tell you that men, young or old, are not as vain as women. Vanity is fully as much an attribute of the sterner sex, the only difference being that men will under no circumstances admit their failings in this respect and, here differing from women, also do their best not to show it. The woman gives herself away through her makeup, her clothing, her accessories and her bearing or attitude. Only when you see a woman whose hair is unkempt, who is devoid of makeup and whose clothes indicate at a glance that their wearer is uninterested in her looks, can you say to yourself: "Here is a woman without vanity." No such snap judgment can be applied, on the other hand, to a man. Many men, in fact, pride themselves on a careless appearance because they suffer from the delusion that any genuine attempt to appear well groomed may reflect on their masculinity. Many men, too, though well educated and well bred, have the unfortunate facility of being quite unable to look well dressed despite the best efforts of their tailors and their wives. Do not, therefore, be misled when a male sitter appears before your camera in a suit that looks as if he had slept in it; it may be a two hundred and fifty dollar outfit, fresh from the cleaners, that he donned only twenty minutes before arriving at your studio.

Younger men, and teen agers especially, pose an even worse problem. It is the modern habit for teen agers to dress sloppily and carry themselves equally so and, going beyond the teens, even those who attend the most conservative of Ivy League universities seem to take a weird delight in apparent disreputability. Consequently even when they do wear well tailored clothes their normally careless demeanor makes it difficult to photograph them satisfactorily. We are fortunate that the subject we have selected for this chapter, a young college man, is far better than average in this respect and yet, despite his every attempt, his coat collar rides up in a disturbing manner in two of our illustrations, *Figures 31* and *38*, in spite of our best efforts to pull it down where it should be. A man in his thirties, starting his initial steps on the executive ladder, would probably notice this and refuse to accept either pose—assuredly his wife would, if he did not—but to the man of less maturity this would be a defect of no importance if he realized it at all.

The younger man is often more difficult to photograph to his satisfaction and yours because, being still on the threshold of life and therefore having undergone few of the mental strains that come with the years, his face is still smooth and lacking in character lines or even minor wrinkles. Even though he may have a scar or two or perhaps a broken nose thanks to football or other athletic sports, his skin will show little more texture than that of his girl friend and yet the one thing you, as a cameraman, must avoid is making him appear effeminate. His mother may still think of him as her "baby" but he likes to think of himself as an up and coming young individual with a mind of his own, and that is the way he must be portrayed if he is to be pleased. Strong, harsh lighting must therefore be avoided or the natural smoothness of his face will be accentuated and you will produce a "girlish" picture instead of the manly portrait he expects from you. Above all, don't make snap judgments, plunk him in a chair and start to shoot. Talk with him a few moments to get him interested, studying him meanwhile to see how his mouth and chin look in repose and also to discover if he has an attractive smile. And be sure to include, among your poses, both serious and smiling expressions.

For school year book purposes, naturally, a reasonably serious look will be necessary but aside from that find out, through some judicious questioning, what specific purpose if any he may have in mind for his portrait. To a prospective employer he should appear as a bright, intelligent, forceful young man; his girl friend or fiancee will wish to see him as good looking as possible; his mother will want to recognize in the picture the boy who is just growing into manhood; to his chums he must be the hail-fellow-well-met youngster whom they know as a pal. Can all this be accomplished in the set of six to eight poses to which we think you should limit yourself with the average young man who cannot be expected to place a very large order? We believe it can. In speaking of eight poses we are allowing for a couple of wasted negatives due to moves or errors of lighting on your part. Once you gain experience you should never have to shoot more than eight negatives of an average subject in order to have six good proofs, well varied, to show. Obviously if you know in advance or learn during the course of the sitting that your subject comes from a wealthy or especially prominent family it would be foolish to be stingy with film but even then you are not likely to increase an order, or add to the subject's opinion of your ability as a photographer, when your added poses show no originality and are little more than minor changes in the position of the head or body.

Let us commence, then, having conversed a few minutes with our young subject, and having discovered that he does have a very winning smile, by seeing what we can do to capture that as something we think will appeal both to his mother and his chums. We have two such smiling portraits, *Figure 31* and *Figure 32*, and one lighting placement (*Figure 33*) will suffice for both. We seat him at a slight angle to the camera and, to give a feeling of action and movement, have him turn his face toward the lens. We place our main source at approximately a 45° angle from the subject, a fairly standard position, and with our ever ready head screen hold back the light on the ear on that side. Our fill-in, some distance farther away on the left and closer to the camera (note that we stick pretty closely to our three to one ratio), is feathered slightly away from the subject because, as we mentioned earlier,

Figure **31** *Figure* **32**

we must be careful not to over light or we will destroy the modeling and flatten out the planes of the face. Concealed behind him is our background light for which, in this case, we have selected a small spot in order to give fairly strong illumination to the area directly behind the head and shoulders. We can well afford to do this because the shape of the head is good and the ears are well formed and close to the head. For some extra light on the hair and to snap up the entire outline we add two spots at the right and left rear, both of them rather high and just barely spilling

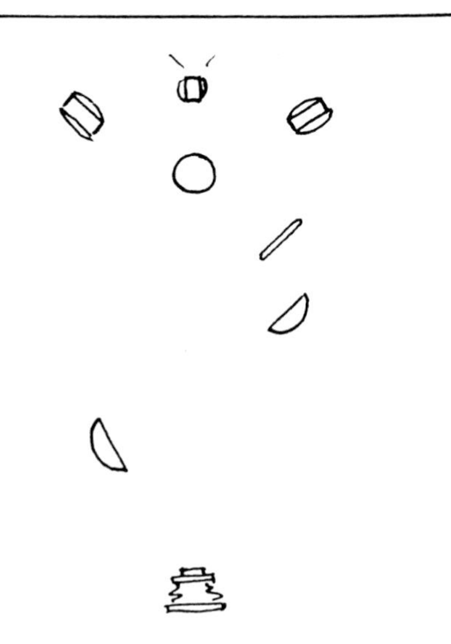

Figure **33**

a little additional light on the forehead on each side. We are careful not to let these spots strike the collar or the neck because we want to hold attention on the face. We having a feeling that mother is going to like this. (*Figure 31*)

The thought strikes us, however, that perhaps the smile was just a little bit "set" and we can get a more genuine and forceful picture. Noticing that our subject's features are more symmetrical than those of most people we decide to try again, but from the other side. All we do is swing him around in the posing chair and again have him look into the lens but this time we make some remark that gets a laugh out of him. It is not necessary to change the lighting at all, so that the same diagram (*Figure 33*) applies, but in order to include a bit more of the figure we pull the camera back a bit, which also reduces the head size. This is always wise when you are deliberately working for a broad smile, one that is almost a laugh. Actually we prefer *Figure 32* to *Figure 31* and while it may not please the subject's mother as much, it surely will appeal to his friends. So much, in any event, for two straight head and shoulder portraits of the "bread and butter" type. Had the expression been serious everything we have said about the lighting and posing would also apply. Portraits like these, serious or smiling, will satisfy the majority of your sitters.

As we have said before, and as we shall continue to emphasize throughout this book, it is not sufficient merely to satisfy those who entrust you with the task of recording their features for posterity. Almost anyone with a camera can do that, including the amateur and sometimes even the veritable beginner. If you are to make a success in portraiture you must give your subjects more than they expect and, if you are a professional and anxious to make more than an average living from your vocation, portraits that will make them—*and* their friends—remember your name in preference to others whenever portraits are under consideration.

Never fail, when a subject's clothes are suitable, to include at least one three quarter length in your set of proofs. We will concede that a three quarter requires a bit more time, more care and the exercise of some originality and ingenuity on your part but, in the final analysis, what have you as a photographer to offer other than your time and your ability? The few sheets of paper, each bearing an image, which you finally deliver actually cost very little, even including the basic films and the processing. Today when every family has at least one camera and often each member of a family has a camera of his own, your subjects are well aware of the comparatively minor cost (from a material standpoint) of the portraits they finally accept from you. They come to you because they respect your competence as a photographer and only when they realize that you are willing to devote some time and trouble to their individual problems will they feel they have received their money's worth.

Bearing all this in mind, and because we intend to present our subject with a set of proofs of sufficient variety so he will be practically compelled to select several, if not all, for finishing instead of just picking out one because all are so much alike, we decide on a three quarter length. We substitute a small table for our posing chair, have him sit on the edge of it and place his left hand in his trouser pocket. We select a magazine of light weight from those on our reception room table (so we can roll it up) and put it in his other hand. In this case, as in most, he will rest the hand in a natural position on his right leg, and if we have to do any rearranging at all, it will be only to move the hand so that the roll it bears will not be directed

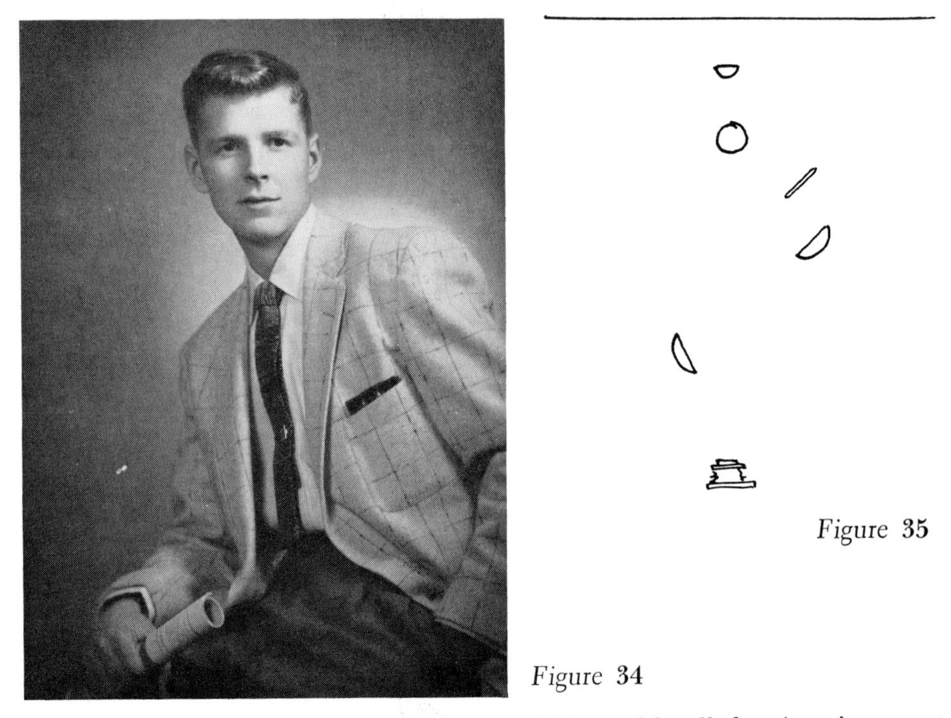

Figure 35

Figure 34

downward to the edge of the picture space, which would pull the viewer's eye out of the composition. We pull down the coat sleeves if there happen to be too many objectionable wrinkles and, because this is a rather conservative pose, we decide we want a serious expression.

Our result is *Figure 34* and, as for the lighting, we substitute a normal background light behind the subject instead of the small spot we used before because now we only want separation from the background rather than an accentuated circle of light. We also eliminate the other two spots because we do not wish any part of the figure too strongly outlined; as we said, this is conservative in nature and we are not seeking any glamourized treatment. So, as in *Figure 35*, leaving our main source and fill-in practically where they were, only a bit higher, we have for our subject a very attractive portrait from a simple two point lighting plus the background light. What was so difficult about all this and why should any photographer hesitate to spend the few additional minutes necessary?

Our subject also has a good profile and whether he realizes it or not his mother, his girl friend and others are undoubtedly aware of it. It will mean a definite change in the lighting and the use of our judgment as to whether we should select the right or left side of the face. Especially when the subject is male, a good dramatic touch can be given to a profile by including one hand and, if we are successful, almost surely this will be another proof from which at least one finished picture, if not more, will be ordered. Merely to satisfy any subject you should show six proofs and if your price scale is similar to that of most professionals you make more money from an order that calls for as few as one print each from six proofs than one which specifies half a dozen prints from one proof. Your material investment is the same in either case so if all you are going to invest is a little extra time, why in the world should you let the dollars fly out of the window as a result of saying: "Look this way," "Look that way" and letting things go at that?

For our profile, *Figure 36*, we bring back our posing chair and add a small table on which the subject can rest his elbow. If he smokes, and most men young or old do nowadays, a cigarette, cigar or pipe is a most logical accessory and a complete and proper excuse for including the hand in the manner shown. We place a background light behind the subject, rather low, to provide adequate separation for the shoulders and lower part of the head. Off to the left we place one spot to outline the back of the head and shoulders, but not too strongly. At right rear and rather high we place another to illuminate the hair, the forehead and throw a splash of light on the near cheek bone, all to provide modeling and add interest. Note that this now becomes our main source light and the former main source, remaining where it was, now serves as the fill-in, being feathered to control the shadow depth. *Figure 37* tells the story and all we need to add here is that care must always be taken not to over light the hand, a warning which applies always to three quarter poses. Referring again to *Figure 34*, too much light on the hand and rolled up magazine would have been ruinous. Hands must always be subdued—in portraiture it is the face that must be the principal interest.

Men, young or old, often look more dignified when garbed for the outdoors, and a hat alone is often no small guide to an individual's personality Many a man will spend more time in selecting a hat than in buying a suit of clothes, and once the hat is his he proceeds to mould it to his own wishes by denting or creasing the crown until its designer would hardly recognize it (or would not admit the fact if he did). At the very least he snaps down the brim in his own peculiar manner. If your subject wears a hat, by all means include it in at least one pose. The choice of including all of the hat, or cutting off part of it to allow room for a larger head in

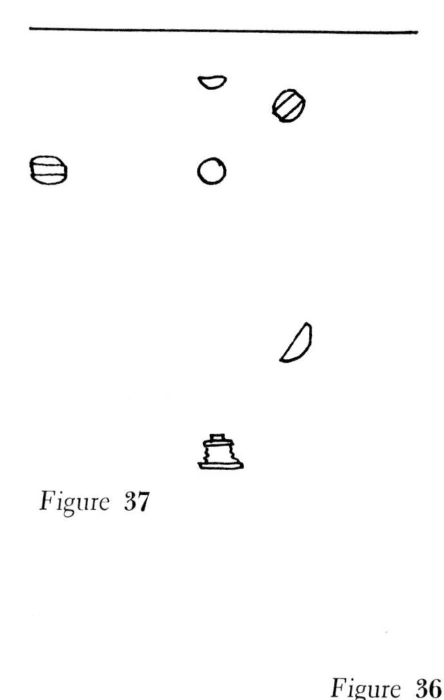

Figure 37

Figure 36

Figure **38** *Figure* **39**

your composition, is yours. Often cropping off enough to leave only the subject's pet tilt of the brim or dents in the crown will enable you to compose a more interesting picture. This is a matter for experiment and practice.

In this case our subject does have a hat and it is one of the more modern flat top affairs so we decide to include all of it so that, in future years, he may have a full record of his college day appearance. This being another head and shoulder pose, we revert to the original lighting setup (*Figure* 33), which we used for the first two illustrations in this Chapter, *Figures* 31 and 32, but with one minor change. Instead of a spot behind the subject to illuminate the background we use an ordinary background light because we want separation from the background rather than too much of an accentuated light area behind him. Also we raise the two spots at left and right rear in order to secure adequate illumination of the hat itself—and always remember that when you do include a hat in a portrait it must have enough detail and tone value to look like a hat and not a shapeless black mass. In addition, because a hat necessarily throws a shadow on the subject's face, we lower both the fill-in and the main source light so that the shadow from the hat, while of course it should be there, will not be an opaque pocket obscuring the forehead and features. The result is *Figure* 38.

Changes of costume, when they are available, are every bit as important when photographing a man as when the subject is a woman; more so, in fact, because to the camera and our monochrome film and paper (with which all of us will deal for many years to come) men's clothes show little variety. There are innumerable details in women's apparel which distinguish one costume from another regardless of color but, to the camera, men's suits are like the old saying that: "In the dark all cats are gray." So, if we want more variety we need something more definite than just another suit and, having already taken advantage of our subject's hat, we bless him mentally for having worn a good looking topcoat. All the time, mind you, we are aiming for six proofs sufficiently different so that he and his family will have real difficulty choosing between them and will, we hope, want finished prints from at least several.

Let us then revert to the three quarter pose once more, having asked him to put on the topcoat and, leaving the lighting just as we had it but raising all lights a little higher, we take away the posing chair and bring in a ladder back chair which we place at an angle to the camera. Asking our subject to stand partially behind it, we tell him to place his hands on it, one grasping the chair and the other holding his gloves or any other handy prop. The disposition of his legs and feet is unimportant (because they will not be included) so long as he is standing comfortably. Deciding that we would prefer to outline the upper portion of his figure we remove the background light and substitute a small spot behind him. In fact, for this portrait (*Figure* 39) we have returned to the identical lighting (*Figure* 33) which we used originally in this Chapter, and therefore are not repeating it.

We can now anticipate one question which, if asked, is likely to identify the querist as one reader who really needs this book! It is: "Why, if the lighting setup for the last two portraits is practically identical with that used for the first two, go to all the trouble of changing the setup for the third and fourth poses and then returning to the original?" In other words, why take the trouble? For the very simple and practical reason that we want to impress our subject with our desire to give him "something special" instead of, as would be the case in so many studios, rushing him through with the least possible delay. We are, as we work, building up a psychological factor in our subject's mind and we are making him, as we proceed, more and more curious to see the eventual results. When he returns home he will talk about what happened and instead of saying: "Well, I had my picture taken," he is going to comment enthusiastically: "You know what? Mr. Soandso not only took me seated but he put me up on a table and then he said I had a good profile and he took that. Next he took me in my new hat and to finish up he had me put my coat on, too. I'll bet he really got something." In such a frame of mind, and assuming you aren't the type of photographer who keeps people waiting two weeks to see proofs, you have him sold before he returns for them.

CHAPTER 6

Men of Maturity

Once a man passes his late twenties or early thirties, he has reached the stage—so far as the photographer is concerned—where he is no longer too good a prospect for portraits. The man who ultimately reaches the distressing—to him—decision that he must have his portrait taken, does so for business purposes or because his wife, close relatives or others have hounded him to the point of no return. Accordingly he enters the camera room with a chip on his shoulder and the ultimate success of the sitting will depend very largely on the cameraman's tactful approach. In at least eight cases out of ten some form of coming publicity due to a promotion, an award or recognition of some kind, election to office—whether political or social—or some type of achievement, has made a new portrait necessary.

Thus driven to the wall, he wants to get in and get out as quickly as possible and plans to spend no more than he has to for the minimum number of glossy prints that will serve his purpose. Usually, the more important he is the harder he will be to handle and the less time he will be willing to allow. Thus he may seem like a most unpromising prospect and yet, once he is before your camera, he presents an opportunity that no sensible photographer will ignore. Your objective must be twofold: to provide what he insists upon and to try and make some additional poses that will please his family. Ordinarily, the first shock of staring at the lens being over, it may be possible to cajole him into permitting you the luxury of several poses; if not your problem is to present him as the rockbound character he thinks he is and yet to include enough human appeal so his wife and children will recognize him for the lovable personality they consider him.

In any event, one bit of advice is appropriate here. So far as is humanly possible or practical, proofs of your male sitters should always be sent to the home. Assuming your own competence as a portraitist this alone will make all the difference in the final order. If your subject calls at the studio for his proofs he will take snap judgment there and then and your order will consist of the precise number of glossies upon which he had previously made up his mind. If the proofs are good and are sent to the home he will have no alternative but to order, in addition, finished prints to the extent specified by the adoring family.

Remembering that most of the men you will photograph will be business or professional people, certain principles must be kept in mind. Their time really is valuable, so do not waste it. Be sure, before you undertake to photograph men, that you have mastered your equipment. As you will have realized by now, there are certain basic lightings which are always good and can be achieved with a minimum of moving equipment around or parading yourself back and forth. Seat him with as few preliminaries as you can and, in many cases, he will immediately adopt a characteristic and comfortable pose. If the pose is reasonably photogenic you should be able to tell with a glance or two which side of his face is the better and, having decided that, touch or move him as little as you can, securing your result by moving the camera and the lights. If he has slumped, wait until you are nearly ready for your exposure before asking him to sit up straight. If his coat collar has ridden up, if he has too many wrinkles in his sleeves, if the tilt of his head is not just right, wait with those adjustments until the last moment.

All of this is pure psychology. He will have seated himself in his most natural and accustomed manner, and the longer he can stay that way the more relaxed he will become. It is those final adjustments that place a subject under tension; once they are made he immediately feels stiff and awkward but, if you are ready to make the exposure almost at once, the momentary unnatural sensation will not disturb him. If you commence by telling a man to look this way and that, tilt his head, pull down his cuffs, straighten his shoulders and so on, and then he realizes he has to hold the position while you (as he will be thinking) "fuss around" with lights and camera, his unaccustomed discomfort will cause him to lose faith in your ability and will certainly be disclosed in his attitude and expression.

What's more, after all that rigmarole he will be mentally convinced that the job is done and will want to be on his way. He will have been waiting for the shutter to click and will accept the sound as a signal that he has been photographed, which was all he came in for anyway. On the other hand, having allowed him to relax before finally spending barely a minute on the last essential details, you will not have aroused his antagonism and a remark like: "Now for something more forceful," or: "Don't your friends ever see you smile?" will find him receptive. The ice thus being broken, and unless he is genuinely in a hurry, you will probably be able to make several more negatives and perhaps even a three quarter or full length. Until you have sounded out your subject, don't make the mistake of chattering incessantly. In fact, the less conversation the better unless you happen to know the man personally or have sufficient information about his business or profession so you can ask an intelligent question or two.

To illustrate this Chapter we have selected five photographs which were made for as many different purposes. From their accompanying lighting diagrams you will readily see that none are beyond the scope of any studio owner or properly equipped advanced amateur. Note also that although each involves a change in the accessory lights the main source and fill-in remain in almost their standard placements throughout. This does not imply, as you must surely realize by now, that you can expect to leave these two basic lights in the same identical spots permanently. Though they retain their relative positions it will become necessary, from one sitter

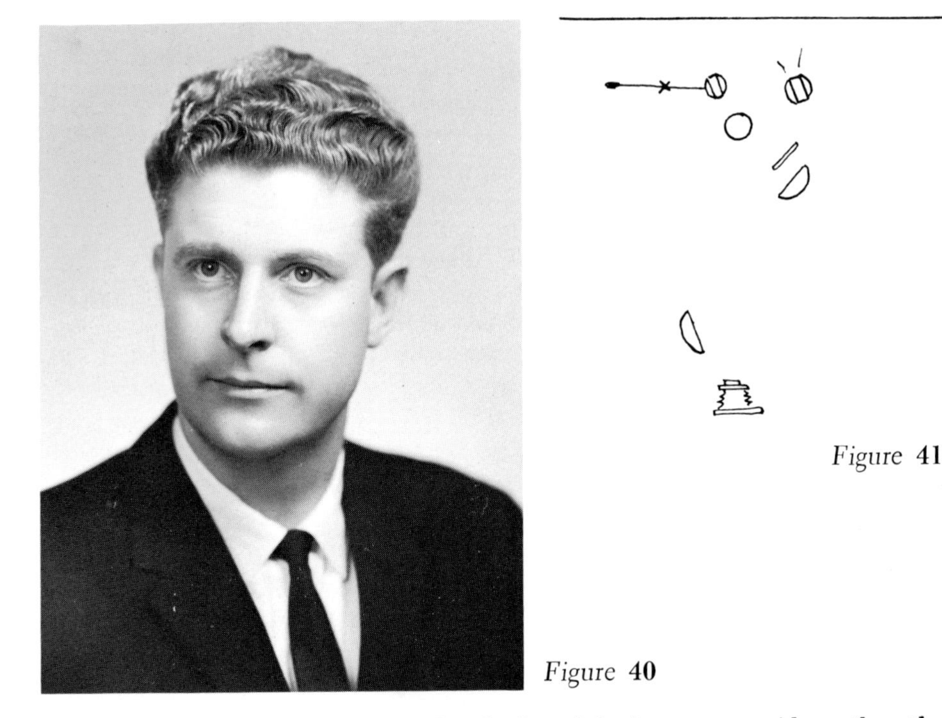

Figure **41**

Figure **40**

to the next, to move them a few inches back and forth or to one side or the other, or even a foot or two. The basic lighting placement remains the same although the actual final positioning of each light will vary depending upon the subject: his size, his coloring, whether his clothes are light or dark and—at times—whether or not he wears glasses.

Let us emphasize one thing more. Men, except when they are being purposely photographed for character studies, do not want to look like backwoods roughnecks. They should be posed in good taste and the negatives must be properly retouched. Some professionals advocate the use of orthochromatic emulsions for portraits of men to make them look more "rugged." That may be all very well for the illustrator who is trying to depict a hunter, fisherman, or other sports devotee, but take it from us that the average man who appears before your camera wants to appear dignified and businesslike. You can secure all the skin texture that is necessary with any of the modern panchromatic emulsions and what you will gain in faithful color fidelity is far more important for your purposes. If you are shooting for amusement or to secure salon prints, then try ortho, but for general work standardize on any good pan film.

Your most common request will be for a portrait for reproduction—a "glossy"—meaning nothing more than a head and shoulders and a pretty straightforward shot at that. So we have *Figure 40*, a plain conventional lighting for which, in view of the stated purpose, a straight into the lens, rather serious expression, fills the bill. Here is a convincing portrait which the subject could use for almost anything from a trade journal illustration to political campaign cards. This is straight photography, a good likeness, a dignified pose, a thoughtful expression. All necessary lines and facial characteristics are maintained, thanks to a thoroughly competent job of retouching. No unsightly reflections call undue attention to the glasses although no attempt has been made to subdue them because they are an essential part of the subject's personality. The set of the shoulders and the fact that both are in reasonably clear focus helps to give him breadth and stature. His family will readily recognize this expression, serious but not unpleasantly firm. He might appear just like this on looking up from his evening paper to decide whether or not Junior can drive the family car that night.

The main source and fill-in and the overhead boom spot to light the hair (*Figure 41*) are synchronized speedlights but an incandescent lamp was used in the spotlight directed on the background in order to assure a soft break of light over the shoulders. When making a portrait for reproduction, always keep the engraver in mind and never permit the shoulders to merge into the background. Good separation is essential. Also, when you know that a glossy is wanted, which often means reproduction by the very coarse halftone screen used by newspapers, stay away from deep shadows, maintain a full tonal scale and deliver a print which has plenty of depth. Remember that the engraver's process accentuates both the highlights and the shadows and that if your credit line finally appears under a halftone consisting chiefly of stark blacks and whites, the fault will be solely your own. Asking your male sitters to moisten the lips just before making the exposure will give them more color and thus a firmer line. It is also usually wise to conceal the bulb or shutter release behind your body and seldom if ever let the subject know the moment of exposure.

We have an entirely different approach in *Figure 42* even though the original purpose of this sitting was also a glossy print for reproduction. This man is an active farmer and a bank vice president. He needed a photograph because he had recently been presented with the highest honor a leading fraternal organization can award.

Figure 43

Figure 42

Certainly, rather than argue, we first made other poses without his hat and coat but we knew, and knew also that his friends and family would realize on sight, that these would not present such a man recognizably to the public. We insisted on the hat and coat—and the smile—because this is the way he appears when attending his many club and farm meetings. Don't ever underestimate the farmer—he is a vital force and much more of a business man than most city folks realize. This portrait gives this man a vibrant personality and cannot help but appeal to his family.

Again a conventional lighting (*Figure 43*) with the main source and fill-in feathered up a bit to avoid over lighting the topcoat. Because of the hat we use two spots from the rear, one on either side, just missing the ears but giving a touch of accent on each side of the face. A small spot, directly behind him, illuminates the background and provides the needed separation. No, the coat collar is not "riding up" in this case; we deliberately turned it up a little to provide a touch of "get up and go." Both main source and fill-in, by the way, were kept rather low to assure sufficient illumination below the hat brim and for that reason they had to be feathered up to avoid too much light on the coat.

Even the clergy now and then break into print and find new portraits necessary although, bluntly speaking, they are not normally good prospects for photographs because of our American predilection for paying ministers as little as possible. Those whose congregations are large and prosperous, and who draw decent salaries as a result, are in the minority. Often, however a good portrait of a popular minister or priest may have sales possibilities far beyond his immediate family, aside from being excellent window display material. So when a member of the cloth makes one of his rare appearances before your camera, accept it as a challenge and put forth your best efforts. The subject of *Figure 44* is a minister and, being a personage of large and commanding stature, a three quarter view is almost a requisite instead

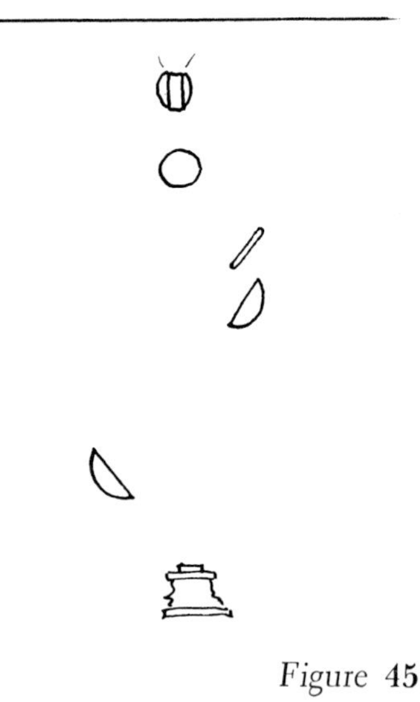

Figure 45

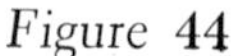

Figure 44

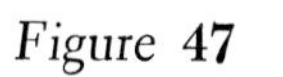

Figure 47

Figure 46

of the customary head and shoulders. Such a subject, accustomed to appearing in public, can be trusted to assume his own pose and only few alterations will be necessary or advisable.

Ministers are more patient than most people, yet they too are busy men and will appreciate seeing that you know your job and can portray them speedily. Correct posture is an old story to them—they know more about how they should appear than you so that your chief task is to watch the little things that make for perfection in the final picture. A pose such as this calls for the most simple standard lighting: main source and fill-in plus a spot behind the figure to bring out the shoulder lines in the manner we mentioned earlier, all as in *Figure 45*. A smiling expression is uncalled for with such a subject—an attitude of interest and sympathy is more in order. The taller the subject the higher your lights should be and to keep the hands subdued so they retain characterization and yet do not clash with the face, both lights should be feathered up. A very simple lighting, requiring a minimum of equipment. If your subject is wearing a clerical collar and vestments, then probably a seated pose will be more suitable but in any event, and even though he specifies a head and shoulder portrait, include at least one three quarter view in your set of proofs. The identical lighting will still apply.

There are times when wrinkles in the clothes are literally part of the subject and if he is to look natural and be recognizable to his friends and associates, aside from the fact that any attempt to straighten them out will practically involve wrestling him all over the camera room, he must be portrayed "as is." That was the case with the subject of *Figure 46*, a rather heavy, kindly man, deeply religious, and the head of a considerable chain of stores. A busy individual, and a bit hard of hearing, he himself had no desire for a photograph but his directors decided a portrait of him should hang in each of the stores and he deferred to their wishes. The last thing they wanted was for him to appear the stern, dignified business tycoon. This

Figure **49**

Figure **48**

was a matter of public relations and it was important to display him as a firm, though kindly, individual, "natural as an old shoe," whose unexpected visit to any store in the chain would not throw terror into the manager and the clerks and whom any customer would be happy to meet.

Seating him, we had him hold a book in his accustomed manner but while resting his hands on a small posing table in front of him, to maintain steadiness. Assuring ourselves that he was quite comfortable we let him severely alone until all was ready, when a request to "look up" was the only thing necessary. The main source and fill-in remain as before, but to illuminate the top of the head and also throw some light on the shoulders we added a boom spot overhead (*Figure 47*). Instead of a spot behind him we used a small background light to provide a more diffused effect. In this case we are not making a portrait for reproduction, but a negative from which a number of finished enlargements are to be made, each to be framed and prominently hung in a store. We can forget about the sharpness so necessary for the engraver and aim for something more pictorial. We have here what might be called a formal portrait with informal treatment.

Let us close this Chapter with a type of subject whom you will find before your camera more and more in the years to come, a college senior who is at the same time a war veteran (*Figure 48*). The "college" or "year book" portrait of a callow youth is not for such as he. He has already been out in the world, has met many of life's challenges and is mentally far beyond the ordinary college senior stage. Men like this, in their early thirties, whose careers have been interrupted by military service, are more serious than the average and what they seek is a good "family" portrait. They want to look dignified, but not too much so, to appear manly and yet well groomed. To give our sitter a touch of masculinity we bring his hand to his chin and while his forehead evidences intellectuality we do not want to emphasize it so we are careful not to place our spot at left rear too high. All we want is a little touch of light on the hair. Again, to keep from drawing attention to the high forehead and rather large top of the head, we use a small spot behind him to keep the light on the background around the shoulders and thus not outline the head as a whole. The diagram (*Figure 49*) speaks for itself. Careful feathering of the lights maintains the modeling of the face. The result is conservative, but neither static nor dull, two points you must always bear in mind when your subject is an older man. Static and even dull he may well be—some men, once seated, seem almost lifeless—but unless you can engender that essential spark of animation your portrait will be a failure. You may at times have to snap your subject out of his lethargy with a deliberately rude comment, for which you can always smilingly apologize when you have clicked the shutter. But, no matter how, wake him up!

CHAPTER 7

The Small Fry

If it were not for youngsters, bless their hearts, photographic portraiture as such would be in a bad way because photography of the small fry represents fifty per cent or more of the total business of the every day professional. While adults on the average, once they have passed their twenties, are seldom photographed more than once each decade, most children are portrayed several times during their first year of existence and often once a year thereafter until they reach their teens. Thus children are by far the largest and most important field for the portraitist and, except for the comparatively few studios that genuinely specialize in adults, woe betide the professional who cannot record, for doting parents, the cute expressions and familiar poses of their offspring.

Far in the minority are those photographers who profess to think of youngsters as "small adults" and believe that, in the camera room, they should be treated accordingly. Such cameramen make no pretense of bending from their accustomed dignity and refuse to—as they feel—"belittle" themselves by attempting to make friends with children, play with them, or make them feel at home. This attitude is usually the result of their own shyness or lack of understanding of children, plus an unrealized mental refusal to attempt the adjustments necessary to accept children as they really are—beings of a totally different world—rather than insufferable little nuisances who disrupt the normal calm of their studios. That such photographers do nevertheless succeed in producing good portraits of children cannot be denied but to them every such sitting is an effort and a strain, with a feeling of mutual gratification on the part of all concerned when it is over. Usually they are men —sometimes women—who do not really like children but, photography being what it is, cannot afford to refuse them as subjects. Such success as they attain in the portraiture of children is accomplished the hard way, and it is all unnecessary because this is a situation which can be corrected.

If you suffer from such inhibitions and want to be really successful in portraiture you will do well to make a determined effort to understand and like youngsters until you can honestly welcome their appearance before your camera. Unless you are a most hardened and determined hater of children, this faculty can be developed but you must work at it until your liking for them becomes genuine and is no mere crust over your real feelings because youngsters can sense your sincere friendship, or utter dislike, instinctively and almost immediately.

Today's children are quite different from those of years gone by once they have outgrown the baby stage. Television and radio, as well as modern ideas in the education of children—and even more so the current parental attitude toward their activities—have caused them to be far more of a problem. It is very nearly impossible today to tell a child arbitrarily to do this or that; the modern child wants to know why and expects to have it explained to him in language he can understand. Yet these facts have been over weighed in our favor by advances in photographic technique. The long exposures of yesteryear are no longer necessary, thanks to modern lighting equipment, faster lenses and films which combine far greater speed with tremendous latitude. It is comparatively easy nowadays to catch in a brief sitting expressions and poses which took earlier photographers anywhere from an hour to half a day.

It is still necessary to retain the attention and interest of these small subjects and that means they must be entertained. Your success as a photographer of babies and children will depend almost entirely on your ability to keep them happy and occupied while they are before your camera. There are undoubtedly as many methods of accomplishing this as there are photographers, ranging all the way from getting down on one's hands and knees and cavorting around the camera room to the use of simple magic tricks and the addition to your stock in trade of live props such as birds, dogs and cats. Baby talk in general is outmoded and will not improve your standing with the parents. Fortunately there is one generally accepted method, open to everyone, of occupying all younger children both mentally and physically and that is by the use of simple toys.

These need not be expensive, rather they should be of a type that you can buy in reasonable quantity, and present as a memento of the occasion to your subject when the sitting is over. Beware, especially when you are dealing with the very young, of toys so small that they can be promptly popped in the mouth and of those with sharp edges with which children are likely to cut themselves. And all must be spotlessly clean. If you do have some available that you can give to the child then you can afford to invest in a few more costly toys as permanent studio props. Bouncing monkeys, swinging acrobats, animals that walk, make noises or whose eyes light up, are all sure holders of attention. Small puppets which you can slip over your left hand and operate with the fingers to hold attention, while you are manipulating the bulb behind your back with your other hand, are almost sure fire. For babies and very small children few toys are better than the almost universally used rubber ball, preferably a bright red. To go into greater detail on this would involve more than our space warrants although we shall offer some additional suggestions in discussing the illustrations. Suffice it to say that you are going to have to join your subjects in playing with these toys if you expect to keep them happy and secure expressions that will please the parents.

When dealing with smaller children your basic lighting setup will not be greatly altered—at least so far as standard poses are concerned—with the exception that

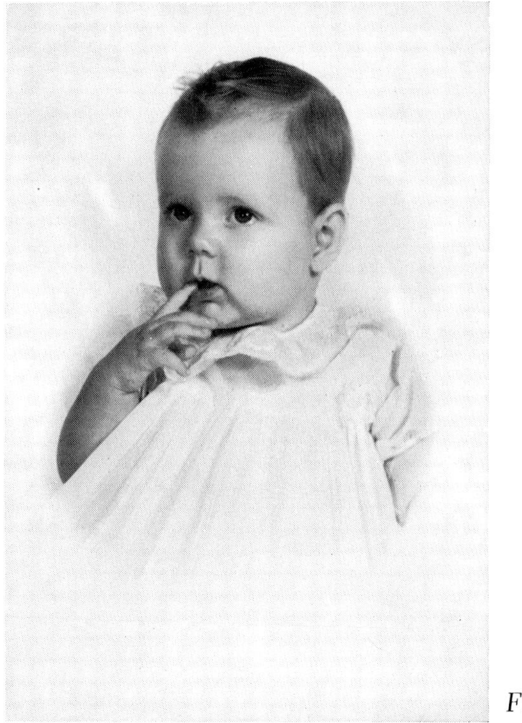

Figure **50**

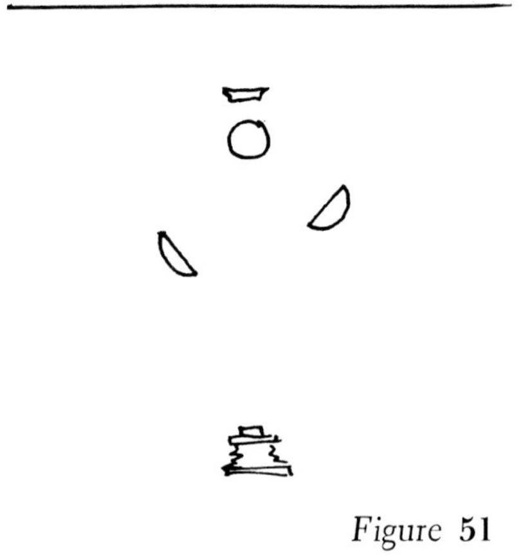

Figure **51**

due to the smaller height of your subjects it will be necessary to bring your lights closer to the floor and adopt a lesser ratio (distance) between your main source and fill-in. Remember that deep shadows are normally out of place in portraits of chil-

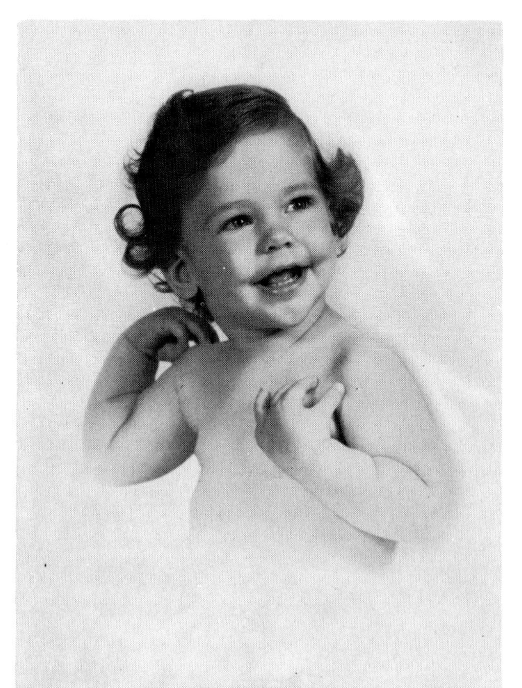

Figure **52**

dren and that working in a high key, plus the maintenance of a somewhat airy atmosphere, is preferable. With adults, because they can hold a pose and follow instructions, it is possible to adjust the lights, move them back and forth and work at a somewhat slower tempo.

Your best method with children will be to place your main source, fill-in and background light beforehand, having established a predetermined position for the child. The problem then becomes simply that of keeping the youngster at that position by holding his interest and attention while watching intently for poses and expressions and being ready to trip the shutter the instant you see what you want. Another reason for placement of lighting equipment in advance is that children tire easily and become bored even more quickly so that once the youngster is in place, the more rapidly you can make your exposures and change your film holders the better. An assistant, to change holders, focus the camera, and occasionally manipulate a particular toy, is most helpful.

High key portraits on white or near white backgrounds seem to have most appeal to the average parent and it is well to bear in mind that if you want your backgrounds to be white and clean you should develop such films about twenty five per cent to a third longer than you normally develop those with gray or darker backgrounds, regardless of the light source you may be using. In this connection you will note that our first two illustrations are darkroom vignettes so, for those unfamiliar with these, a word or two about how they are produced may be helpful.

Children in general, certainly those very small as well as those who are most active, cannot be posed in the customary manner as we have already explained. Consequently it often happens that an exposure may result in a very pleasing expression or body pose but that the extremities—hands or feet or both—are quite unsatisfactory or perhaps show a move. The experienced photographer can still work up such a negative into a good print by "vignetting out" the displeasing portion. There are several devices on the market for making darkroom vignettes, but a very simple method is to lay over the negative a sheet of not too thick red paper and outline in pencil thereon that part of the subject you want to retain, then cutting out with scissors the outlined portion. The balance of the sheet, with the opening remaining in the center, is used as a mask.

During projection printing (enlarging) it is held between the enlarging lens and the paper on the easel; when contact printing it is placed *under* the plate glass top on the printer, the thickness of the glass usually being sufficient to avoid the edges of the mask from printing in too sharply. In projection printing it is wise to keep this mask moving slightly to avoid a sharp cutting off of the image, this movement achieving the same purpose as the thickness of the glass when contact printing. If you over develop as suggested you will not have to be too precise about moving the mask. The whole idea is to secure a very gradual blending of the image into the white background. It goes almost without saying that the photographer who wants to deliver really appealing portraits of children will make practically all of them against white or light backgrounds and of course that is imperative if you know beforehand that you expect to vignette, because vignettes of children against dark backgrounds are not too pleasing.

Even a vignette on a light background should be worked up with a "sketch effect" on the finished print to break up the severity of the plain light ground. No vignetted

Figure **53**

Figure **54**

portrait on a white background will have a really finished—or professional—effect unless this is done (See *Figures 50* and *52*) to bridge the otherwise sudden transition from the image to total whiteness. While this sketch effect does require a bit of skill, practice on a few discarded prints will soon afford you the necessary dexterity. It is done with what professionals call "crayon sauce" which is made as follows. Secure from your photo supply dealer or any firm dealing in artists' materials a small quantity of dry black pigment such as ivory black or lamp black, and mix that with any inexpensive white talcum powder until you arrive at the shade of gray you want. Using a small pad of dry cotton batting, apply the mixture lightly to the surface of your print around those parts of the image where you feel the treatment is desirable and wipe off any excess with another clean dry pad of cotton batting. This will leave a gray tint around the image. Next, using a clean eraser, work in your sketch effect by eliminating parts of the gray tint and leaving whatever shape or design you prefer. If, as will probably happen with your first attempts, what remains stands out too sharply or is too deep in tone, you can cut it down and soften it by gently rubbing it down with another fresh clean dry pad of cotton.

Do not accept it as an axiom that a smile is essential to every child portrait. *Figure 50* is an excellent example of a nonsmiling portrait which captivates because of the serious, thoughtful expression. This was caught on the spur of the moment because we thought the finger in the mouth was what really made the picture. It was a moment of hesitation while the baby coyly wondered what we were about to do next with the toy we were showing and the result is a sort of "age of innocence" picture that parents will keep and cherish. A portrait with such an expression will be looked at time and again because it has far more appeal than a smile, however attractive. As the lighting diagram (*Figure 51*) indicates, we have here the simplest form of a standard lighting, consisting of nothing more than main source, fill-in and background light, all of them much closer to the floor than in the case of an adult subject, and with the fill-in brought closer to the young sitter. Notice the bit of sketch effect (already explained) worked into the background to break up the otherwise severe treatment of a straight vignette.

The subject of *Figure 52* is a year old little lady with a smile that no true lover of children could resist. The lighting placement is the same (*Figure 51*) and again the vignette has been softened by just a faint sketch effect in the background. This interested upward look was the result of bouncing a monkey (a ball or anything similar would do) on the floor and catching it rather high in the air. We were primarily seeking an open mouthed smile which we had noticed earlier but the subject unexpectedly cooperated by raising her arms and we were Johnny-on-the-spot with the bulb. You must be eternally watchful when photographing children if you expect expressions like this and, we might point out, your watchfulness should commence when you first see the child because that is your opportunity to note, while the youngster is not on guard, any particularly appealing expressions or poses so that later, before the camera, you may be able to recognize and record them.

In *Figure 53* we come to "Miss Personality", a well behaved little miss of not quite four. To hold her attention and secure this interested expression we required the services of a mechanical kitten, in this case operated by an assistant. We told this little miss we knew she was a "big girl" and could hold the little parasol just the way we wanted her to do. Flattered at being treated as an individual, as children of this age usually are, she was more than willing to cooperate by accepting that important—as we made it appear—responsibility. This youngster really had personality and we felt it essential to produce a portrait that would adequately display it. Parents will not readily tire of a picture like this. Because this young lady was so

Figure **56**

Figure **55**

agreeable it was possible for us to elaborate on our lighting (*Figure 54*) by adding two spots at left and right rear which added translucency to the parasol, held it in sufficiently light key to act as a frame for the head and also provided enough light through the parasol on the hair to avoid any blocked up shadows. Note also that, this being a three quarter and the subject somewhat larger, it was possible to return the main source and fill-in lights to their normal positions.

Moving on in our age brackets we have in *Figure 55* a ten year old who has reached the stage where clothes are beginning to be consequential. Not yet a teen ager, she is at least in her own estimation "growing up" and thus her hat, gloves and pretty dress are a matter of real concern to her. At this age, with girls in any event, toys and other devices as a means of keeping the subject in place are not only unnecessary but an insult to a child's intelligence. You can go to some trouble in posing such a child and feel assured that the pose will be held because the youngster is fully as interested as her parents in a portrait that will do her justice. Getting the right expression is what is important here and while the subject will be only too anxious to cooperate she will tend to be self conscious and you will have to be on guard for an expression that is genuine and not "put on." Conversation must be your chief dependence in dealing with children like this and you will have to make an effort to learn something about subjects which are important to them. By all means do not "talk down" to them, or they will lose respect for you. School, pets, boy friends and the like are most apt to evoke the expressions you seek. For this effect a standard lighting is sufficient with a boom light at right rear to pick up the hat —important to the child—and hold the outline and detail of the hair. This, incidentally (See *Figure 56*) is not a boom spot because when dealing with children we do not need as intense a light as a spot produces. Instead, while affixed to the

Figure **57**

Figure **58**

Figure **59**

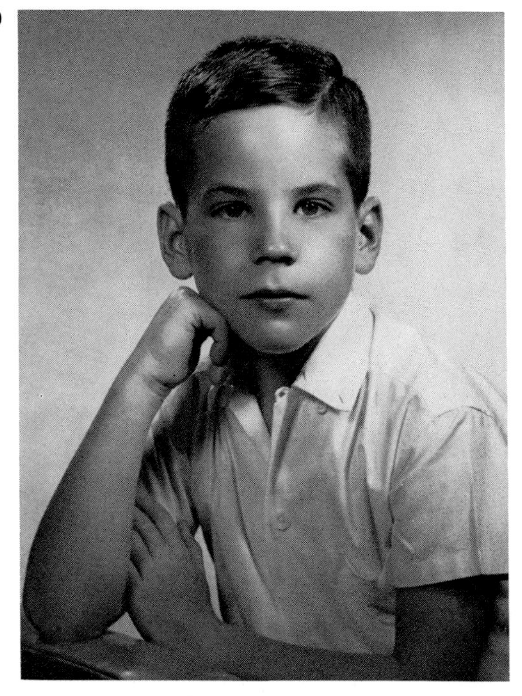

boom for convenience, it is a small light in a reflector, of the type known as a "highlighter."

Active young boys such as the fifteen month subject we have in *Figure* 57 are often rather difficult to control. Most of them are "all boy" and if your portrait is to be at all realistic and to show the youngster as his parents know him any attempt at "taming him down" will destroy the very feeling of exuberance you want to convey. To keep him interested you will have to "put on an act" and keep chattering away. For a subject like this you will have to take snap judgment as to what you think will work out best, arrange your lights and have everything ready before you place him in position. Having decided in advance on the effect we wanted, we added to the standard arrangement of main source and fill-in a boom light (not a boom spot) at left rear (*Figure* 58), seated him on a low bench and, keeping constantly in action, awaited the appropriate moment. In this case we were using speedlights which, whenever you are dealing with an active youngster, are a life saver and enabled us to "catch him on the wing." It is an absolute waste of time to try and pose arms and hands, legs and feet when your subject is a vivacious boy in this age bracket. Spontaneity is the only answer and in addition to producing portraits that are full of life, the avoidance of attempts at deliberate posing will save you many an ulcer in later life.

You will be fortunate indeed when your subject is an older boy with a mind of his own, like the handsome young chap we have chosen for *Figure* 59, an eight year old. A young chap like this will really get into the spirit of things if you and his parents will only give him the chance. Our first pose of this boy portrayed him more formally, in accordance with his mother's wishes, but without creating any disturbance about it he made it clear that what he really wanted was to be shown in his shirt, with his collar open. He was so polite about it that we promptly won his whole hearted support by assuring him we would make a picture exactly like that. We went on to explain that we would have to pose him and it would be necessary for him to be patient and still, to all of which he agreed. Again we called into play a boom light and, having won his confidence, were able to arrange his arms and hands just as we wanted them. Except for some slight adjustment of the lights, and a bit more feathering away from the subject of the main source and fill-in, their placement is identical with *Figure 58*, and the result is something both he and his parents will enjoy for years to come. This is a portrait we like to think of as presenting a Typical American Boy, sturdy and strong minded, but not overbearing, which latter we implied by not letting him clinch the hand at his chin into a fist.

CHAPTER 8

"Novelty" Poses of Children

There have been certain developments in the fields of advertising and illustration during the past several years which have indeed been a blessing to the studio photographer in his work with children. We have in mind the original and amusing portraits of youngsters which have appeared in book form and have also been syndicated in newspapers throughout the country by Constance Bannister, as well as the use of child subjects in advertising illustration by Ruth Nichols, to mention two of the most noted specialists in this field. They have done much to broaden the general concept of child portraiture because parents everywhere have seen examples of their work in magazines and newspapers, and because every mother is convinced —and this is perfectly natural—that her own offspring is "every bit as cute" as those she has seen on the printed page, she is far more receptive to the idea of including in a set of proofs one or two poses which depart from the customary. Except in the rare cases where a child has some natural deformity which the photographer will have to conceal or subdue, more likely than not she herself will bring up the subject and ask for something "cute."

This should pose no serious problem because nearly every small subject sooner or later develops some particular trick, stunt or antic which the parents proudly show off upon the slightest provocation. In fact both Miss Bannister and Mrs. Nichols are frank to admit that they are not blessed with any specially talented youngsters as subjects and their secret lies solely in their willingness to spend the time necessary to induce each youngster to perform, an effort which the parents eagerly abet. Often securing an exceptionally appealing pose or expression may be the purest accident but in any event the cameraman must watch his subject like a hawk, ready to pounce upon opportunity whenever it presents itself. The illustrations we have selected for this Chapter are direct examples of what we have been saying because none of them were especially posed for this purpose except the last (*Figure 67*) which was planned though not deliberately "posed." All, in fact, were selected from existing negative files and in each case prints were delivered as part

Figure **60**

of a regular order. Pictures like this have what the advertising fraternity call "stopping power" and if the reader is a studio owner he will find that no window or showcase display he can prepare will draw as much attention and comment as one built around chidren's portraits which have, like most of these, a humorous touch.

Primarily, however, you must remember that poses like these are the frosting on the cake, so to speak, and that is the reason why these appear in a separate chapter. First, as we explained in Chapter 7, your effort must be for a direct likeness and —by all means—the "smile" that every mother wants. Devote your attention first to portraying the youngster before your camera in the typical poses the parents expect, making mental notes while you work of poses or expressions which seem to have added possibilities. Once you are sure of a good standard set of proofs, by which time you should have secured the child's confidence and friendship, go a little beyond what the parents anticipated and try for something a bit off the beaten track.

As a professional you should know—or will soon learn—what your average revenue must be from every sitting if you are to pay your bills, allow yourself a reasonable salary, and show a business profit in addition. Any competent professional has a well founded understanding of what can be expected, in the form of an order, from a good set of proofs. It is the sale of prints from added poses which the

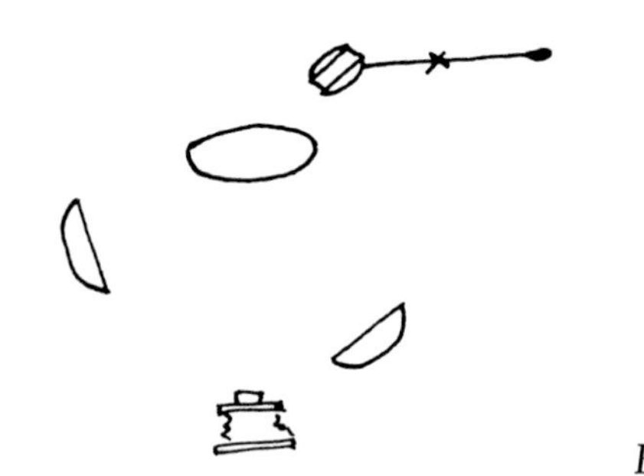

Figure **61**

parents were not expecting that will "put the jam on your bread," because your studio overhead goes on relentlessly and a certain portion of it is chargeable the moment a customer enters your door. Your aim must always be to increase the average revenue per sitting and, with children as your subjects, out of the ordinary poses are the most certain method of accomplishing this.

If, having accumulated a fair quantity of such photographs, you do decide to make use of them in a window display, you will find that catchy or amusing titles will add greatly to their interest and because these illustrations were at one time used in just that manner, we are quoting in connection with each the title that we thought appropriate. These, of course, are only suggestions but they will perhaps aid you or your receptionist when the time comes to show your proofs.

All of us are only too familiar with the standard pose of a baby, usually in the nude, lying on its tummy on a blanket or fur rug. As a rule the child is shown facing the camera with the head seeming much too large for the body, a situation exaggerated because a child's head is in any event much larger in proportion to the length of its body than the head of an adult. In such a pose the child is badgered until it looks up at the camera with considerable strain on its neck and probably with a rather dazed expression. The little tyke is thoroughly uncomfortable, wonders what it is all about and wishes it were over. Why not, instead of posing the baby in a manner which will be an unfailing source of embarrassment in later years, leave its clothes on—after all the mother is probably proud of the layette—and permit it to disport itself in a perfectly natural manner?

Consider *Figure 60* in which the baby, comfortable, safe and unhampered, lies on its back on a large cushion or other padded surface and is photographed from the side. At that age and in that position a baby will almost automatically play with its feet and, to give its toes added attraction, we remove one little stocking and bootee. While thus pleasantly engaged and seeking attention as babies always do, it will look at the photographer but without any visible strain. "Look What I Found" is a title that comes immediately to mind and what mother, no matter what other poses have been selected for the assorted relatives, will not insist on at least one finished print of this for herself? Our two chief lights (*Figure 61*) appear in approximately their customary positions, but their function is reversed because the one near the camera is now the main source and the other becomes the fill-in. In addition, because in this case we have a horizontal subject and must preserve its roundness and three dimensional effect, we need some top and back light. For this, above the baby and somewhat to the rear, a boom spot is just the thing but because we are dealing with a baby and should never, with such a subject, use a powerful light close by, a 150–watt lamp is ample. Also, as soon as you have satisfied yourself as to your modeling with that spot, turn it off if you have any other adjustments to make and do not turn it on until you are ready to make the exposure.

The "bread and butter" part of your sitting over, if you are dealing with a small child not too greatly out of the baby class, it is sometimes well to place a piece of child's furniture such as a small chair or table in place in the set, give the youngster some small toy and suggest that it be placed on the chair or table. Knowing what you have in mind you will already have focused on that position and all you then need do is to await developments. The small, pudgy arms and legs of children are always graceful even though their actions may at times be awkward or perhaps ludicrous. The little girl shown in *Figure 62* is very carefully following her instructions and what gives this picture its humorous touch is her serious concentration on what she is doing, all unaware of the little bulge of panty she is exposing. The title "Oops! My Slip's Showing!" resulted in many smiles over this print. The lighting placement (*Figure 63*) is simple indeed, with the main source at the right and the fill-in by the camera, with a spot to illuminate the background. To concentrate interest on the figure the upper corners were burned in during printing.

The term "burning in" will not be new to most of our readers, but for the others a brief word of explanation is advisable. This is really just another form of "dodging" while enlarging. Ordinarily the purpose of dodging is to hold back certain portions of an image so they will not print too lightly. Burning in is the reverse. Using a card, roughly trimmed to the right size and affixed to a piece of wire, the major portion of the image is covered so the light only strikes the corners of the print or whatever portion it is desired to have a bit darker. The card is of course kept in slight motion to avoid any sharp line or falling off at the edges of the burned in portion. Ordinarily that will require as much again as the original exposure but because this depends entirely on the effect desired—and sometimes only a slight touch of added tone is wanted—no hard and fast rules can be established. You will have to experiment with your own negatives and enlarger but it is a simple trick and proficiency will come to you very quickly.

Our next two illustrations, *Figures 64* and *65*, are very typical of the baby pictures we already mentioned, popularized by Miss Bannister, and show how easy it is for any photographer to produce portraits of youngsters which are sufficiently different

Figure **63**

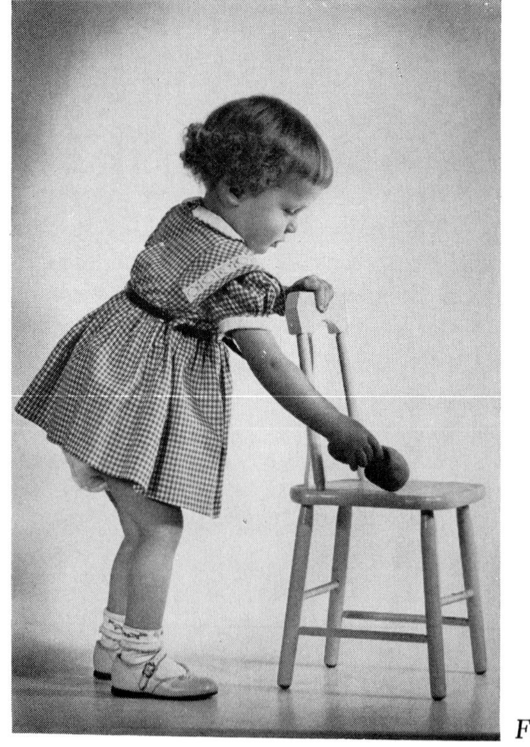

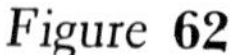

Figure **62**

Figure **64**

Figure **65**

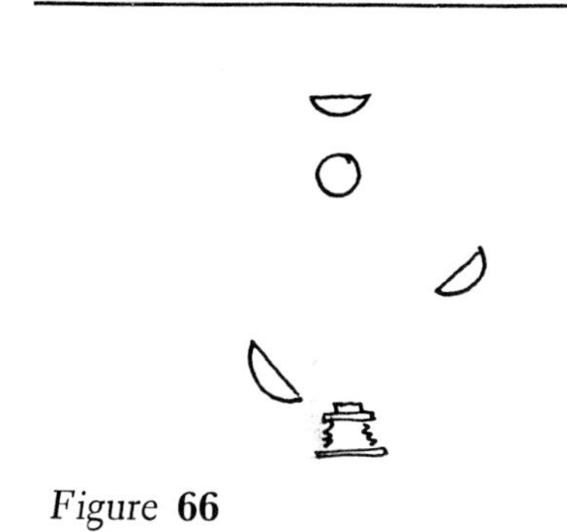

Figure **66**

Figure **67**

and amusing to appeal to even such normally *blasé* individuals as newspaper editors. The photographer who can accumulate a number of these not only has material for window displays but can often sell the editor of his local paper on the idea of running them as a series under a standing head and over the photographer's credit line, an inexpensive method of securing the finest type of publicity. Of course in every case a written release must be secured from the parents but once such a series starts that photographer will almost certainly find himself being approached by other parents who are anxious to see their children similarly publicized. Again the lighting could hardly be simpler and in the case of these two, although they were made of different youngsters and months apart, one diagram (*Figure 66*) will suffice for both. The main source and fill-in are in their accustomed positions and in each case a background light is placed behind the small subject. Note that the corners of these were also burned in during printing. We titled *Figure 64* "That's Too Embarrassing to Think About" and *Figure 65* "I'm More the Executive Type."

Two youngsters in one photograph are, obviously, more interesting than one, although much more difficult to catch on film in a pose which does justice to both.

Figure **68**

Children in any event are so active that every child portrait is to a certain extent a compromise. One soon learns to disregard minor errors of composition, and even an occasional move of a hand or finger, when an expression or pose is otherwise so obviously natural and pleasing that it would be folly to discard it. Rarely is one able to plan a composition when portraying a child, and with more than one child success in such an effort must largely be attributed to good fortune.

Figure 67 was deliberately planned. Having satisfied the parents with several groups in customary arrangements, we found these youngsters to be such an affectionate young couple that we decided to take a chance on another film or two. We told the little girl that if she would kiss her brother—they were sitting side by side on a small bench—we would have our monkey puppet (an accessory which had greatly aroused her interest) kiss her. She obliged so quickly that we completely missed the first exposure and had to ask that she repeat, which she seemed happy to do. The parents were delighted with this photograph, which we later titled "Aw, Shoot! They Caught Us!" and which still attracts attention each time it is displayed. As the diagram (*Figure 68*) indicates, our lighting was reversed, the main source being now close in on the left with the fill-in at the right of the camera. A background light behind the figures, and burning in the corners while printing, completed this unusual little group which finds its charm in the little girl's watchful eye and her brother's suppressed smile, without which combination the title we selected would have been meaningless.

Let us concede before we leave the subject of children that the illustrations in this and the previous chapter, thoroughly satisfactory though they are as examples of professional child portraiture, would not in most cases "make the grade" when it comes to winning ribbons or awards in convention picture exhibits or photographic salons. The average mother has not the slightest interest in your achievements along those lines; what is important to her is your ability (or lack of it) to produce portraits of her children that will please her. Accomplish that and so far as children are concerned you will have few worries. If your craftsmanship is equivalent in quality to what we have shown here we can assure you that it will be at least as good as your competition and in most cases better.

CHAPTER 9

Posing and Lighting: The Bridal Portrait

The uninitiated reader, especially if he has looked ahead and discovered that two chapters, which follow very shortly, are devoted respectively to three-quarter and full-length poses, will wonder why it is necessary to devote still another chapter to the portraiture of brides, who are, ninety per cent of the time, portrayed full length or in a three-quarter position. Professionals so thoroughly recognize bridal portraiture as a problem in itself that in their contests, convention picture exhibits, and the like, it is always set up as one of the five main classifications in portraiture, *i.e.*: men, women, children, brides, and groups. There is a very logical reason for considering a bride—in her wedding gown, of course, because we are dealing here with formal bridal portraits—as a photographic problem quite different from the average female subject.

No other event in a woman's life is as important to her, and her family, as her wedding. And, from the woman's viewpoint at least, nothing connected with her wedding—and we include the groom—is as important as her wedding gown and veil. The bride and her mother (assuming the latter to be living, and if not, her closest female relatives and friends) will have spent not only hours but days of thought and worry in the consideration and selection of her wedding finery, and in many cases the gown will represent the largest single financial investment in connection with the entire affair. Consequently, the photographer is expected to produce not only a portrait that will make the bride appear as charming and attractive as possible, but a picture of the gown, veil, and headdress which will enhance them to the fullest extent.

The style of the gown, its embroidery or other adornments, and its train, if any, must all receive not only adequate but fully accurate consideration. If there is a lacy, sheer overskirt, it must be lighted to disclose the heavier fabric beneath. If the gown is satin, its shimmering sleekness must appear in the photograph, while if it is brocade, the picture which does not make the fact readily recognizable will be a failure. In other words, a formal bridal portrait must be two things: a portrait likeness of the wearer, and what really amounts to a commercial illustrator's appreciation of the gown.

There are two schools of thought with respect to the portraiture of brides. Some professionals feel that a bride should always be photographed against a white or very light background, basing their judgment on the theory that the airy atmospheric effect thus obtained is more suitable to such a joyous occasion. On the other hand, if the chief reason for a formal bridal portrait is to provide prints for eventual appearance on the society pages of the local newspapers, a dark or black background is far more suitable. The photographer must bear in mind the reproduction problems inherent in the coarse screen engraving process necessary, due to the fact that newsprint is perhaps the most unsuitable material extant on which to print a halftone engraving. Few if any of the fine halftone engravings used in this book, for example, would look like more than smudged black areas if they appeared in a newspaper. For newspaper engravings a certain amount of contrast is essential, and a bride and her gown will appear to best advantage if a black or dark background is used.

For that reason, the two full length pictures used to illustrate this chapter (*Figures* 69 and 71) are both made against black backgrounds. They could have been taken just as easily against white backgrounds with practically the identical lighting arrangements. But then the backgrounds would have had to be thoroughly illuminated, not as we have shown heretofore with one light behind the subject, but with two spots or broad lights directed against the background from either side of the subject, in order to assure allover even lighting. Care would also have had to be taken in the use of the other lights shown in the diagrams (*Figures* 70 and 72), to avoid overlighting or "burning out" the edges of the gowns and veils (here silhouetted against the black backgrounds), in order to avoid their

Figure **69**

Figure **70**

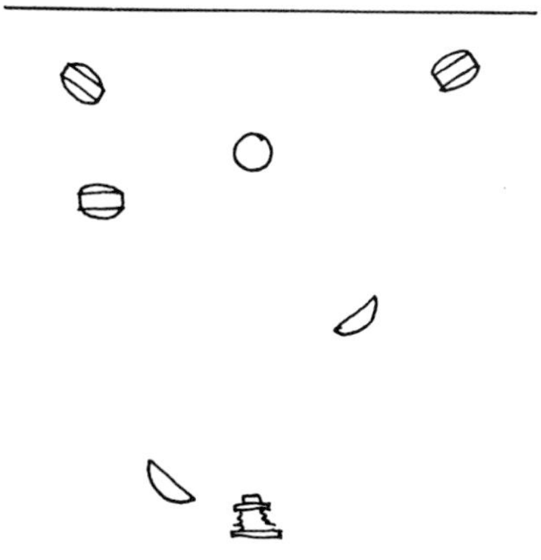

merging into the white background and becoming lost. The fact is that the photography of white costumes against white backgrounds is one of the more difficult effects to produce properly, and can only be achieved as the result of considerable practice and experiment. Therefore, we are not discussing it in detail in these pages. For all practical purposes, the illustrations and diagrams we are presenting will give the reader what he needs for immediate results, and the rest is necessarily up to him.

A few additional factors warrant emphasis before we concern ourselves with the illustrations. Remember that most bridal gowns are white in themselves and that any ornamentation—often considerable—will also be white. Overlighting the gown and veil, therefore, will result in disaster because the all-important details will be lost. To avoid this, make sure that your main source and fill-in lights are well feathered *up*, so that what you have is an allover soft illumination instead of a flood of direct light. Sometimes you will find that a little added "punch" or emphasis is needed to accentuate folds or draping by adding a bit more shadow or pattern. If so, at right or left front of the subject, add a small spot opened for a broad light and direct this across the gown as a "cross lighting," but be sure to feather it away from the gown, so that this cross lighting does not result either in burning out the material, or in heavy, blocked-out shadows.

In so far as the bride herself is concerned, an almost invariably good rule to follow is to keep the body edgewise to the camera. This tends to give the pose a feeling of action, and in addition is normally more flattering because the body and waist will appear slimmer, always a matter of importance to the bride. Remember, too, that a wedding is a joyous occasion, a truly big event, and that a sober or studied expression is out of place. "How sweet she looks!" is the comment that a successful bridal portrait should elicit, so that what you should aim for facially is a gentle, happy smile.

Figure 69 illustrates at once two of the points we have just mentioned. This young lady has a nice slim waist so we have posed her sideways to the camera to emphasize it, and to bring out its small size even more, have avoided concealing it by having her bring her arms up above, with the hands clasping a small Bible. Notice the careful posing of the hands, much as it is explained in the chapter on that subject. Notice also that since the girl is rather tall, we have had her tilt her head slightly, because a bridal gown has a tendency to make any subject look even taller than she already is. The lighting in *Figure 70* is in no sense complex, with our main source and fill-in lights approximately in their customary positions, although a bit farther away from the subject than normal because of the full figure. In bridal portraits it is very important that the veil appear translucent and not solid, and this is accomplished by means of the two spots at left and right rear. Both the main source and fill-in, as advised earlier, are feathered up to avoid overlighting the gown, and to make sure the lace of the overskirt is not lost against the white underneath it, we have used an additional small spot at left for the needed cross lighting. No light is thrown on the background, which consists of wide black seamless paper drawn from a ceiling roll. Wide seamless paper of this sort is a rather modern development, but today can be secured, in many colors, from almost any dealer in photographic supplies.

A glossy print from the negative of such a session can be submitted to any newspaper with full confidence that the reproduction will not only please the

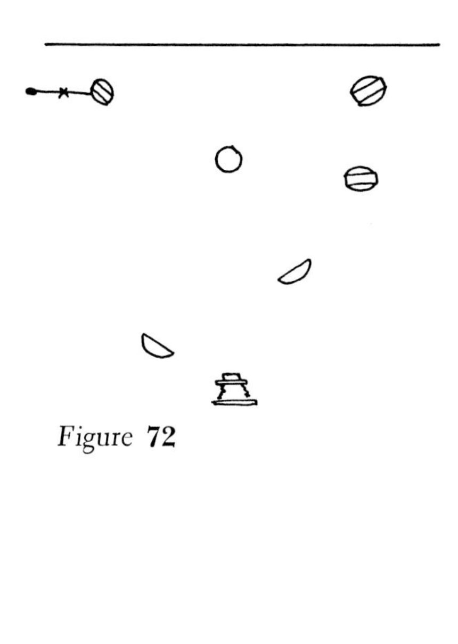

Figure 72

Figure 71

bride but will do justice to your credit line. It is, we might add, quite all right to cut off a small part of the skirt, as at the right, when it would be obviously impossible to include it all without pulling the camera so far back that the figure would be much too small. This gown, like that in *Figure 71,* does not have a train. When a gown does have a long train—and these are seldom seen nowadays except at the most elaborate high society weddings, and seldom if ever in the average community—that train must be included. This is usually accomplished by swirling it around in front of the figure, or by taking a horizontal instead of a vertical photograph, although then the figure will necessarily be somewhat smaller.

As the arm itself discloses, in the case of the bride in *Figure 71* we are dealing with a young lady who is not quite as slim as the other, but who, on the other hand, happens to have a very sweetly smiling and attractive profile. The arm is very graceful, with a nice dimple at the elbow, so we place it with a bouquet, both to conceal the waist line and also to give us an additional accent to break the otherwise monotonous and uninteresting front line of this fairly unelaborate gown. Never let an arm and bouquet hang straight down along the side of the gown, because the result will be an accent in the center of your composition which will draw attention away from the face. Our lighting arrangement for *Figure 72* leaves our main source and fill-in much as they were in *Figure 70*—remember to feather them up—but the other lights require a few changes. One spot remains at the right rear to illuminate the veil, but at left rear we have placed a boom spot to provide an edge light on the profile, and at the right we have placed a small spot, feathered away from the subject, for a cross lighting on the gown. Again the wide black seamless paper serves as a background. All quite simple, but very effective.

Now for a situation which arises frequently in the smaller communities where

Figure 73

Figure 74

the newspapers—and remember that a primary reason for formal bridal portraits is "to get them in the paper"—are reluctant to publish too many such pictures and frequently set a limit on the size halftone they will use, often nothing more than what is called a "single column cut." The reader, if he is a professional, will know this from past experience, and if not, should make it his business to find out. When a full-length portrait is reduced to column width (little over two inches), the face will be almost lost, to say nothing of the detail of the gown. It is not always easy to convince a bride and her parents of this, but it must be explained tactfully if you are to retain their good will. One solution is to submit to the paper a glossy print showing only the upper portion of the full-length pose, which will mean submitting an enlargement from that part of the negative. If you do not do this yourself, but submit the complete print, the paper's engraver will either reduce the entire print, or will crop out the head and shoulders as he sees fit, which may be far from satisfactory.

Much more preferable, if your subject is cooperative and willing to stand the slight additional cost, is to make a special head and shoulder portrait, such as that in *Figure* 73. This will at least include the headdress, veil and a reasonable portion of the gown, will reduce satisfactorily without too much loss of detail, and will appear in a manner creditable to both you and the bride. Because more dissatisfaction arises, in bridal portraiture, from poor newspaper reproduction than from almost any other cause, we had better explain this problem more fully. You must realize that the importance of the wedding to the average bride is such that if it does not become a satisfactory permanent record in the local paper, it will not be the paper that is blamed, but yourself. Many, if not a majority, of the newspapers in the smaller communities cannot afford the cost of halftone engravings made by an outside photoengraver, and nowadays make their own on plastic materials by purely mechanical means, instead of by the expensive hand operations which were formerly the only means of producing photoengravings. In the hands of competent operators, the plastic plates made on these machines can be quite satisfactory, but because the process is automatic the machine is often in charge of a minor employee, and the finished engravings are something less than desirable. Consequently, the easier you can make the engraving job, the better, and you will be more certain of good results if your prints are a bit on the soft side, not contrasty, and not falling away too rapidly from one tone to the next.

A portrait such as *Figure 73* should reproduce well by any engraving method, and will reduce satisfactorily to a very small engraving, while retaining good detail. This is a "camera vignette"—how to make these is fully described in Chapter 20—taken against a background of wide seamless paper of a pink shade. For this particular portrait a soft focus lens was used, but the softness has been kept within limits that will not affect its reproductive possibilities. In other words, it differs only slightly from a normally sharp portrait. For a normal head and shoulder pose we would not want anything as elaborate as the use of the Bible and the bouquet at the bottom of the picture area, but because this is a bridal portrait, it is essential that they be included. At the same time, we want to include as much detail of the gown as possible in our limited space, and if we raised the subject's hands, too much of the fine detail would be obscured. The lighting for a pose like this requires a bit more care than usual, but the result is well worth it. As the diagram (*Figure 74*) indicates, we return to our customary main source and fill-in positions as we would for a normal head and shoulders, the fill-in being so placed that no light is cast on the vignetter. To bring out the translucency of the veil properly, we use two small spots at right and left rear, and for our light ground

Figure **76**

Figure **75**

and vignette effect, use a small spot behind the subject as a background light. And, as we like to do with most of our head and shoulder portraits, we bring back our favorite accessory, the head screen.

There are times when your subject, or you yourself, may want to depart from the standard or accepted poses and try something a little different, and so we offer *Figure* 75. Here we have a bride with a contemporary style of hair-do and veil, a pretty gown, and we want to give her something different in the way of background. We used a plastic railing at floor level and hung a decorative plastic panel in the background, and kept both considerably out of focus. While this may not appeal to some, it does get away from so many of the plain effects you see today, and tends to give the effect of "depth" to the portrait. Brides spend considerable amounts on their gowns, and they will be much happier with photographs that show them in detail and in their entirety. A setting such as this, with appropriate filters over your lights for background illumination, would work beautifully for a direct color portrait.

As a rule, formal bridal portraits are by appointment, taken some days prior to the wedding, and the groom is seldom present. He does not normally come to the fore unless an entire wedding party visits the studio just before or after the ceremony, although he will of course be much in evidence if candid photographs are taken during and after the ceremony. When the wedding party does come to the studio, the purpose is largely for a group portrait of the entire party, and usually, also a portrait of the bride and groom. Sometimes, for anticipated newspaper publicity, the groom will accompany the bride to the studio for prior formal portraits, but in most cases the picture of the couple is one which has to be taken amid considerable confusion and merrymaking and—unfortunately—in a hurry.

Figure **77**

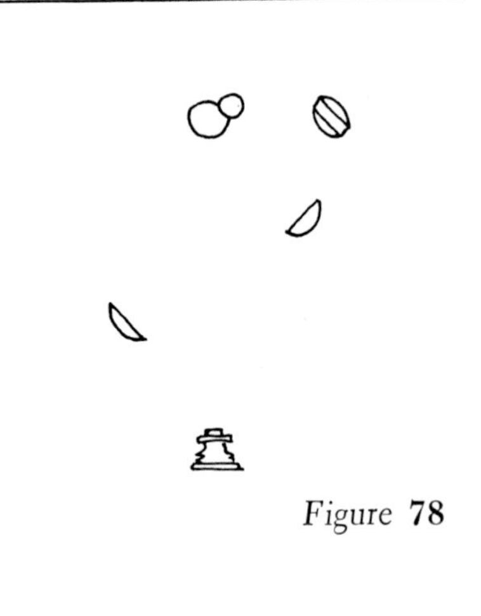

Figure **78**

Figure 77 is a typical example of such a bride and groom portrait. Even though the groom is included, the gown is still, to practically all concerned, the matter of chief interest, and he takes his place behind it. Any light or gray background may be used, the one in this case happening to be a wide seamless pink paper which, depending on how it is illuminated, can be made to appear as anything from almost white to a fairly dark gray. Too often, the groom's arm remains hanging at his side in a rather awkward position; we chose to place it as if he were supporting the bride, making the pose less formal and also more natural. Both heads are turned slightly away from the camera, instead of looking directly at the lens. Note that the main source of light (*Figure 73*) has been brought rather close in to the groom, in order to give some detail and modeling to his dark suit, which all too frequently, in a picture like this, appears as a solid black mass. With a spot at right rear directed on the ground, adequate separation and relief are obtained. The groom, though subordinated to the bride as he should be, is certainly not neglected, and a group like this should be good for the sale of several extra prints. With no loss of detail anywhere, and no merging of either figure into the background, this is another picture which will reproduce excellently.

CHAPTER 10

Family Groups

We are inclined to think that as a general rule professionals care less about making groups than any other portrait subjects that come before their cameras. The reasons are fairly obvious: it takes more time and more effort to achieve a suitable and harmonious composition; it is often difficult, especially when some of the subjects are children, to hold their attention and interest; care must be taken to secure expressions, whether serious or smiling, that are genuine; there is always the possibility of added expense due to wasted films caused by moves. The last should be of least importance because, if the photographer will only stop to think, the cost of a few extra films is one of his smallest expenses in connection with any sitting. The reader should think of a group as a challenge instead of a chore and as an opportunity which, if properly handled, will mean a considerably larger order than can be expected from a sitting of just one individual and—perhaps more important—a chance to display his ability as an artist with the camera. Good groups are not only profitable subjects but also offer the spice of variety for the window display and reception room sample albums. True, they require more careful lighting and more retouching, but a reputation for being a good photographer of groups is well worth having.

Most professionals, and we among them, attack the lighting problem very much as if we have one individual under the lights instead of several. Most of the time we will use two lights, a main source and a fill-in, changing the setup in the case of a larger group so that our two lights are each pretty much to the side in order to provide a cross lighting. The illustrations, we believe, are sufficient evidence that this is a practical—and simple—method of securing proper balance of light and shade on all the faces as well as all necessary detail in the clothing and—let us emphasize—without burned out, staring whites in collars, shirts, blouses and other light or white areas.

One important factor in the composition of any group is that it be cohesive, that the figures be "tied together" by a community of interest disclosed by their looking in the same direction, whether that be toward the camera, to one side or the other or, in the case of a large group, perhaps at some person or object in the center. Except where all heads are, as just mentioned, turned toward the center it is a serious error when they look or face in different directions because immediately the cohesiveness of the group is lost and frequently one result is that you have two or more groups of persons, each of which could be trimmed out to make a composition by itself and whose only apparent connection is that they happen to be on the same sheet of paper. Also, while we are discussing composition, a simple and practical way to handle larger groups of six, seven or more persons, is to build up two groups, facing somewhat toward the center or at least toward the camera, and then to complete and unify the whole by placing the last person or two in the center. In the case of a group of two, and except when you are dealing with two youngsters alone, it is never wise to have two heads at the same height. One should always be above the other and, if the subjects are a man and a woman, the man's head should always be the higher of the two.

Figure 79 is the sort of group of two with which every photographer is often confronted, a "natural" so far as a motive for a group picture is concerned. A Fiftieth Wedding Anniversary portrait is not only an occasion to be commemorated for the couple themselves but of which their children, their grandchildren and all of the relatives will want prints. So, today, will the newspapers which, in small towns and large, are only too glad to give space to such photographs with a paragraph or two about the accompanying celebration. Such a picture should therefore always be made with the possibility of halftone reproduction—as discussed in Chapter 9—borne in mind. Another point which must not be overlooked in this connection is that any anniversary is news on the day it happens, and of no interest whatever to a newspaper twenty four hours later. In other words, in the case of such a sitting, get

Figure **79**

Figure **80**

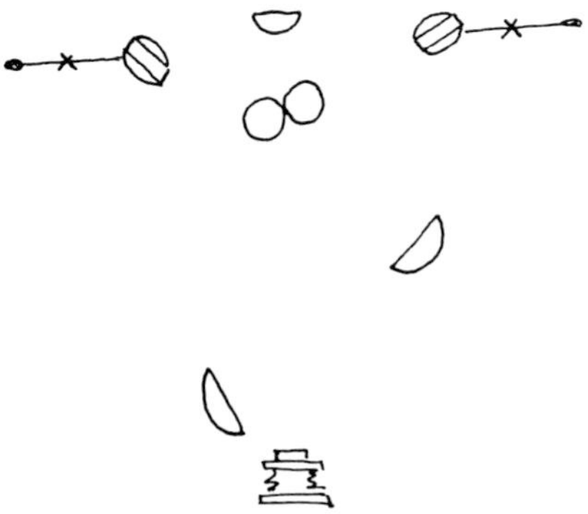

your glossy prints out and to the papers without delay.

Compositionwise there is not a great deal that can be done with a group of two other than to make sure you do not have two heads uninterestingly on a level with each other and that if one is a man he normally gets the preference. For the best effect the couple should be seated, close together of course, with their bodies turned about three quarters toward the camera. As with almost everything that has to do with portraiture, there are exceptions to this rule, chiefly if your subjects are heavy in which case they should be turned, as much as possible, so their sides are toward the camera, to avoid that appearance of bulkiness. Posing a group of two so that both bodies face the camera is unwise, even if the people are slim, because this automatically spreads the heads too far apart for suitable composition on a vertical print, which is what most people prefer. This is practical, however, even with a larger group, if your intention is to make a horizontal such as *Figures* 83 and 87. You will also find the use of a camera vignetter (See Chapter 21) very helpful when working with groups, even of only two people, if your subjects are stout or have heavy arms, in order to conceal or modify such tendencies; also when a youngster's bare legs, in a group, such as *Figure* 83, are likely to become too prominent. Sometimes a bit of burning in when printing, as in *Figure* 79, will be easier and fully as satisfactory as vignetting.

An anniversary couple will almost surely be wearing flowers, orchids or some other spray on the shoulder of the lady, and a *boutonniére* in the man's lapel. These, if the subjects' and the donor's feelings are not to be hurt, must be included and so it will be wise to pose the couple as in *Figure* 79 with their left sides toward the camera. Reversing the pose will silhouette the flowers against the background and make them far too prominent, as you will quickly discover if you will do a little experimenting with a couple of complaisant subjects. Your group will have a little more action and interest if the subjects do not look directly into the lens. With an elderly couple like this, work for a soft lighting effect and avoid contrast, not only because such a lighting is more flattering in subduing the lines and marks of age but because it will greatly reduce the amount of retouching necessary, and enough of that will be required in any event.

With our fill-in and main source in much their normal positions (*Figure* 80), but with great care taken not to over illuminate the man's collar and shirt and the flowers (note that there are no flat glaring whites whatever in *Figure* 79) we add a background light to provide relief and separation from the background. Because we are dealing with gray hair on the lady and fine white hair on the man and must not ignore either, we need some top and back lighting for which we use two boom lights (not spots) at right and left rear. These must be carefully handled or the hair will be burned out completely or, in the case of the man, made to appear like white wool or cotton.

As a piece of general information we should add at this point that in a group of two the man should always be closer to your main source light. You can avoid over lighting his head and ears either by feathering the main source or by using a head screen, while the slight difference in distance of the woman's head from the main source will cause just enough fall off in the intensity of the light so that her normally lighter skin tone will remain in suitable balance, thus eliminating a lot of dodging when printing. Portraits like this deserve your utmost care because they represent

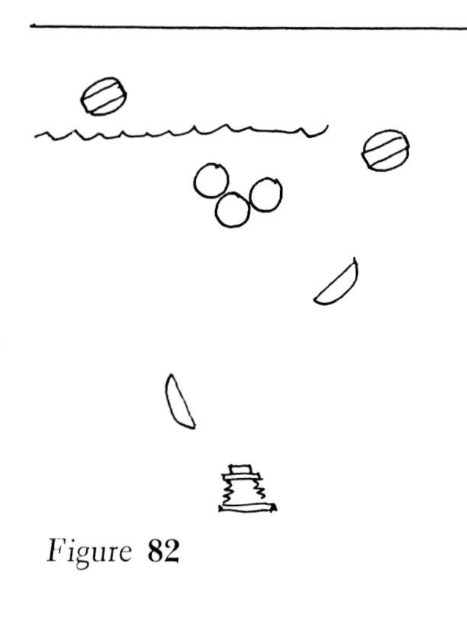

Figure **82**

Figure **81**

your true obligation as a portrait photographer. Not only are you dealing with people who have braved the storms of life for many years but it is highly possible that this is the last portrait that will ever be made of these two together. This may well be the final record for their family and friends to treasure and you are therefore being entrusted with a great responsibility.

Odd numbers in groups are always easier to handle than even quantities and with a group of three (*Figure 81*) the most logical arrangement is to place the heads in any one of innumerable triangular compositions. For the very reason that, in most cases, the cameraman will place the apex of his triangle at the top and usually pretty much in the center of his picture area, we have chosen to depart from this and invert the triangle which, still being a triangle, nevertheless rises to a high point with the girl at top left. With any such composition it is important that all lines in the picture lead the viewer's eye to the main feature—the three heads—and so while we have not resorted to anything so obvious as straight lines of the arms to accomplish this, nevertheless the arms of all three subjects have been so placed that they carry the eye up to the three faces. The skirts, too, have been lightly pulled out and straightened to aid in accomplishing this result. On the other hand, as a deliberate foil to the triangular composition we have purposely retained vertical pleats in the length of glam'e cloth which hangs before the light toned background.

This glam'e cloth, which is translucent, is fairly close to the subjects (*Figure 82*) so there is ample room to place a spot behind it to illuminate the background itself, the whole giving us a pleasant, airy effect which we have accentuated by burning in the upper corners of the print. The main source is a bit farther distant from the subjects than usual and the fill-in slightly closer, and both, to avoid burning out the detail in the costumes, are carefully feathered up. A spot at right rear, in front of the glam'e cloth, provides the necessary relief for the arms and also gives some added

Figure **83**

illumination to the hair. All three of these young ladies have dark, almost black, hair and unless such a spot is properly directed the hair will show as little more than a solid black mass. In a group of this sort, where all gowns are formal, it will require some thought to dispose properly of the arms and hands but if the arms are placed, as already explained, so they complement the basic triangle, it only remains to make certain the hands are gracefully arranged—see Chapter 17. Above all the hands and arms must look as if they had dropped naturally into position and while that is not true of the hands and arms of the young lady in front, her raised hands are quite consistent with the interested expression of all three girls as they gaze at something outside the picture which has quite obviously attracted their attention. For any group of three you will never go wrong if you base your composition on a triangle.

The only other acceptable alternative, when posing a group of three, appears in *Figure 83* with the heads in a diagonal row, either full face or in profile. Such a composition, however, will require a horizontal photograph and is not, for a smaller group, as desirable as a vertical. The horizontal format, on the other hand, is almost

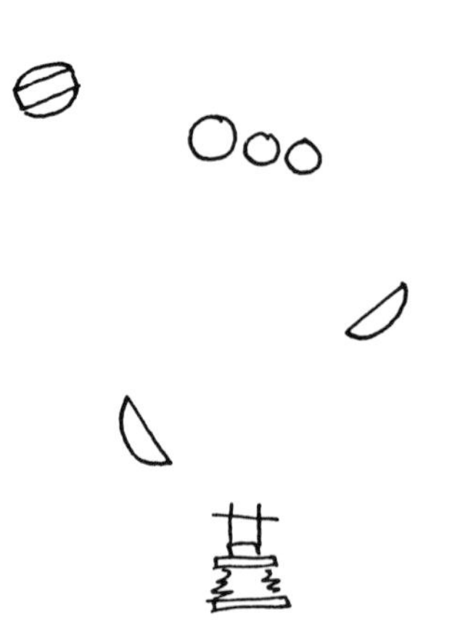

Figure **84**

unavoidable for any group larger than three as we will see shortly. In *Figure 83*, having a bit more space to work with thanks to the horizontal format, we have not, as is usual when planning a group and essential when the picture area is vertical, crowded the figures together but have given them ample room and have actually left a slight space between the two boys. There is one compensation in a composition like this which is that, all three faces being on the same plane, the problem of keeping all in focus becomes much simpler. Perhaps some remarks on the posing of this particular group may be of help when you are confronted with a similar situation. All are not seated on one piece of furniture. The mother is on a standard posing stool, the younger boy (in the center) is sitting on a small table and the older boy is standing. This not only enables us to adjust the three head heights to our satisfaction but also discourages the desire and ability of the younger boy to squirm around and out of place, particularly because the mother's arm, not shown, is holding him firmly.

Although the mother is, in this case, the largest and most important figure in the group, we have placed her farthest away from the main source light (*Figure 84*). The reason for so doing is not a matter of skin tone, because there is little if any difference between the complexions of the mother and the youngsters, but because of the large area of white of her blouse, which had to be subdued in tone so that its detail and tone value might be retained without totally destroying the balance of light and shade of the whole composition. Thus all the white clothing has been properly controlled, a satisfactory balance of light and shade has been maintained, and we still have nice modeling of all the features. The only other light needed is a spot to illuminate the background. We have in this case used a vignetter to tone down undesirable arms, legs and other extraneous details at the bottom which would otherwise detract from the composition. Having selected a rather dark background and lightening the area behind the figures by means of a spot sufficiently to ensure separation, no burning in of the corners is necessary.

Now what to do with a group that presents two problems? In *Figure 85* we have four individuals, an even number most commonly considered to be the most difficult to compose attractively, and in addition all are youngsters of disparate ages with no parents in the picture to maintain a sobering influence. To trip the shutter at just the right time when four active young people are all gazing in the same direction, showing the mutual interest that gives the group the cohesiveness we mentioned earlier, while avoiding moves and retaining good modeling on all the faces, is quite an achievement. What will interest the younger members will only bore the older ones and vice versa and it will require both patience and understanding on your part before you will succeed in getting all of them interested in the same thing and looking in the desired direction. For such a group you will find it almost imperative, as we did, to have an assistant do the entertaining while you remain at the camera ready to seize the inspired moment.

A profile view is best because it enables you to keep the figures close together and in this case happened to be necessary because the mother had expressed a desire to show the older girl's pony-tail hairdo. We think this alternating of the taller and shorter children is far more attractive than the easier and more common solution of placing them in an orderly row by height. This group was taken with speedlights, which of course helped immensely, but because we were using speedlights we re-

Figure **85**

quired an incandescent spot of greater strength than normal to maintain a lighter tone on the background. Otherwise the lighting (*Figure* 86) is much as usual. With smaller children this combination of speedlight and incandescent would be unwise because of the danger of having "ghost" images, due to the difference between shutter time and speedlight exposure time, caused by possible moves. For the finished print the upper corners and bottom were all slightly burned in.

For our final illustration (*Figure* 87) we offer one of the most common types of "family" groups—father, mother and several (in this case three) youngsters. You will be called on frequently to make such groups and any inability on your part to do so satisfactorily will only mean that your customers and prospects will go

Figure **86**

Figure **87**

elsewhere, permanently. At least one such group—and it should be changed frequently—should always be prominently included in your window display. Fortunately the average couple will have two chief desires in mind because, for one reason or another, they have become convinced that they need a pictorial record of the entire family. They will be entirely satisfied with any reasonably good arrangement which includes good likenesses of all. When it comes to groups of five and more the usable compositions are endless and it would require a dozen or more illustrations merely to indicate the possibilities. This is one case where nothing can take the place of experience because so many different factors enter into the arrangement

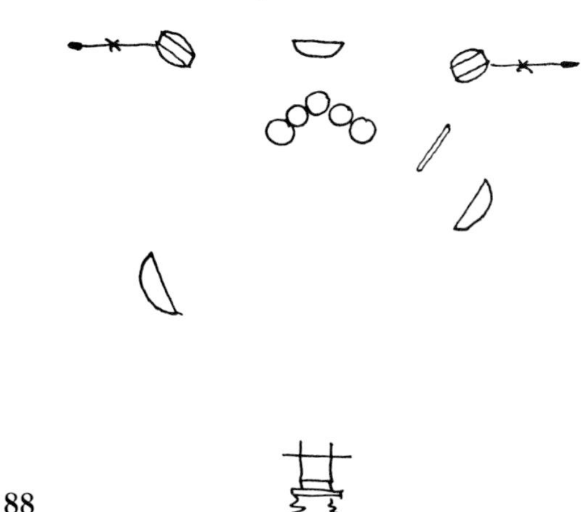

Figure **88**

of each specific large group. We therefore limit ourselves to this one illustration as—and we emphasize—a point of departure. This, we concede, is straight "bread and butter" work, but due to the careful modeling of the faces, detail of the clothing and control of light and shade, a better than average group which will more than please the majority of your customers.

We have placed the father and son closest to our main source light for the reasons explained earlier, even though the boy is wearing a white shirt, because their facial tones are darker than those of the mother and daughters. Placing the boy somewhat behind the father has aided us in screening some of the light intensity from that shirt, and we have also helped things along on that side somewhat by means of the head screen (*Figure* 88). One reason for the uniformly good expressions is that this is entirely a speedlight picture, but while the main source, fill-in and two boom spots were all working at 50 watt-seconds, we set the background light at 100 watt-seconds, twice the intensity of the others, to assure us a light toned background. Notice here the difference in placement of the main source and fill-in lights, both more to the side than normal and with the fill-in farther away from the camera, so that the two act as cross lights. It is this use of the two lights that has given us the good modeling on all the faces and retained all the tone value and detail of the white clothing. There is fine tonal gradation throughout, the only pure white being the father's collar (which even at that is not flat white paper although we doubt if the engraver will be able to retain the effect) with no solid blacks anywhere. To subdue the foreground we not only used a gray vignette but also burned it in slightly when printing, doing the same with the upper corners. The two boom spots were "highlighters," just strong enough to accent the hair on all five of the heads but without burning out any of the detail.

Unless you are blessed with a fairly large camera room, you will have to allow for some compromises in your lighting when working with groups. Most professionals find themselves restricted to rather narrow camera rooms which make it impossible to pull the main source sufficiently far to the side and are consequently forced to work with a little flatter effect than is normally preferable. You still, under such conditions, will not find yourself with undesirably flat lightings if you will use care in placing your main source and fill-in so that you maintain an agreeable ratio between them. In all of our lighting diagrams we have tried to indicate the angle of direction of the lights in relation to the subjects. Beyond that diagrams cease to be helpful, even if we were to go to the extent of including their distance from the subjects in feet and inches because, as we stated in the Introduction, no two subjects (and much more to the point no two photographers) are identical. With respect to groups, however, if you are to avoid negatives that will require a lot of dodging during printing, it will be necessary that there be some overlapping of the illumination from your main source and fill-in lights.

CHAPTER 11

The Three Quarter Figure

More can be accomplished in portraiture, artistically from the standpoint of composition, and practically with respect to the true rendition of character, with the three quarter pose than almost any other. Largely this is because the hands, which are necessarily included, immediately become an important factor. In Chapter 17 the posing of hands as such, arrangement of the fingers and the like, will be discussed in detail but at this point we shall confine ourselves to the over all figure, considering the hands as merely compositional accents which, while they are an integral part of the composition, must remain subservient to the face at all times.

The possibilities of posing and arrangement are almost beyond description and we shall limit ourselves to four illustrations of a rather simple nature rather than confuse the issue. Once you have experimented with a few three quarter poses and have learned to appreciate the far more interesting possibilities they make apparent, what you can yourself develop thereafter will depend solely on your own imagination and such suitable items of furniture as you have or obtain for your camera room. Don't get the impression from the accompanying illustrations that such poses are limited to having your subject seated on a chair or posing bench. Frequently a characteristic and relaxed pose of a man will show him perched somewhat negligently on the edge of a desk or table, and a small table itself, as shown in part in *Figure 93*, is an extremely helpful accessory on which a subject may rest one or both arms or even one or both elbows with one hand supporting the head and the other extended or raised in some accustomed position.

Such a table should not be too large and if on casters so it can readily be moved around will be even more useful. Frequently when you are working with a man, seated on your posing chair, and have completed your customary head and shoulder poses, extremely characteristic positions and expressions will result if you suddenly wheel a table before him and ask him to rest his arms on it. He may well have felt stilted and formal until then, but will promptly relax and proceed to "feel natural." So by all means, if you are accustomed to limiting the number of exposures you make per sitting, reserve at least a couple for the moment when your sitter, thinking the worst is over, leans forward with a sigh of relief at sight of the table. The same will be true whenever you are dealing with a woman who is active in civic or other affairs, or who—and their number is steadily increasing—is a business executive, because she too will be accustomed to dealing with others, whether in her office or from a speaker's platform behind a desk or table.

But, and particularly when your subject is seated on a chair of any kind, be careful that the act of relaxing is not accompanied by a slump of the body. While such a slump will not affect the average head and shoulder pose, it becomes a serious matter when you are dealing with the three quarter figure where it is necessary that the subject present a suitable aspect of dignity. When your subject is stout this is extremely important and only too often the stout subject, given the least opportunity, will sag into some accustomed position which, natural and comfortable though it may undoubtedly be, will be most undesirable for a permanent record. When dealing with a nervous or irritable subject this is something you will have to watch carefully, but handle most tactfully, and probably the simplest way out of the difficulty is to complete your composition so far as hands, expression and the like are concerned and then, just before you click the shutter, say pleasantly: "Will you straighten up just a moment, please."

Your principal field for portraits in the three quarter style will be among your more mature customers. This does not mean that younger men and women, and even an occasional teen ager, will not also be pleased with such poses, especially when they happen to be especially well groomed in the case of men or, when women are concerned, are wearing obviously new gowns of which they are proud or particularly noticeable accessories such as furs or expensive handbags. Older people, because of their greater years, have a better knowledge and understanding of art and because of that broadening can better appreciate the compositional value and added character rendition that the three quarter pose makes possible. They want something more than just a likeness and can usually well afford to pay for something better than what they are accustomed to seeing in every studio show window. Study the pictures in the big national illustrated magazines and you will find that, more and more, people of importance and standing are presented in the three quarter pose. Whether your purpose is to make pictures that will please your friends, appeal to judges if success in salons is your aim, make a hit with editors if you are free lancing in the field of journalism, or open the pocketbooks of your sitters if you are a professional (whether working from your studio or in the home), do not underestimate the importance of the three quarter pose.

As a rule a three quarter will be a vertical composition but when the subject is attractive and is also wearing a gown she is anxious to display a horizontal may be more suitable, as well as a welcome change, as we see in *Figure 89*, one of the examples where a three quarter is not only suitable but highly desirable for a younger subject. In this case a studio posing bench was used, but any type of love seat such as found in many a home would serve as well. Notice the triangular composition and the concealment of the one hand in order to avoid an accent at that side which would pull the viewer's attention away from the face. Another alternative might have been to place that hand in the lap, but it would have been most unhelpful to the composition. As it is the graceful lines of that arm carry the eye directly to the face and help to give the portrait a feeling of action. The other arm, bent at the

Figure **89**

elbow, avoids a too obvious triangle and gives us an opportunity to display a pleasing arrangement of hand and fingers on the rolled arm of the seat. Some readers may not care for this position of the arms but it does depart from the conventional (and if we cannot get variety into our portraits occasionally we are not likely to go far in portraiture) while still being quite correct compositionally.

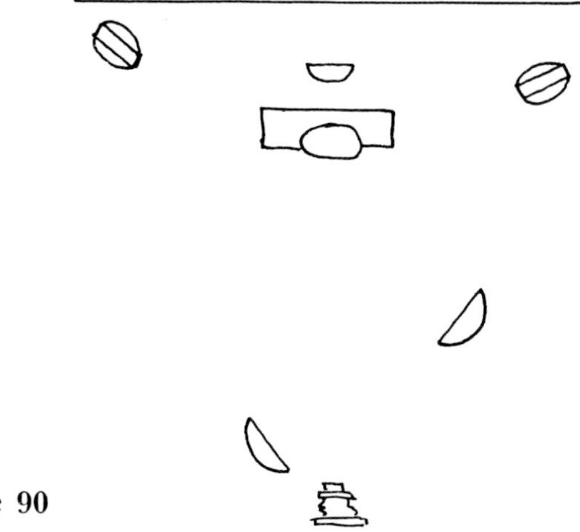

Figure **90**

Figure **92**

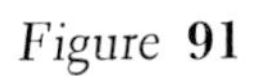

Figure **91**

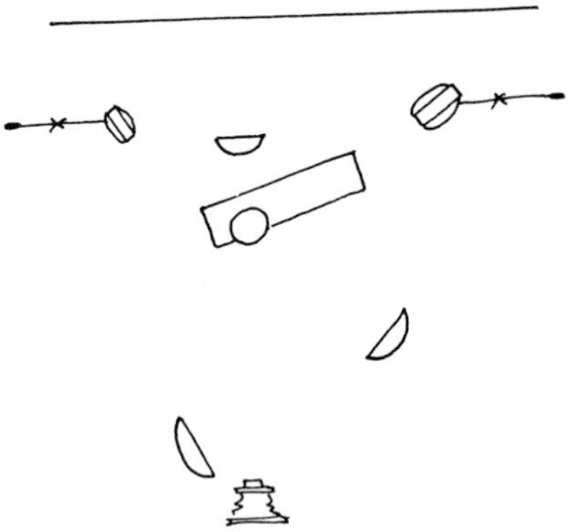

Our main source and fill-in (*Figure 90*) are in approximately their customary positions but for relief from the background we have added a small light behind the subject, being careful to direct this light rather low against the background so that the illumination is not much above the subject's waist line. For proper lighting

Figure **93**

of the hair two small spots were used, one on either side at the rear, with particular care taken just to "touch up" the hair and bring out some of the detail of a very attractive hairdo without over lighting, which would have drawn attention away from the face. The main source, which is of course the one closer to the subject on the right, was at about a 45° angle from the subject and carefully feathered up because too much illumination on the gown would have destroyed the airy detail which constitutes its chief charm. The fill-in was at about the height of the subject's head and directed pretty well into the figure. Being sufficiently far away it has illuminated the shadows and given us nice roundness and flesh tones with no harsh effects. With a little burning in of the upper corners the result is what might be called a somewhat low high key portrait.

Let us consider now, in *Figure 91*, the mother of this same young subject. Here we have a charming lady, perhaps prematurely gray, whose personality we have definitely tried to project in a manner we think could not have been done nearly as well in the customary head and shoulder pose. When a subject appears before your camera as carefully gowned as this lady, why neglect the opportunity of achieving a portrait that will really show her as she is instead of eliminating much of what adds to her character and appearance? You may be sure that any woman who has pride enough to dress well and equip herself with appropriate gloves and other accessories is not going to resent the suggestion that you both attempt something of greater appeal to her family and friends. You can, in fact, be almost certain of enthusiastic cooperation. We asked her, therefore, not to remove her hat and gloves, and we seated her on the same posing bench but first turned it to a rather sharp angle to bring the high end curve toward the camera. This gave us a suitable and at the same time comfortable spot on which the subject could rest her arm and hands, thus displaying the gloves and—with the one arm—disguising any slight tendency of heaviness at the waist. Though not necessary in the case of this subject we emphasize the point as one worth keeping in mind when, as so often occurs, extra weight must be concealed.

This portrait was made with synchronized speedlights but the lighting placement (*Figure* 92) can be duplicated with any type of equipment. Having placed a small light behind the sitter to illuminate the background, and with our main source and fill-in very nearly in the same positions as they were for *Figure* 89, we placed a boom spot at the right rear and another small spot at the left rear, keeping both of these on low watt settings. To insure sufficient illumination on the background we used a medium watt setting for the small light behind the subject but we kept that light directed low because we did not want any halo effect around the head or body. The main source, at right front, was feathered off the face a little and the fill-in was feathered up a bit, both of these being on medium watt settings. There is, you will see, a complete absence of harsh contrast. One thing to remember with a subject in this age bracket is that the hair must not be over lighted or the result will be white hair with no detail at all instead of the beautiful silver gray which we have carefully retained here and which, thanks to the two rear lights, shows a definite outline even through the translucency of the hat.

Still moving up in our age bracket we come to the sweet little old lady who is the subject of *Figure* 93, and for whom we have provided a table such as mentioned earlier in this Chapter. Here we have a subject who, though blessed with quite a few years, is still right on her toes and fully aware of all that goes on around her, in other words a bright, snappy older person like many one meets today, and who must be portrayed with all the pep and energy she possesses. A grandma-with-her-hands-in-her-lap pose is not for her. All who know her love her and one reason is that she refuses to sit quietly in a rocker and just twiddle her thumbs but is vivacious and constantly on the go. You should have no difficulty in recognizing such a subject and should be wary of posing her in any lackadaisical or contemplative attitude. We think we have successfully captured her personality in her expression and added to it by the pose we selected. Most women of this age delight in little trinkets that friends have given them—beads, ear rings, lace collars and what-not, so it is wise not to overlook such accessories but to play them up. Any props selected should be appropriate to their interests and what these may be can easily be elicited in the course of conversation. For this lady, a very active church worker, nothing could have been more suitable than a Bible.

In discussing *Figure 92*, the lighting diagram for *Figure 91*, we remarked that while it consisted of speedlights it could readily be duplicated with any other equipment and to prove our point we require no lighting diagram for *Figure 93* because, although this old lady was photographed with incandescents and not speedlights, the basic lighting placement is as nearly identical as lighting ever can be. To emphasize her personality we wanted a snappy, but not contrasty, effect. We wanted to hold the detail in her lovely white hair (which she had insisted on having done just like this "for her picture") and we again used a boom spot at right rear and a small spot at the left rear. Because we did not want too great a spread of the background light we cut it down with a snoot and then, to break up the monotony of the ground and give the picture a little added pep, resorted to the trick of holding back, while projecting, the two places in the background where light areas have resulted. The spot at right rear was directed downward somewhat in order to illuminate the Bible and give a touch of backlighting to the hand. In this case the main source and fill-in were not feathered.

Now for a man, before we leave this subject of three quarter poses, and to make things really interesting we have selected as our subject a friend of many years who has a long narrow head which is accentuated by an almost total lack of hair except on the sides and back where it is of little help to the cameraman. This man has reached the age where he has time to read and enjoy life and has long passed the stage—if the matter ever really disturbed him—of having any self consciousness about his lack of hair. In fact, and we have found this to be true of many men who are really bald, he is secretly a little proud of it because it is distinctive. Under normal conditions, faced with such a condition, the cameraman will try every dodge he knows to conceal the top of the head. Certainly he will not use any spots or top light of any kind. He will feather his main source and fill-in to the limit to avoid having light strike the top of the head. He will try, with an extra heavy head screen placed well up, to cast a shadow over that white expanse. If his subject has a presentable hat and is one of the many who, while unwilling to wear a toupee, nevertheless resent their condition and want to hide it, the photographer will ask him to put the hat on. It isn't too easy, but a bald head can be subdued by one or another or a combination of the lighting tricks mentioned. Beyond these, or rather in conjunction with

Figure **95**

Figure **94**

them, the best advice we can offer is to work always for a soft lighting effect, exposing fully but being careful not to over expose, and specifically to avoid over development. This—the bald head—is another one of those situations which can only be met satisfactorily by experimenting under your own lighting conditions.

Fortunately, as we have stated, the subject of *Figure 94* is not in the least vain and has no desire to have the top of his head rendered in shadow. It's his head and it suits him but at least one thing we can do is to resort to a three quarter pose so his head will not be the totally dominant feature of the picture area. We asked him to seat himself naturally in a comfortable chair and to hold in one hand the cigar without which he is seldom seen, and we let the matter ride with an almost standard placement of main source and fill-in. Both of these were feathered up, incidentally, but not because we were trying to keep the light away from his head; we wanted to be sure that his hands, while necessary to the composition, would not be so light in tone that they would completely draw attention away from his face. We needed background illumination around the shoulders but not surrounding the head and so we again used a snoot on the background light, all as shown in *Figure 95*. We brought back our friend the head screen, not to shade the head or attempt to conceal the top of it, but to make sure of retaining modeling and roundness.

Finally, and this is another little trick worth knowing for various purposes, still more to draw attention away from the head we worked in a little background effect. To do this, tape the negative, emulsion side up, to the smooth side of a sheet of finely ground glass and work in the sketch effect on the ground glass with a stump (bit of cotton on a stick) which has been rubbed in powdered black. The result is somewhat similar to that achieved by working on a print with an eraser, explained in an earlier chapter, but in this case inasmuch as the background effect becomes part of the negative all prints, contact or projection, made from it will be alike.

CHAPTER 12

Full Lengths

Do not be misled, due to our selection of illustrations for this chapter, into the common but quite erroneous assumption that a full length portrait necessarily implies a standing figure. In photographic language there are three generally accepted types of poses, no matter who the subject may be: the head and shoulder, or bust (to which, because it far outnumbers all others, we are devoting the greater part of this book), the three quarter, and the full length. More properly, this should be spoken of as the full figure, because the subject may be seated, reclining, or even on the floor (as shown in *Figure 102*), and the only real essential of a full length is that the entire subject, from head to foot, be included. This being primarily a book of fundamentals, we have chosen as illustrations subjects most likely to confront the reader, who, in our opinion, when he first attempts full lengths will find the standing figure not only easier but most called for. For the same reason we show no full lengths of men here, because in the everyday work of the average photographer such portraits will be few and far between; and additionally because, should such situations arise, the lightings shown here will be equally applicable.

Inasmuch as a full length portrait ordinarily includes one or both hands and one or both feet, it does bring up certain compositional problems which are the main reason why this type of pose is avoided, whenever possible, by many portraitists. Yet, because the full length has an appeal all of its own, and can therefore be an important source of added income to the photographer, we hope that you will make a definite effort to become proficient in this field. Your greatest challenge will lie in the posing of the body and the proper placement of hands and feet so that they act as compositional accents and do not detract from the face (for that must always remain the dominating feature of any portrait). So far as lighting is concerned, the full length is far from complicated. Your principal illumination will still come, unless you are deliberately working for some special or unusual effect, from your main source and fill-in lights. Both of these, however, will have to be raised higher from the floor and will have to be pulled farther away from the subject in order to assure adequate all over lighting. Spots, too, when directed on the hair or upper portions of the figure, will have to be raised from their accustomed positions.

One advantage of the full length is that it enables you to call your imagination and originality into play with respect to accessories and props. Pieces of furniture and decorative adjuncts of one kind or another—a bookcase, a mantel, a pillar, or a drape—placed beside or behind the subject are helpful if not essential because, with a few exceptions, the eye is not accustomed to seeing a standing figure alone against a plain background. It is more or less accepted that a bride is being photographed in order to display her gown, and the fewer objects in the picture area that may detract from it, the better. The same is true of a man in uniform, particularly if he is in the armed services and happens to be well beribboned, because the uniform, the decorations, and his military bearing speak for themselves without extraneous props. Accessories, though, such as a swagger stick, crop, or pair of gloves, will add an appropriate touch. Ordinarily, you would not want to show a standing subject in a static pose, but these are two acceptable exceptions.

There may be several legitimate reasons for making a full length, aside from the purely commercial aspect of being able to show a subject a proof or two somewhat different from what was originally anticipated, in the hope of the eventual sale of additional prints. When dealing with women, a beautiful gown or a fine full length coat—especially if the latter is fur—offers opportunities that should by no means be ignored. Similarly in the case of men: a judge, an educator, a cleric, if wearing his distinctive robes, should always be photographed at full length, whether seated or standing. People in show business,

Figure **96**

Figure **97**

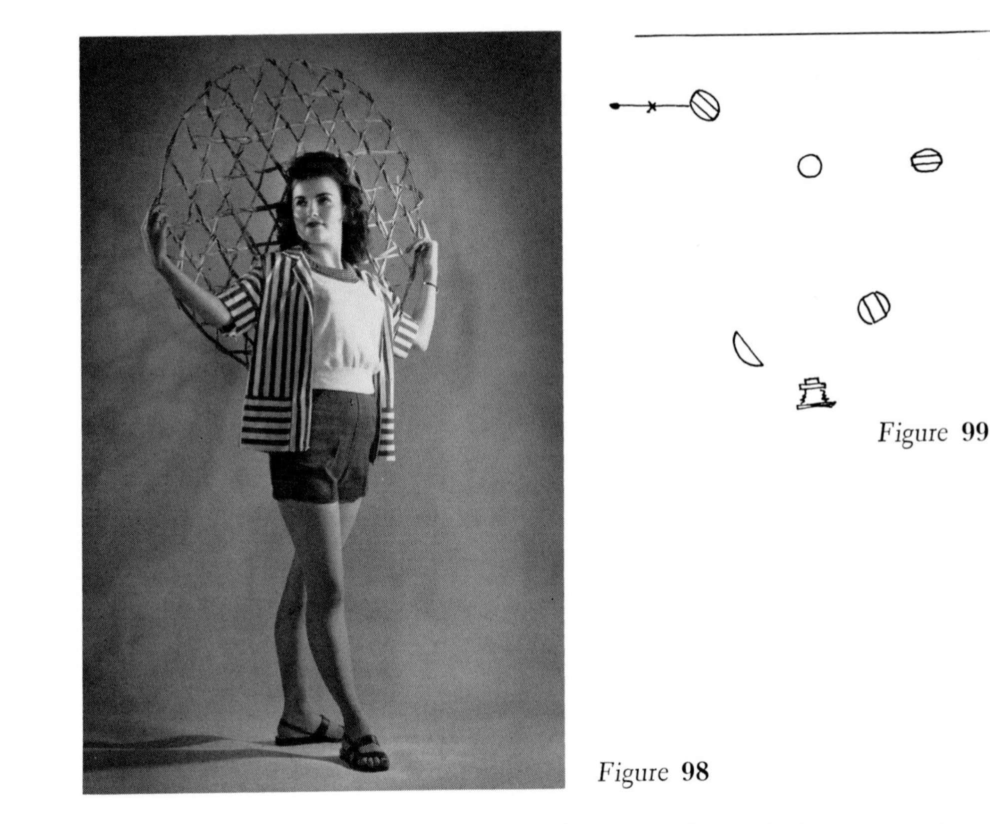

Figure **99**

Figure **98**

and others who have to appear before audiences, will usually insist on at least one pose that will display them as they customarily appear on the platform or the stage.

When you happen to know that a male subject is a devotee of hunting, fishing, equestrianism, or some other type of outdoor sport, try to induce him to bring a suitable outfit along so he can change into it at the studio. You are not only assured of an added sale, you will probably make a friend of him for life. All of this applies equally to the occasional woman who excels in similar avocations. Also the full length is sometimes the only way to bring out successfully in a portrait those avocations or vocations which lie in artistic activities, because only in such poses can you adequately include their "tools of the trade." The painter at his easel, the sculptor at work at his table or pedestal, the pianist or cellist at his instrument, and many others, will welcome your effort to present them as they and their friends are accustomed to seeing them.

In our attempt to make this book as instructive and practical as possible, we felt it necessary, in view of all that has been appearing in photographic periodicals concerning shadowless backgrounds, the use of existing (or available) light, and "bounce" light, to include here one full length (***Figure*** *96*), which equals any of the results thus obtained, but is produced with the same basic lighting we have been emphasizing, plus a few accessory lights. Here we have a portrait with all cast shadows in the background eliminated, with a full rendition of detail in the face, figure, accessories, and props; and with a complete scale of tones without heavy shadows or contrast in the image itself. Mind you, this full length of an artist at her easel is from a contact print, made without dodging, holding back, or burning in. It warrants considerable study and a serious attempt on your part to duplicate the effect.

Our background was pink wide seamless paper, brought down from the usual roll near the ceiling and extended on the floor toward the camera, well forward of the subject, who, with her easel, stands on it. Thus background and "floor cloth" or floor covering are one, without any horizontal line where commonly the floor and wall or background would meet. As the lighting diagram (*Figure* 97) indicates, we have flooded this entire strip of paper with illumination, using one light at left rear which was feathered up, another at right rear which was feathered down, and a spot to the left of the subject which was focused on the background, level with the subject's midsection. In other words, to all intents and purposes we have "washed out" the background and floor cloth with light, leaving only enough effect of shadow below figure and easel to avoid the feeling that they are suspended in the air.

Our main source of light, at about 45° angle from the model on the right and just out of camera range, was approximately nine feet from the floor. The fill-in, approximately two and a half times as distant from the subject as the main source, was reasonably close to the camera. Since a bit more "punch" was necessary, we placed a small spot at the right, directing it at the lower part of the figure, but feathering it away somewhat to avoid too pronounced an effect, in order to secure separation between the legs of the slacks, which otherwise would have tended to appear as one solid mass of gray. Finally, to add a little snap to the gray hair and retain its nice modeling and detail, we added a boom spot at the left, high enough so it was shooting over the spot placed in approximately the same location to illuminate the background. This boom spot was also well feathered.

All of this, as is so often the case when lightings are explained in print, was far less complicated and time consuming than it sounds. The chief point to remember when making a picture of this type is that if you want a good even background tone, you must light the whole background uniformly. That was the reason for feathering the two lights first mentioned and for then adding the spot in the center—to even out and blend the entire effect. Judging the uniformity of light is largely a matter of experience. If you have difficulty with this, the solution is to add a good light meter to your equipment, and then adjust your lights by moving and/or feathering them until the meter reading is the same at all points.

In view of the popularity of sportswear for summer, we show (*Figure* 98) a young woman in a sporty outfit, holding a rattan hoop. Again, we used our seamless pink paper as background and floor cloth. Indeed, it comes in so handy as a background material for full length and often three quarter poses, that we would be lost without it, and sometimes wonder how we managed before it came into use. At this point, we ask that you compare this background effect with that in *Figure* 96. Note the versatility of this material; whether it photographs light or dark, vanishes entirely (as in *Figure* 96), or provides a soft gray background with attractive shadows depends entirely on how you illuminate it. Where before we deliberately washed out the background with light, this time we have thrown no direct light on it whatever, and the only illumination is from some "spill" light from the spots. By this we mean that we have purposely allowed some light from the spots to "spill" over onto the background to create the interesting shadow effect.

From the diagram (*Figure* 99) you will see that in place of our customary main source we have substituted a spot at right front, rather more toward the center than usual. That position was selected so that the spot would also throw the shadow on the left of the background. This spot was therefore placed rather high, because we did not want too much light to strike the subject's legs. Since there already was ample detail in the composition, it was important to concentrate the interest on the upper part of the body and especially on the face. The fill-in, at left front near the camera, was about on a level with the subject's head and was not diffused. We might add that our floods, which we normally use for main source, fill-in, and occasionally for other requirements, have deflectors in front of the bulbs so that the illumination they throw is not really a direct beam of light, but rather a bounce effect from the main shell of the reflector. A small spot was used at the right of the subject to outline the legs against the background, but was feathered away to prevent that light from becoming too strong. A boom spot at left rear, to outline the hair and the arm on that side, completed the effect. The positions of her head, body, and hands all combine to give a feeling of action, and to avoid any dull, static result.

A pretty young girl in her first formal, as in *Figure 100,* unquestionably calls for a full length portrait. A few successful pictures of this type will do wonders for your reputation, or if displayed in your window, for your "walk-in" business. A first formal is a highly important thing in any girl's life, and a suitable prop

Figure **100**

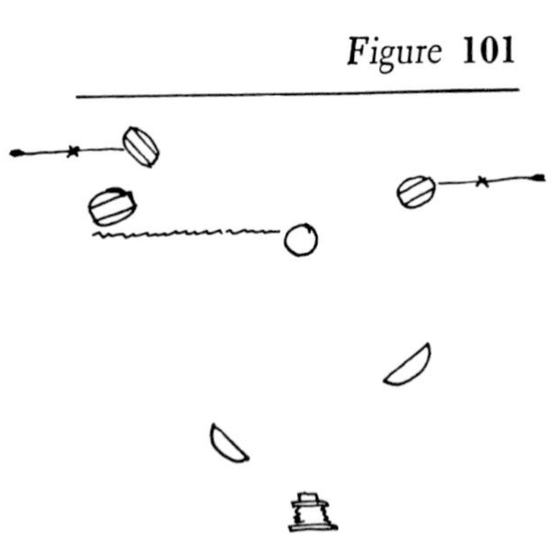

Figure **101**

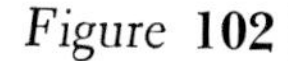

Figure **102**

such as, in this case, a drape of plastic, will add to the glittering, glamorous effect and make your subject that much happier. You may have other and more sedate drapes of dark or heavy material, but they would not be suitable for a young girl. We have introduced, as our only posing accessory, an antique pedestal and vase, to give the young lady something on which to place her hand and to add variety to the pose. The feet—and more about these in a later chapter—are so placed as to imply action. A white wall was our background and, as *Figure 101* shows, the plastic was hung directly behind the subject and some distance in front of the background. The spot at far left, behind the plastic, was directed at the background, to give us a lighter effect where it would accentuate the subject's small waistline. Two boom spots, one on either side at the rear, were needed to bring out the full beauty of the blonde hair, the one at the left behind the plastic and directed through it. Also that at the right just touched the cheek and shoulder sufficiently to add sparkle to the lighting. The main source, at right,

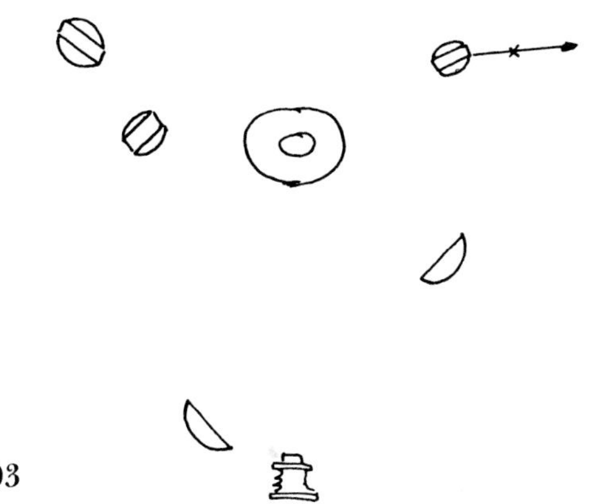

Figure **103**

was feathered up to avoid overlighting the gown, and the fill-in was raised a bit above the subject's head.

For a very different version of a full length we have, in *Figure 102,* a young blonde, whom we have now seated on the floor, which is again covered with our pink paper. An effect like this is, of course, out of the question unless your subject is wearing a very full skirt. When the subject is appropriately costumed and does not object to sitting on the floor—some may on the basis that it is too undignified for a photograph—the result can be lovely indeed. For such a pose you will have to go to some trouble in spreading out the skirt to a full circle, while at the same time retaining enough pleats or draping effect to avoid monotony. The posing of the hands and arms is also quite important, because your composition will necessarily be triangular, and yet real angularity as such must be avoided. Also, and this is extremely important, your subject must look quite comfortable. In *Figure 102,* the lines of the arms carry the viewer's eye to the face, without being obvious, and the skirt frames the whole composition. Placing the head at an angle adds action and interest. Few young subjects, not to mention their parents, would fail to enthuse over such a picture.

Notice that, as shown in *Figure 103,* there is very little light thrown on the background. In fact, almost the entire airy effect results from spill light from the main source and fill-in, plus the spot at left. This spot was directed just below the shoulder, and produced a small triangle of light between the arm and waistline, and then struck the ground behind the shoulders and back. To pick up the hair (we are firmly of the opinion that a blonde should look like a blonde, and not be shown with dark hair, as many cameramen appear to overlook completely), we used a spot at left rear and a boom spot at right rear, handling both with the greatest of care to avoid any danger of burning out the detail. The main source, at right, was feathered up to avoid overlighting the skirts. The fill-in, at about the height of the subject's head, was feathered slightly away from the face. Careful feathering, for a result like this, is essential. Had we been making a fashion shot, for example, direct light would have been necessary to bring out the full detail of the pattern and material of the dress, but we wanted a soft effect with emphasis on the face.

Except when a full length is made in the home, or props are purposely included to give the effect of a home portrait, you may often find yourself left with a considerable expanse of uninteresting background. While we have already assumed that you are a reasonably competent printer, it will not hurt to take this opportunity to show what can be done with an average picture to make it into a more finished looking portrait. Study therefore *Figures 104* and *105,* which are from the same negative, but clearly show what can be done to add interest and atmosphere with a bit of judicious burning in. The lighting diagram (*Figure 106*) is of course the same for both pictures. The prop which our subject is using for a support is the plastic balustrade shown in the bridal portrait (used vertically), with our white wall again used as background. The main source and fill-in were placed as usual for a full length, and the background was given a medium spread of light by the spot behind the balustrade. The main source was feathered up and the fill-in was about two feet above the subject's head. To pick up the hair we added a boom spot at left rear.

The result (*Figure 104*) was attractive, and we felt it did justice both to the

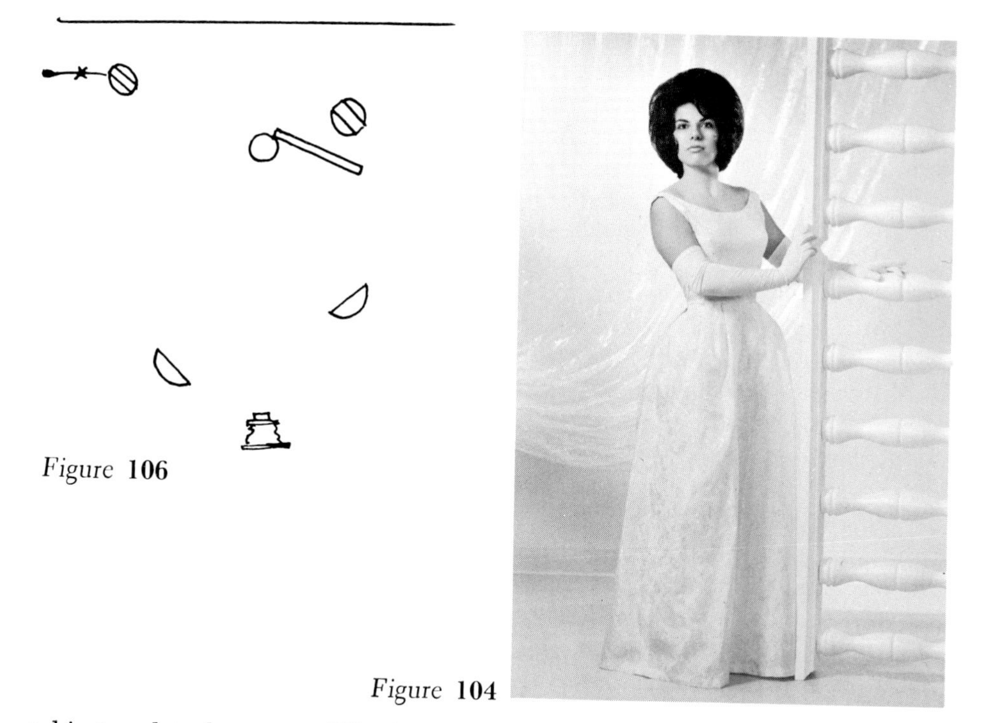

Figure 106

Figure 104

subject and to her gown. We did not doubt she would be satisfied with it, but still, it was "just another photograph," too much a record of the gown, with no "oomph" to it. We felt that it lacked atmosphere, that it needed to have more interest centered on the figure, that the balustrade was competing too strongly

Figure 105

with the face for attention, and that the lower right corner was rather drab. We decided to correct all this in the printing, by dodging (covering) the central area of the composition with an oval shaped paddle. Having given the negative the normal all over exposure, we gave all but that central area as much exposure again. Keep an assortment of dodging paddles, in various shapes handy, and you will find you need fewer props and less complicated lighting arrangements when you are working with full lengths.

Certainly we should not overlook the small fry while discussing full length poses because, if you photograph many children, these will frequently be requested. The little subject of *Figure 107* is three years old, fully as active as might be expected. A timely tip right here will save you many headaches when your aim is a full length of a child: pre-focus your camera, or if this is not practical, have an assistant keep the subject in one spot until you have completed all camera adjustments. Make a mental note of that spot, or rather, small area, because you will have to allow a certain amount of leeway around the figure. You can then forget about further manipulation of the camera, other than the final procedure of making the exposure, and feel free to proceed with securing a suitably vivavious pose and expression. Patience and the ability to recognize instantly what you want will be your chief essentials.

You will be better off with a simple lighting, which will enable you to concentrate on the subject. We advise (as in *Figure 108*) an almost standard placement of main source and fill-in, with nothing else. However, in this case we kept the main source well to the side, so that part of the illumination fell on the

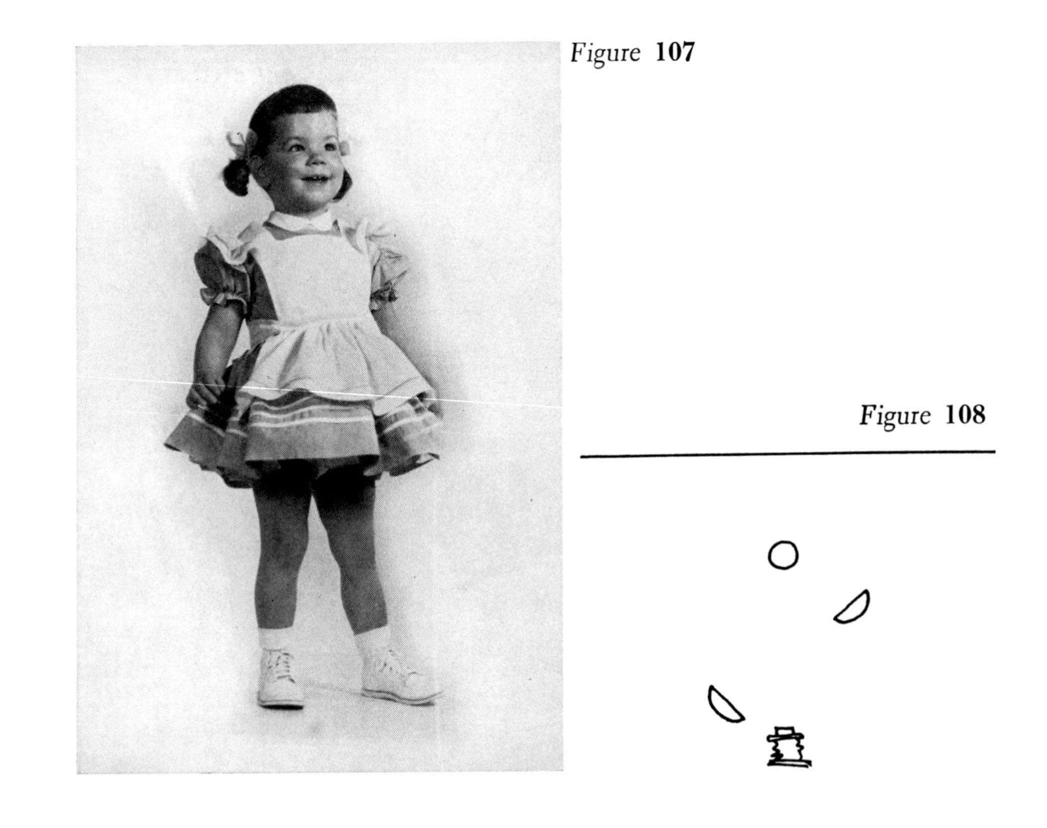

Figure **107**

Figure **108**

light background, keeping it light and dispelling the shadows. The fill-in, by the way, was placed rather high and directed down on the subject—or rather the place where we finally succeeded in catching her. As shown here, this is a vignette—not a camera vignette, but one made in the darkroom—because it means less to worry about in the camera room. The sketch effect was worked in with powder, cotton stump, and eraser, as described in an earlier chapter, to relieve the severity of a plain vignette. The purpose of the vignette should be obvious: even though you have focused on a restricted area, the pose may still cast an unexpected and undesirable shadow on the background. What you want is the figure, and the vignette enables you to center all your interest on that alone.

CHAPTER 13

The Profile

Few people are accustomed to seeing themselves in profile. Women do so more frequently than men, because of their greater use of three-way mirrors while "putting on their faces," but even to them a profile portrait will look a bit strange. For that matter, none of us are ever wholly pleased with a portrait, because it never looks to us exactly as we appear to ourselves. A photograph, you know, is the only way we can ever see ourselves as we appear to others. Being unable to see through their eyes, we depend upon mirrors, and therefore must always view ourselves in reflection, and not directly. A profile portrait is therefore doubly strange, and consequently being far more of a novelty, attracts immediate attention in any group of photographs. Thus, to the photographer who wishes his work to stand out from the commonplace, the ability to produce well lighted, well modeled profile portraits can be a valuable asset.

More to the point is the fact that many professionals neglect to seize the opportunities presented by the profile, even to the point of dodging the issue whenever possible. This is due largely to the erroneous belief that profiles require complicated lightings, which is far from the case, as we propose to make clear in this chapter. Most assuredly, profile lighting can be accomplished in much less time than is required for almost any type of portrait of a child or, for that matter, a plain head and shoulders of a cantankerous or obdurate adult. The principal difference, in so far as lighting is concerned, is that a spot or other light, at the rear or the side, replaces the usual main source light.

Before we discuss the illustrations in detail, let us clarify one other point. Excellent though the profile portrait may be as an attention getter, or to add a touch of variety to a set of proofs, we do not suggest that you attempt profiles of all who come before your camera. The profile is the most revealing view of any subject's facial characteristics. Receding or bulging foreheads, over large or misshappen noses, bulging eyes, protruding lips, lantern jaws, and weak or double chins are all immediately accentuated in a profile view. In fact, in a profile these cannot be concealed or disguised in any way, whereas in the customary view of a face, angled slightly to one side or the other (because only a few of us are blessed with the almost symmetrical features of true beauties), any competent professional can make the most homely individual look at least presentable. Study your subject first, and only suggest a profile if it will be pleasing, if not flattering. Do not, if you can avoid it, make profiles of persons wearing glasses. It can be done, and sometimes beautifully, but is something only the experienced—and expert—cameraman should attempt.

On the other hand, when the subject before you does have a good profile, you overlook a golden opportunity if you let that subject get away from your camera without making at least one profile. People do not buy profiles in quantity, but making one definitely means an added sale, because it presents the subject in a manner that is unexpected. Don't get the idea that people who do have good profiles are unaware of it, because they will have been told of the fact many times by their relatives and friends. Indeed, if you as a photographer, considered an authority on faces, do *not* comment on the beauty of a fine profile, your reputation as an artist will suffer in so far as that subject's opinion of you is concerned. But don't go overboard. Fulsome flattery is neither necessary nor wise. Just tell a woman: "You have a beautiful profile," or say to a man: "Yours is a strong profile," and add that you want to take "just one more picture." The suggestion will be welcomed, the more so because chances are good that you will be the first professional photographer to have made it.

Babies and children nearly always have attractive profiles, and one sure way of pleasing a mother is to make at least one such negative. The more poses of a youngster, the better in any event, because, if they are sufficiently varied, mothers and relatives find them irresistible; your order will grow from the sale of extra prints. Suppose we commence, then, with just such a subject for our first illustration. *Figure 109* is of a sweet little girl decked out in her "Sunday dress and hat" in a manner which can only be described as "cute." First—and don't overlook this—we made our customary full face poses from various angles and then, the youngster being just as cooperative as she was sweet, this one. For a child we want just a faint edge light, to bring out the features, and this is provided by the boom spot at the right (*Figure 110*), somewhat to the rear of the subject. This spot is really our main source, and the fill-in, to right of the camera, gives us the necessary soft illumination and modeling of the features. Without that fill-in, of course, the result would be a silhouette.

Neither the boom spot nor the fill-in help at all with the back of the figure; so, to avoid a heavy shadow on that side with consequent imbalance of light and shade, we use a small boom light (not a spot because too much light will be disastrous) to add detail to the hair and the back of the dress, while at the same time bringing out the shape of the hat. While the spot is about on a level with the face, the second light is rather high. A back light behind the figure takes care of the background and is feathered downwards so that the lighter area hardly extends above the shoulders. To avoid any deep shadows on the face, undesirable in the case of a child, the fill-in is directed rather more into the face than would be normal were the subject an adult. This picture, it happens, was taken with speedlights, but it could easily be duplicated with any light source.

Figure 110

Figure 109

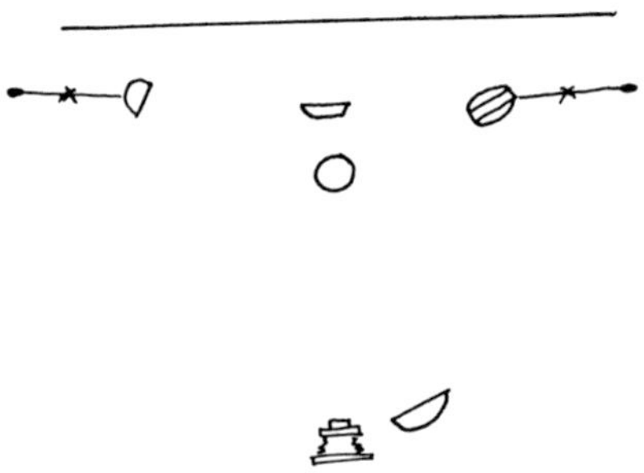

Whether a profile is directed toward the right or left is purely a matter for your own judgment. Usually, one side will be preferable, as you can quickly tell by having your model turn the head first one way and then the other. Doing this during an actual sitting, incidentally, will promptly display your own inexperience, because in your initial poses and lightings you should have had ample opportunity to form a judgment. Occasionally, some facial blemish will necessitate showing the opposite side, and infrequently a profile will be equally good from either. For *Figure 111* we had our young subject face to the left, and this, by the way, happens to be a case where a profile was specified. This young girl was to lose her prized pony tail before the start of the swimming season, and her mother wanted a portrait to mark this particular phase in the life of her daughter. How to include the pony tail without making it the dominating factor of the portrait? Obviously, by making a profile.

Since the subject had not quite reached the "formal" stage, we used a piece of net material from our stock of accessories, creating a rather soft drape effect over the shoulders and bust—and more about this important subject of draping in Chapter 21. Not wanting too much emphasis on the drape, since we were not dealing with an adult, we decided on a vignette, with the use of a translucent vignetter on the camera (to be explained in detail in Chapter 22). Studying the diagram (*Figure 112*) you will first note the background light behind the figure, thrown full onto the background to keep it light in tone. Our boom spot, on the left, was rather high and a little to the rear, its purpose being not only to outline the profile but also to throw some light on the forehead and the near cheekbone. On right is a boom light—not a spot—to illuminate the pony tail and the line of the shoulder on that side, which otherwise might merge into the background. The spot is the main source, and, for a lighting like this, it is good to adjust the other light—the boom light, or as it is sometimes called in profile work, the "kicker"—to about half the brilliance of the main source. Failure to do this will result in too equal a light on the profile and the back of the head, and of course we must not detract from the lines of the features, which are the main interest. The fill-in is close to the camera at left, but throws no light on the vignetter. It is feathered away from the face rather more than usual, care being taken to retain the modeling.

Before we leave *Figures 111* and *112*, we suggest a couple of experiments. Asking your subject to hold this pose, with all the lights in their exact positions, and using the same exposure that you did for the complete profile, try three more takes. First turn off all the lights, except that which illuminates the background; the result will be a silhouette, and while silhouettes are only occasionally saleable, they are excellent novelties for window display use, particularly if your subject happens to have a truly fine profile. Next, leaving the background light on, turn on the fill-in also, and you will have a semi-silhouette, a very attractive effect and one not often seen. Finally, turn off the fill-in again, leave on the background light, and add both the boom spot and the boom light. A print from this negative will be quite dramatic, although probably not saleable, but simple experiments like this will aid you greatly in learning to "read" light. Only in this manner can you discover for yourself, with your own equipment, to what extent one light adds to or cancels out the effect of another, which is what is meant by the term "reading" light.

Our purpose in presenting *Figure 113* is to acquaint you with a profile produced more in the style of what is called a "line" or "edge" lighting. The difference between this and ordinary profile lighting is that there is no carry over, from the spot which serves as the main source, onto the cheek which faces the camera. Interesting though line lighting is, and although it can be unquestionably dramatic

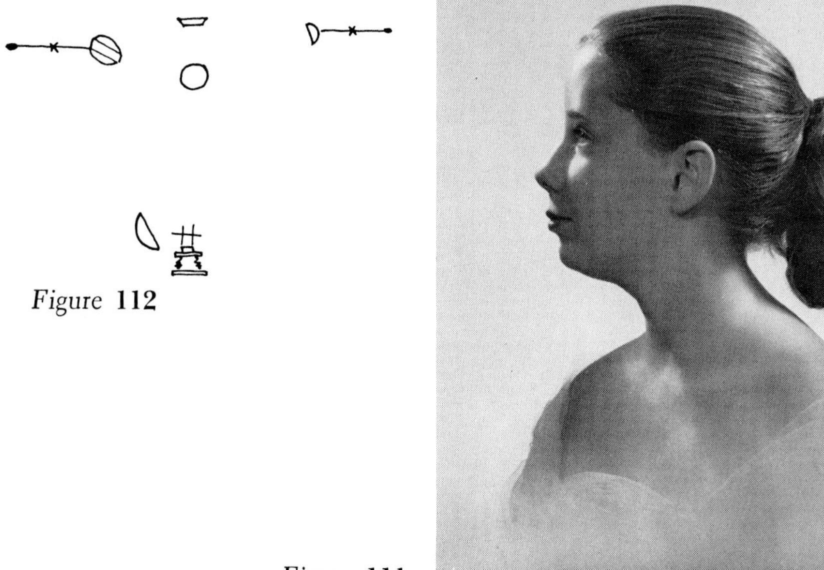

Figure 112

Figure 111

and forceful for a limited few, we neither advise nor recommend it. In plain language, it has nothing like the sales appeal of the other examples we are showing. The lighting shown in *Figure 114* is simple indeed, consisting of a fill-in, feathered up to provide a soft illumination of the visible side of the face, and two spots at right and left rear. The spot at the right, directed on the face (and again this is the main source), is kept well back. Care must be taken in its placement to be sure no light strikes the lens. Dramatic effect aside, and this is the sole purpose of line lighting, in our opinion a smaller amount of light on the back and top of the hair would be equally acceptable, perhaps more so. However, this will show what it is, and how easily it is accomplished. You will also notice that the two spots have provided all the relief necessary, so that a background light would serve no purpose and is therefore omitted.

Returning now, in *Figure 115*, to the type of profile lighting which we prefer and have found to be more generally acceptable to the public, compare the appeal of this with *Figure 113*. For one thing, the ratio of light on the hair to that on the face is much less, holding the interest on the features. The carry-over of the light from the spot to the cheek, mentioned before, produces a pleasing roundness, and at the same time, a better likeness. This light is produced by the boom spot (*Figure 116*), which is now at left rear, inasmuch as the subject is facing left. Be careful, though, that you do not bring that spot too far forward or you will overaccentuate the cheekbone. This spot should also be kept fairly high, so that the shadow thrown by the nose will pretty much follow the normal line of the cheek from nose to mouth. It is also well to let this shadow fade off gently, rather than having it end in an abrupt blob of black shadow on the cheek just above the upper lip. The light on the profile itself, plus this touch on the cheek, provides all the emphasis necessary to give this portrait life and interest, and heavy contrasting shadows are not required.

Figure 114

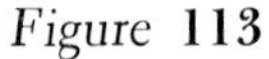

Figure 113

Figure **116**

Figure **115**

Looking again at the diagram (*Figure 116*), you will see the intentional absence of a background light. This is done so that the ground can be kept in an all over soft gray, so as not to draw attention away from the profile. The boom spot—the main source—on the left illuminates forehead, nose, lips and chin, as well as the cheek, and even spills over a little onto one hand and the other arm. Handle that spot carefully, because these extra touches of light, if properly placed and handled, give a welcome touch of relief while leading the viewer's eye to the face. Should they become too strong, the result will be just so many unrelated splashes of strong light, all competing with the face for attention and destroying the portrait. We have illuminated the hair and the subject's back with a boom light on the right, also brought a bit more forward than usual because we are including more of the arm in this picture, and it needs sufficient illumination to insure roundness. The fill-in, to left of the camera, and feathered up slightly to keep the lower part of the picture area subdued, provides just enough light for nicely balanced flesh tones and a pleasing, softly modeled result.

As a final illustration, consider *Figure 117*. We present this profile of a young man, as we feel that all too often the profile is left entirely for the feminine subject. If your subject is a smoker, you have every excuse to make a very interesting portrait using the pipe, cigar, or, as in this case, the cigarette held in the hand (but be sure its held naturally). If you keep your background lighting subdued, yon can easily get the smoke—if it isn't visible, a small bit of chewing gum placed on or in the tobacco will produce prolific smoke, but will spoil its use.

This type of portrait will make a "stopper" in your window display, will please a great percentage of your subjects, and really is not at all difficult to produce. Referring to *Figure 118*, you will note a background light, kept low to break just over the shoulders, and thereby not overilluminate the background. A boom spot lights the front of the face and acts as your "point-light," and a boom hair

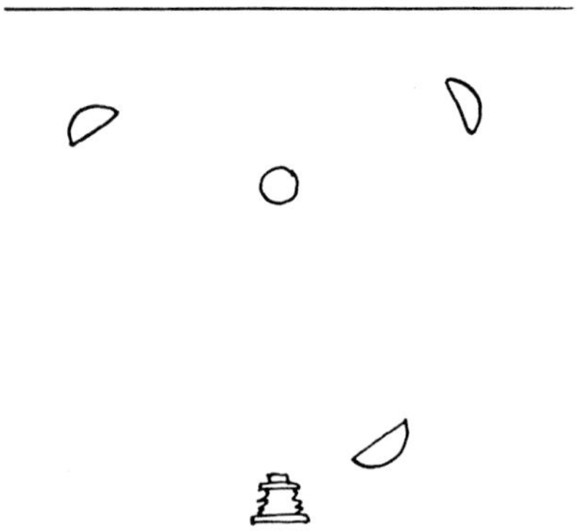

Figure 117

Figure 118

light back of the head and at right angles to the body gives some light to the back hair line. Your fill light is used to the right of the subject and feathered so as not to overilluminate the shadow, or camera, side of the face.

In summing up the chapter on profiles, bear in mind that not all people have good profiles; we never make them of people wearing glasses with heavy frames. But, when a person with a good profile comes to you for portraits, do not let him leave without making at least one profile to show with his proofs; you will be giving a service that too many photographers overlook.

CHAPTER 14

Essentials of Glamour Portraiture

By this time the reader may well have come to the conclusion that there is "too much of a sameness" to the illustrations we have shown, and to a certain extent that is true, and with good reason. After all, this book as its title indicates is a text—a manual if you will—with the specific purpose of teaching you how to produce, day in and day out, portraits that will appeal to your sitters. That involves primarily certain fundamentals of lighting and posing which, to be quite honest about it, do not vary greatly regardless of the age or sex of those who come to you for photographs. Photography is like any other art, profession or trade in that, before you can attempt to assert your own personality in your portraits, you must first know the basic requirements of what constitutes the making of a good portrait. Not until you know the rules, and how to apply them, can you safely undertake to depart from them. If you have mastered what we have offered in the preceding chapters, which we might well call a "bread and butter" course in practical portraiture, you are now ready to advance to something more interesting and—to some of your subjects though definitely not all of them—more appealing and even more saleable.

In other words, we are now ready to discuss "glamour" in portraiture, a term for a while so sadly abused that for a long time many professionals preferred to avoid this type of work entirely. Largely due to the influence of the excessively theatrical illustrations appearing first in the big circulation movie magazines and later in those devoted to television, both photographers and the public came to accept any portrait as glamourous that was a sufficiently startling departure from the conventional. While there is a place, and in fact a demand, for portraits of individuals who seem to be all but falling out of the picture area; harsh, contrasty effects with heavy blocked shadows; faces grotesquely enlarged until they completely fill the picture space and show every pore in the skin; others which show hardly a trace of retouching—these, believe us, are not glamour. Their purpose is solely to attract attention and stop the viewer.

We should also stress the fact that entertainers and others in show business require a—shall we say—revealing type of photography which you, as an average photographer, should avoid rather carefully when dealing with the girls and young women who come to you for portraits in the course of your normal activities. They will want something unusual and different, striking and appealing, but seldom are they seeking the deliberately sexy effects that appear to be what so many photographers have in mind when they speak of glamour. On the rare occasions when your average subject really wants something of that sort, she will tell you frankly and you can then safely "go to town" but otherwise use good judgment and remember that glamour can be fully as attractive and still remain in perfect taste. Your purpose is to attract more sitters, not to drive them away.

True glamour should evidence just as careful attention to correct lighting and composition as the most standard portrait—it is only the effect, the treatment, that varies. Glamour does require more care and attention to technique, but it does warrant that extra effort because, first of all, there are far too few professionals willing to go to the necessary trouble, and second, because there are in any community many persons ready to pay well for such portraits. With one exception our illustrations for this Chapter are limited to younger women, because only once in a blue moon will you be confronted with—unless he is in show business—a man who wants to be glamourized in his picture. Glamour portraits like those which follow offer genuine possibilities, not as an exclusive field but as an adjunct to your regular type of portraiture.

As with every branch of photography, even glamour has certain basic factors which you must take into consideration. You must select your prospects for such portraits judiciously. Those who are not trim and neat both in their clothing and personal grooming are not suitable subjects and probably would not be interested in any event. Subjects need not necessarily be beautiful so long as they have charm and grace, in fact it is surprising what can be done with many a sitter whose face, in repose, is ordinary to the extent of being almost unattractive. Those who wear glasses and who suffer from the affliction of buck teeth are best overlooked. For that matter, even if your subject has beautiful teeth they should not show prominently and smiles with the lips closed are far preferable. A brilliant display of teeth may be fine for an advertisement of dental products but no matter how fine the portrait may be otherwise, the subject will soon tire of it. You must seek to get expression from the eyes and, in general, your aim will be for the "come hither" look, usually accompanied by an upward tilt of the head. You must be careful that lip rouge is applied properly and that the hair is well groomed. Trivial though some of these bits of advice may sound, they must be borne in mind before you start to work because they all add up in the end result: satisfying the subject.

So far as technique is concerned, having reached this point in these pages, you should know how to make a good basic lighting, lacking which understanding you should not even attempt glamour. You must expose your film correctly because you want detail in the highlights and most certainly need "open" shadows. Your negatives must be beautifully retouched; in fact in glamour work you will seldom find anyone complaining about over retouching provided the likeness is not destroyed. Finally, in printing, you must record the entire scale of tones of your negative—chalk and soot are not glamour as your subjects will expect it.

Most of your glamour subjects will be in their late teens, twenties and early

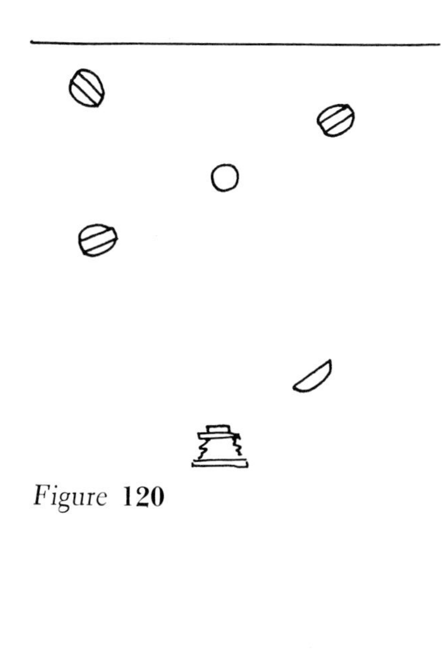

Figure 120

Figure 119

thirties, but now and again an older person will prove to be an excellent prospect and so for our first illustration, *Figure 119,* we have selected a portrait made some years ago of Mrs. Falk when she was about thirty eight, just to show that glamour is by no means limited to the young. Notice that the shadow of the nose "bleeds off" rather than stopping sharply on the face. Thus attention is not drawn to the nose, of which she is conscious though not over sensitive. The lips do not smile but the eyes certainly do in that "come hither" effect we spoke of earlier. Basically, except that we have substituted a spot at left front of the subject for our customary main source flood (*Figure 120*) this lighting differs very little from many that we have already shown you. About all we have done is to throw a touch of highlighting on the hair and the edges of the hat by means of the two spots at right and left rear, just as in many previous illustrations. We haven't even thrown a light on the background!

The saucy tilt of the shoulders, keeping the chin well up, and the expression, are what really give this portrait glamour. The hat, the flower and the veil all help of course and while the flower and veil might well be studio accessories (they were not in this case) the point we want to make is that here is glamour without a lot of time spent in "dressing up" the subject. What is important is the ability to recognize on sight the possibilities of such a hat, for example, when its wearer walks into your camera room, and to visualize what you can do with that subject if you break away from the conventional poses which you first—and quite properly—make. Accessories or no accessories, never forget that any reasonably attractive, well dressed woman has personality which, with a little imagination and a few deft touches on your part, can quickly and easily be converted into glamour.

Figure 121 is another example of a glamour portrait which results almost entirely from posing and expression, plus a very simple lighting—*Figure 122.* Here is a young

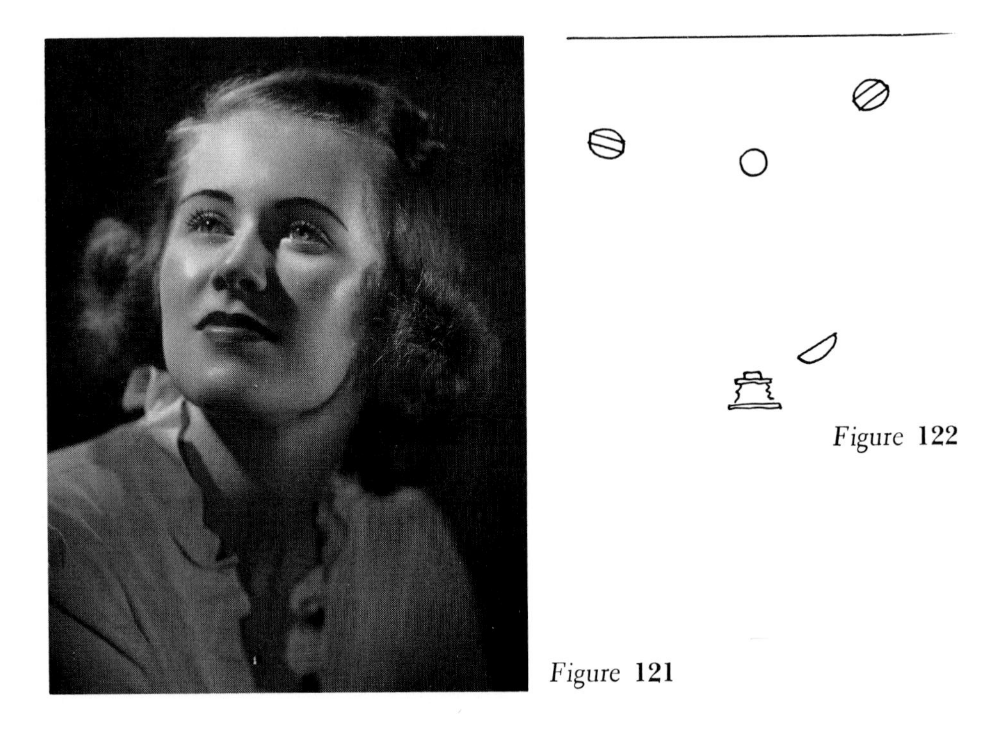

Figure 122

Figure 121

sorority president, a girl with a lot of poise, a full share of good looks, but a sweet simplicity about her whole attitude. Such a subject might confront you any day in the week and the last thing in the world she would want would be a dizzily lighted, freakish portrait. Certainly she has boy friends and she wants to look as glamourous to them as possible, but she doesn't want to "knock them for a loop." So, with no accessories whatever, we give her glamour by raising her chin, catching an introspective expression and taking full advantage of a pair of lovely eyes. The fill-in is at the camera as usual, slightly feathered away, and for a main source we use a spot, high, at the left. To throw the figure in relief against, mind you, a perfectly plain background—into which of course we must not let the hair merge and disappear—we use a spot at the rear on the other side. This is not a picture that will do for the college year book and it will probably not be chosen by her parents and relatives, but it is one that she, her boy friends and a few chums will treasure—and it means the sale of extra prints.

Now we will change, with *Figure 123*, to an entirely different type of lighting (*Figure 124*) which some professionals call "butterfly" although we prefer not to name it at all. The term is derived from the shape of the shadow thrown directly beneath the nose and while this lighting has its purposes, and can be very effective in glamour work, it must be used with caution. If the subject has a nose which verges toward the large, having this shadow below the nose will draw too much attention to it. It is most appropriate for those subjects who are blessed with comparatively symmetrical features, whose facial structure runs toward the square or rectangular, and who carry out the effect with a rather symmetrical hairdo. Given such a combination the lighting can be highly flattering.

First we place two spots at right and left to illuminate the hair and bring it in proper relief against the background which, again, is plain and dark. Our subject, incidentally, is seated on a couch on the high end of which she is resting one elbow so that her hand can rest against her head. We are going to need something up there to balance a corsage we expect to place in the lower right. We have made up a drape effect for her, using glam'e cloth. Over the high end of the couch we first throw a white fur piece—a handy accessory—on which her elbow rests and on which we have placed her other hand, below her chin. This time, you see, we are going to a bit more trouble to secure our glamour result. Next, for our main source, we place a boom spot almost directly in front of the lens and just slightly to the side of the lens-to-subject axis, and raise the spot high so the light is thrown directly down on the face. Immediately the butterfly shadow appears, and note also that just enough of this light, which also strikes the shoulder, spills over onto the background to produce the same effect we would have from a very weak spot placed low behind the subject.

We now add the corsage which appears at lower right and give our attention to the hand in the foreground. The fingers, we see, are not too prominent and while our boom spot does strike the back of the hand it does so unobtrusively. If all of the back of the hand were showing it would not be attractive—the back of a hand seldom is—but we have been careful to conceal much of it with the fur. Our real purpose in placing the hand there was to show the ring, a bit of attention to detail that you must cultivate until it becomes second nature. Any woman is proud of an engagement ring and the idea is to include it without the fact becoming too obvious. Enough of the light from the boom spot has struck the ring to give it just the right sparkle and so our portrait is all set except for one thing.

The front of the hair shows almost no detail, there are heavy shadows in the eye pockets, the butterfly under the nose and the shadow under the chin are almost solid black. All of this, for the photographer who does not appreciate the difference, constitutes glamour, but it isn't the kind of glamour that we want so now we turn on our

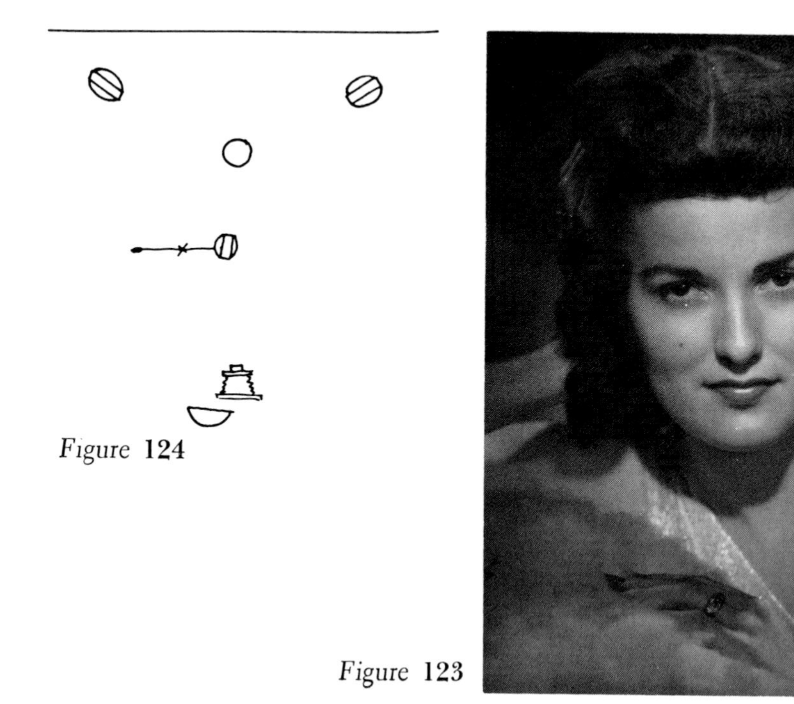

Figure 124

Figure 123

fill-in, moving it beside and almost to the rear of the camera, quite high and feathered up, and just about on a line with the boom spot. Our unsightly shadows now have luminosity and detail and we are ready to make the exposure. Consider the expression of the eyes and merest hint of a smile around the lips. Our subject has become a sultry siren with no need to resort to *decolletage* or similar implications. Cover the hand and corsage with a piece of card and you will see that the eyes, mouth and expression are what provide the real glamour. The rest, while it helps to make a pretty picture, is little more than window dressing but was required because we did want to include that ring.

Some readers may argue that *Figure 125*, a portrait of a college girl taken in a rather simple drape made from a black *mantilla*, another studio accessory which can be used in many ways and is an extremely helpful item, is not actually glamour. From a lighting placement standpoint, see *Figure, 126*, that may be very true because we have our two rear spots, a fill-in and a main source all in approximately standard positions. Note, however, that the two rear spots are in this case high up and directed downward and that we are using another spot—a boom spot—as the main source. It is exactly this use of the spots, resulting in more pronounced shadows although they are still transparent and not dead black, plus the expression and the drape, that moves this portrait into the glamour classification.

The background is deliberately black and severe so that, by contrast, it concentrates all attention on the girl's features and a pair of lovely shoulders, the latter of course emphasized by the downward light from the rear spots. The shadow effect on the face is certainly not what would be expected in a conservative portrait and as for the drape, cover it with a couple of pieces of cardboard so it has the shape of a standard V drape and note the far less interesting result. As we must keep emphasizing, much of the difference between glamour and standard portraiture lies

Figure **125**

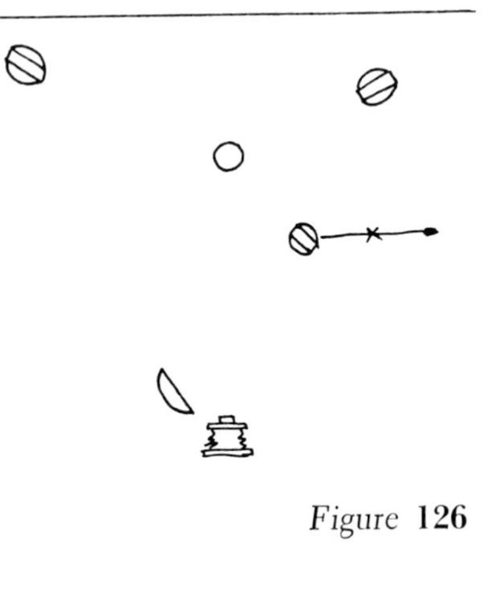

Figure **126**

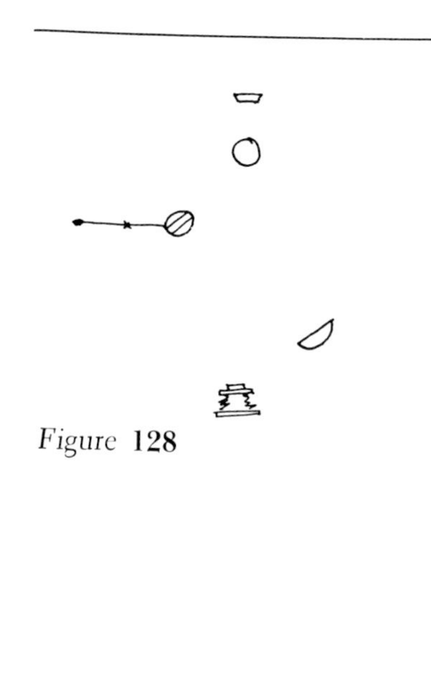

Figure **128**

Figure **127**

in your ability to click your shutter at just the right moment of expression of eyes and mouth. Thanks to the fill-in, beside the camera in normal position, all the shadows have tone and modeling and just enough detail is brought out in the *mantilla* to prevent it from looking like a solid black mass. No light was permitted to touch the background.

In *Figure 127* we have gone almost to the other extreme and have depended considerably on a studio accessory for our glamourized result, although eyes, mouth and expression remain the key to the situation. This is interesting also because it represents a departure from our earlier advice not to attempt glamour portraiture when subjects wear glasses. This girl had very fine eyes and, even though she had short hair, we thought her features were of an exotic type which might lend themselves to an unusual effect. When, at our suggestion, she removed the glasses we were convinced that we could glamourize her in a manner that would be truly striking and so, again drawing on our stock of materials, we draped a piece of mesh cloth around her head, partly for its Oriental effect but more necessarily to conceal the hair.

We placed a background light behind her in *Figure 128* to lighten the background although, in the final printing, we felt it preferable to concentrate interest on the face and therefore burned in the corners. Because of the illumination of the background we needed no spots at the rear inasmuch as there was ample separation and depth without them, but for a main source placed a boom spot, not directly in front as we did for *Figure 123*, but a bit to the side although the spot was quite high and directed downward to secure the same socalled butterfly lighting. The tone of her skin being somewhat darker we moved the fill-in somewhat closer in order to emphasize the detail of the mesh, and give it an effect of bulk below the chin without mass or solidity.

Our chief purpose in this Chapter has been to prove that glamour is not necessarily a matter of accessories but to a much greater extent a problem of the right pose or tilt of the head plus the facility to secure a particular type of expression. While making your first and more conventional poses you must learn to watch your subject's facial changes and especially those which are more animated, making quick mental notes of those you will later wish repeated should you decide you have before you a possible glamour prospect. Then you must later build your glamour pose and lighting around that expression and, when all is ready, by means of conversation or cajolery, bring it back. In brief: eyes, mouth and expression—those are the essentials of glamour. Too many photographers labor under the impression that glamour implies what is crudely spoken of as sex appeal. Nothing could be farther from the fact, as is demonstrated by the illustrations in this and Chapter 15, which follows.

CHAPTER 15

Helpful Accessories for Glamour Effects

If you are really to establish a reputation in the glamour field you must find someone among your assistants who will be willing to make a study of draping. If you operate alone we think it would be a serious mistake not to become at least reasonably expert in the use of drapes yourself. Anyone can quickly toss around a subject's shoulders the commonplace type of V drape, frequently required for school portraiture and sometimes for older women, but you or an assistant must be able to create what really amounts to a new neck line for a girl or woman and thus produce the effect of a formal gown with little more than a length or two of fabric and a piece or two of inexpensive costume jewelry. We mention this here because we must speak of drapes frequently in connection with glamour, although draping is sufficiently important—and not only for glamour portraiture—that we discuss it in detail in Chapter 21.

It is, as we have already explained, entirely possible and sometimes much wiser to glamourize a subject without adding accessories of any type. More commonly, however, and so that the average subject may more easily differentiate a glamour portrait (for which as a rule there is an extra charge) from the more conventional poses and lightings, it is customary to make use of drapes and accessories in connection with the bust and figure and further to embellish such portraits with special background treatments. Accordingly, in each of the illustrations selected for this Chapter something extra has been added. What you may care to do along these lines is a matter for your own discretion and while it is well to have available some lengths of assorted fabrics, a few pieces of costume jewelry, some artificial flowers and perhaps a bouquet or two as well as some sprays of foliage or other gadgets for casting background shadows, plus some larger lengths of material for background use, it is not necessary to invest any large sum of money.

Particularly is it unwise to embark on an immediate shopping spree with the intention of accumulating all at one time whatever you may be likely to need. Almost surely you will spend more than you should and will find yourself saddled with

Figure **129**

Figure **130**

items which, in your initial eagerness and enthusiasm, seemed most desirable but which probably you will seldom if ever use. Take your time in selecting props and accessories and let experience dictate to you what will be most suitable and generally applicable for the type of subjects you normally photograph. And also, if other photographers in your vicinity or of your acquaintance show glamour portraits in their displays, make a point of studying these and securing entirely different accessories and props from what they use. One advantage of glamour portraiture is that it enables you to add your personal touch to your sittings, and the last thing you should do is to slavishly copy the work of others.

Our first illustration (*Figure 129*) you will recognize as another portrait of a young lady we glamourized somewhat more elaborately in Chapter 14 (*Figure 123*). We have worked with the almost conventional lighting shown in *Figure 130* for a very soft effect on the face to secure well modeled features with no deep shadows. This example shows that even with a comparatively flat lighting, accompanied by proper exposure and development, fine roundness and proper projection of the features can be secured. We have used spots at right and left rear to give the hair ample illumination without burning out the detail and of course these spots also provide the necessary separation from the background. Our main source and fill-in are much as we would place them for any conventional lighting. Note, however, the spot at left which is directed on the background through a piece of woven rattan about three inches square to provide the interesting shadow effect, which breaks up the background but not too evidently and without any sharp pattern to detract from the face. A piece from the seat of an old cane chair, if not too tightly woven, would do instead.

The accessory is a simple black V drape which, let us remark, is not just the customary yard or two of plain velvet but has been lined with a light colored material that gives the material more body and adds greatly to its usefulness. Permitting it to fall slightly off one shoulder emphasizes that shoulder by contrast and its curving away at neck and bosom, showing the light lining, adds to the come hither effect. Plain, unlined velvet merely clings to the figure. The pose is important here, too. We have the tilt of the body which is so much associated with glamour work, but we have nevertheless included enough of the figure at the bottom of the picture space so there is a base and we do not have the feeling that our subject is going to fall forward. Despite everything else, much of this effect results from the expression of the eyes and the lines of the mouth which we have been careful not to break with a smile. One other point: be sure your fill-in is so handled that there is at least a suggestion of texture or feeling to the drape, which should not appear solid and heavy.

For *Figure 131*, to show how the same background and almost the identical pose can be used for a blonde as for a brunette, our two spots at the rear remain in very nearly the original positions, as does the spot which throws the shadow on the background, but from that point on as *Figure 132* indicates, our lighting is entirely different. Because this subject is blonde and has the fair complexion that accompanies such hair, we need a bit more contrast between face and hair and therefore want to accentuate the shadows on the face. We want to define them more plainly but still keep them under proper control. So we select for our main source a boom spot which we place high but, because we do not want a butterfly shadow under the nose to emphasize it (this one is a little tip tilted), we place the spot somewhat to the side to allow the shadow from the nose to bleed off the face. The fill-in, at the camera, lightens all our shadows without destroying them.

Aside from the background treatment, which plays no small part in this glamouriz-

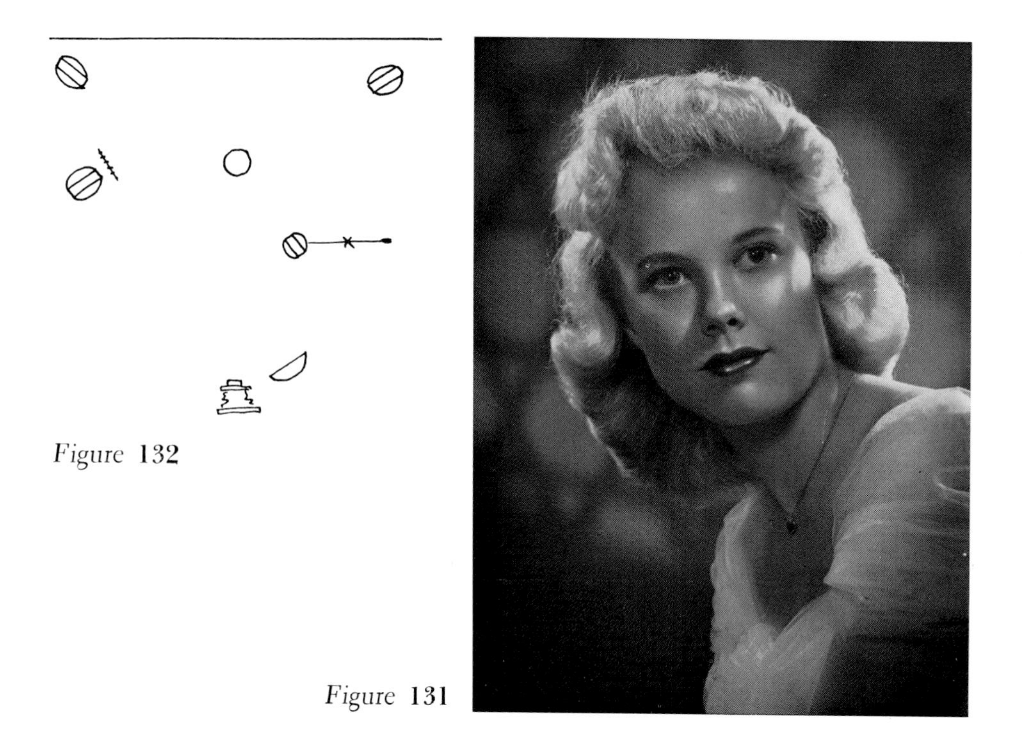

Figure 132

Figure 131

ing assignment, we have used only one accessory, again a drape. Now you see why you need several such pieces of material, because here a black drape would be quite unsuitable. This is a length of white tulle—any pastel shade would do, but to give it body and add an interesting touch of roundness to repeat the lines of the hair (repetition often adds to a composition) we have rolled it loosely instead of placing it flatly over the shoulders. When dealing with a blonde you must use your rear spots with great care to bring out the fluffy lightness of the hair and hold its detail without destroying its beauty by heavy shadows. So many times in socalled glamour pictures the hair is so dark and blocked out that it is impossible to discern whether the subject is blonde or brunette. We are firmly of the opinion that a blonde should be portrayed as a blonde and have little patience with the cameraman who is too lax or too incompetent to accomplish this. Aside from that, blondes are inordinately proud of their hair and, having become rather sadly accustomed to the fact that it usually photographs dark, will tell their friends about you if you make them look as they really are.

Now for something a bit more sophisticated. Our subject in *Figure 133* was wearing a very lovely gown and we felt we could best do her justice with a three quarter pose. She had all the attributes necessary for a first class glamour portrait and we went to some lengths to see what could be done about it. First, some distance in front of our regular background we hung from a standard an ample length of glam'e cloth, the material being not only long enough to reach the floor but voluminous enough to allow us ample leeway to hang it in soft pleats. We asked her to stand in front of that and, not wanting too great an expanse of bare arms, draped a marabou stole (from our stock of accessories) around her arms just off the shoulders. Deciding we needed a little additional accent in the background, so the play of

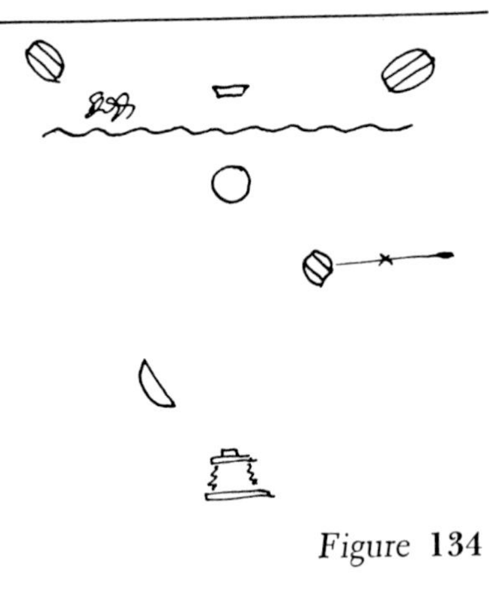

Figure **134**

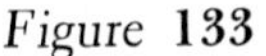

Figure **133**

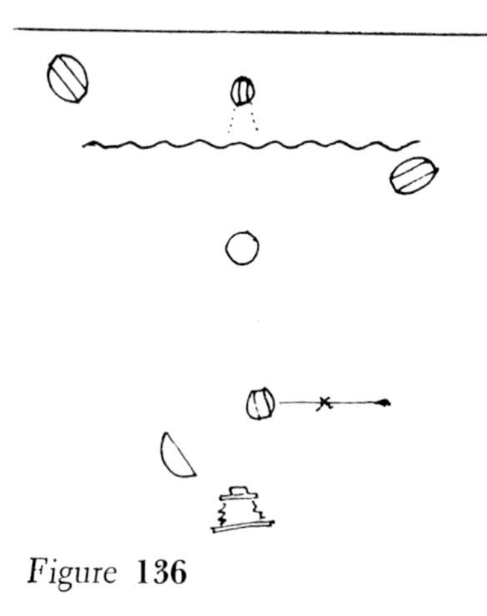
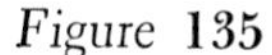

Figure 136

Figure 135

light on the glam'e cloth would not be too monotonous, we hung a spray of leaves at upper left, behind the glam'e.

This glam'e cloth—which is not expensive—is very translucent, with just enough body so it picks up light in a most interesting manner. We wanted that light effect around the edges of the picture area but not cutting directly against the figure so, behind the glam'e (and the subject) we placed a background light directed, not against the glam'e but, at the regular background in the rear (*Figure 134*). This brought the shoulders and the stole out in good relief. Then, to illuminate the hair and bring out the detail at the sides of figure and gown, we put our two spots at right and left rear, though behind the glam'e so their light was directed through it to retain the soft, airy treatment we wanted. For our main source we again used a boom spot, directing it from the side to bleed off the shadow of the nose and feathering it up slightly to avoid any strong lighting on the chest. You will see many portraits of this type where careless handling of the main source has thrown so much light on chest and bosom, sometimes even burning them out, that they overpower the face. Instead, as here, they should always be gently modeled and retain the full value of the flesh tones. Finally, the fill-in, not quite as close to the camera as usual, to illuminate the shadows on the face and bring out the detail of the gown. A lot of trouble, you may say, but well worth it from the standpoints of pleasing the subject and convincing all to whom she shows the finished print that when it comes to glamour, you know your business.

For our last illustrations we have selected two portraits of the same young lady, using identical accessories in each case but altering the pose slightly and the lighting considerably. *Figure 135* is an example of a soft lighting on the face, carefully controlled to let the cheeks recede but still retain the modeling, a condition which often does not obtain when this socalled butterfly lighting is used. For this (*Figure 136*)

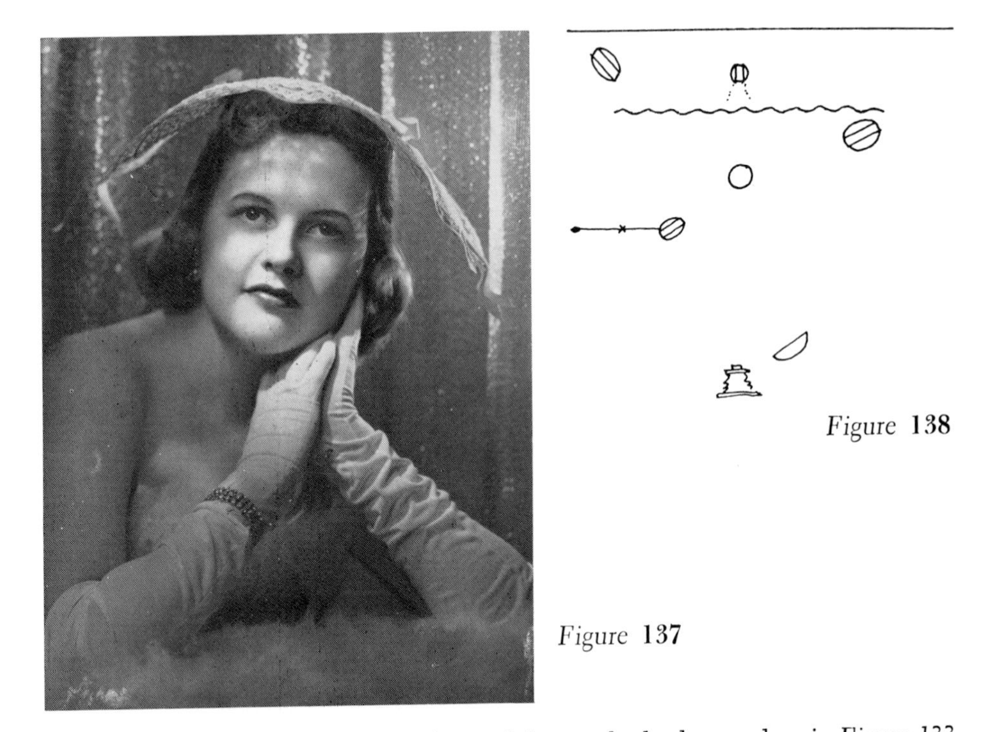

Figure **137**

Figure **138**

the drape of glam'e cloth is used in front of the regular background, as in *Figure 133*, but this time our subject is seated at a small table covered with a piece of fur, on which she is resting her arms. Because we must have separation of the shoulders from the background, we place a small spot behind the glam'e and direct it at the figure. Our left rear spot is also behind the glam'e cloth to bring out the hair on that side and not lose the hat which, like the glam'e, happens to be translucent and requires careful handling.

Because the gloved hands and arms are an important part of our composition we move the right rear spot in front of the glam'e but feather it away because we want the hands to remain in shadow. If they were not, in their position some distance from the face, they would draw attention from the face and instead of being an asset to the picture would be a detriment. Our main source is a boom spot, high and almost directly over the head, shooting down but kept on the face and off the hands and arms. Our fill-in, at left of the camera, is feathered away from the subject and up because we do not want too much illumination on the lower part of the figure or we will have too great a multiplicity of detail. As it is, the lines of the shoulders, the arms and hands, all draw attention to the face which remains the center of interest. The streaks of light on the glam'e are the only other competition, but only sufficiently to add interest. If, in addition to those lights, the hands and arms were lit and there were much illumination on the lower third of the picture space, the face would be lost.

In the other portrait (*Figure 137*) we have made a slight change in the pose. The subject's body now faces the camera more directly and her head is tilted so it rests on the hands. Because the hands and arms are now in direct relation to the face they can be, and properly should be, illuminated. Were they left in shadow the head would seem without support and as now placed they are integral with the main center of interest—the face—and no longer compete with it. With everything else remaining the same we depart from the butterfly lighting and (*Figure 138*) move the spot, our main source, to the other side where it now casts a bleed shadow of the nose across the cheek and our whole lighting on the face becomes more forceful. The fill-in, likewise, moves to the other side of the camera and is again feathered up to avoid too much illumination on the lower portions of the arms and the top of the table.

The purpose of these two illustrations is to show how, once a rather elaborate arrangement of props and accessories has been prepared for a glamour portrait, it is possible, by means of a rather simple change in the lighting, to secure two different poses and thus, without a lot of the manual labor involved in moving props and lights, show the subject an additional proof. With respect to both we might also add that the bracelet is a fortunate accessory and the wrinkles in the long gloves have deliberately not been smoothed out. Both the bracelet and the wrinkles break up, and add interest to, what would otherwise be a long, rather dull, expanse of the arms. Had the subject not been wearing long gloves we might well have decided against either of these poses because arms, if too prominent and no matter how well shaped and cared for, are not too interesting in any portrait, glamour or not.

CHAPTER 16

When People Ask for "Something Different"

Occasions will arise when a subject, perhaps bored with portraits that all look more or less alike, but more probably with some specific purpose or requirement in mind, will tell you flatly that nothing in the way of poses or lightings you have shown is "just what I want." Usually she, because most frequently the objection will come from a younger woman, can give you no more help than to say she wants "something different." We are not thinking of those in show business because not only do they know what they need but they gravitate to a number of specialists in theatrical photography who are fully aware of the problems and requirements. If yours is a university or college town, however, you may well be asked to produce a portrait that will indicate some particular talent of your subject, who may be semi-professionally in the entertainment field or perhaps an author or lecturer, who approaches you hopefully rather than undergo the expense of traveling to some nearby big city solely to be photographed. Perhaps such a picture may be needed for a divider page in a year book or for use on a Christmas card. In any event the problem is in your lap, you are—or want to be considered as—an expert in your field and it is up to you to produce that "something different."

Variations from the conventional in lighting and posing are without limit and we cannot, in the one chapter which is all we can allot to this subject, do more than offer a few suggestions and then only in the hope that they will stimulate your own originality. We can hardly do better than cite a few examples from our own experience which, over the years, has exactly paralleled the career of the average studio owner and will, assuming you are just on the threshold of a lifetime in professional photography, almost certainly duplicate what will happen to you in the years to come. Techniques, processes and materials change constantly in photography, although the basic rules of composition, lighting and posing do not. Nor do people. Talk with any professional about the idiosyncrasies of his subjects and you will find that whether he is located in a big metropolitan center or a small cross roads community, whether he deals with the "carriage trade" or plain Tom, Dick and

Mary off the street, people in the mass are much alike. So, when the demand for "something different" confronts you, don't reach for this book with any hope that it will give you an immediate answer. Instead look over these illustrations once again and accept them solely as a fillip to your own imagination.

Let's take something easy first, like the case of the popular young lady who, engaged in many activities, with a host of friends and a well-to-do father, has been photographed any number of times. For some reason she needs a new portrait but she doesn't want a head and shoulders, and she has full length pictures, and she's just so fed up with being photographed that if you can't show her "something different" she's going to get Daddy to take her to New York or Chicago or wherever it may be, and get a *good* photograph! And she's been glamourized too—perhaps by yourself. First you calm her down and tell her there are any number of poses in which she has never been photographed (which will intrigue her and arouse her interest) while mentally you are beating your brains out until—comes an idea! You then suggest: "Let's go into the camera room. I want to try a pose I saw the other day in *Vogue*, or *Harper's Bazaar* or any other famous fashion magazine that comes to your mind. Don't say you want to try something you saw at a convention because that means nothing to her, while a fashion magazine does.

So, proceeding into the camera room, you draw a chair—preferably of the ladder back type—in front of the background and before she has a chance to tell you again that she wants "something different" you say: "I don't want you to sit on it" and move it sideways to the camera, asking her to stand behind it and rest her hands on the top as in *Figure 139*. Then you say: "Now lean back, away from the chair and turn your face toward the camera." By that time she will be interested and ready to cooperate so you move your main source and fill-in to their customary positions (*Figure 140*) and slide a head screen into place to hold back the light on the arms and hands and front of her dress. For a pose like this you need definite relief from the background and you also want to accentuate her waist line so you illuminate the background with a small spot behind her, but keep the light directed fairly low. Next, to illuminate the hair and assure separation from the background, which is to be darker in the upper portion, also to give a bit more "pep" to the light on the one side of the face, you add two spots at right and left rear. The spot at left is a bit more open than usual because you not only want a touch of light to outline the back of the skirt but a little should spill over as an accent on the chair. Lastly, when you print, burn in the corners judiciously. A flattering result and definitely different, but don't make the mistake of using that same chair in exactly the same recognizable manner with a lot of other girls!

While we have this subject before the camera, let's see what else can be done that will be truly novel, to her anyway. For the result in *Figure 141*, we remove the chair and slide into place any piece of furniture which has a surface or back of sufficient length to bleed out at both sides of the picture space, and enough height so our subject can place her hands on it without leaning forward. Throw a blanket or length of fabric over it to disguise its lines if necessary—all the finished print will disclose will be that she is standing behind some horizontal object. We are going to take her from the back, with her face in profile, and can do so because she has a nice back and arms that have graceful lines. We ask her to stand close to whatever it is, rest her hands on it lightly and turn her head to the right.

Figure **139**

This pose of course will change our lighting (*Figure 142*) completely, except that the spot thrown on the background can remain just where it was. For our main source we select a boom spot and place it at the right, somewhat to the rear, but enough toward the camera so we do not have an edge lighting but one of the type

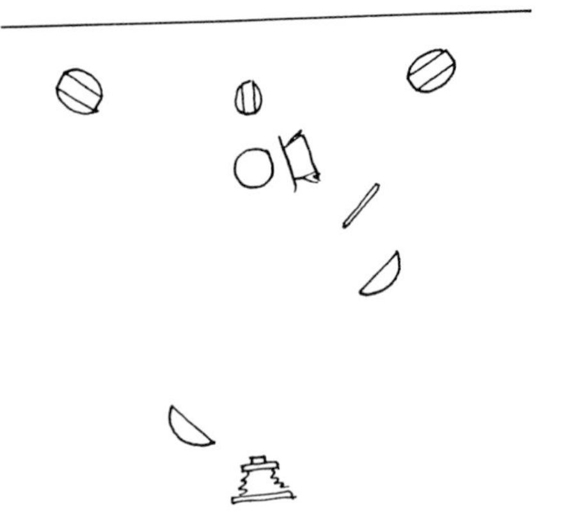

Figure **140**

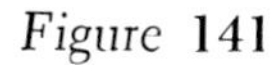

Figure 141

we discussed in Chapter 13, the light falling past the nose and on the cheek. Now the triangular composition formed by the lines of the arms draws the viewer's eyes up to the face where the lighting holds the attention. We need to balance this with illumination on the back of the hair and the other shoulder, as well as the skirt

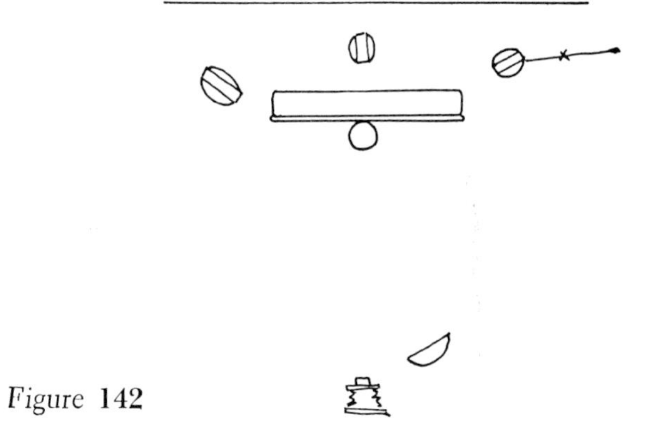

Figure 142

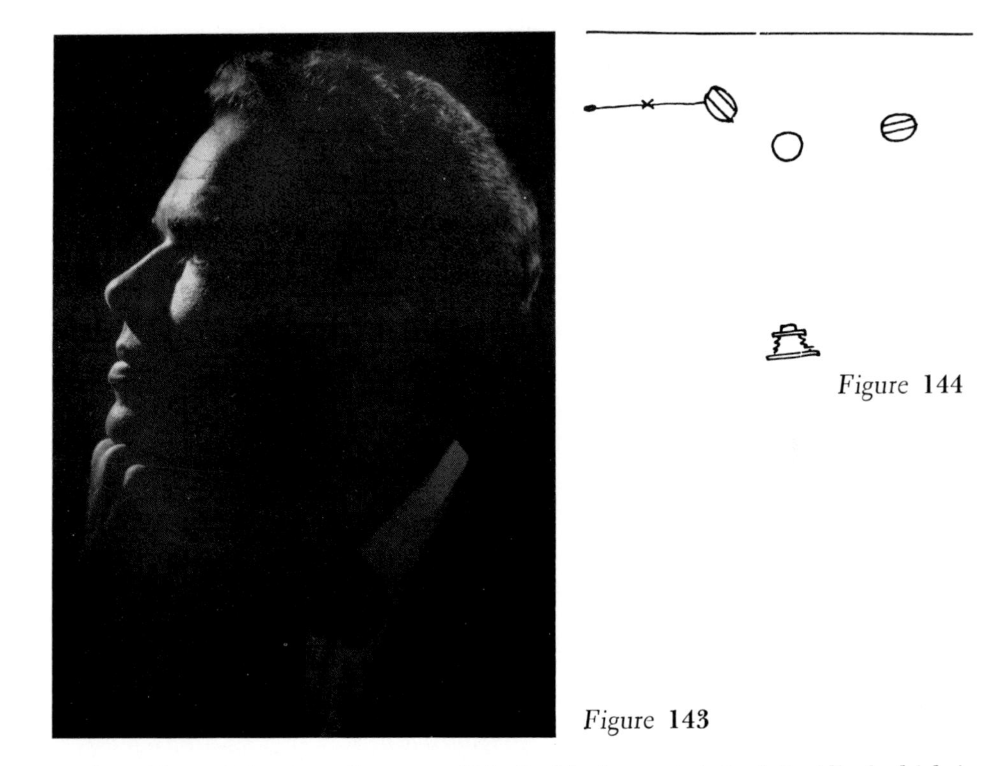

Figure **144**

Figure **143**

on that side, and that is easily accomplished with the spot at the left. All of which is fine as far as it goes. We have an interesting composition and a nice profile but we still do not have a portrait. We turn on the fill-in, at left of the camera, feathering it up carefully because we want the hands and lower parts of the arms in shadow and want no emphasis whatever on that piece of furniture. Now we have nice flesh tones and modeling and all the detail we require of the dress. The light on the background outlines the figure and, while strong, is well balanced by the light on the face. Try this, and *Figure 139*, and work out your own variations on them, and the "something different" wail will no longer be a problem to you.

So much for the ladies, and now what to do when a man comes in and explains that he does not want an ordinary head and shoulders, not due to vanity but for a very excellent reason. This too can happen to you because nowadays even the smallest community has its "little theatre" group if not several. The subject of *Figures 143* and *145* is an art and dramatic coach and needed portraits to "sell himself" to just such organizations. In view of his training he was quite capable of modeling the poses he desired and explaining the somewhat weird effects he had in mind. Could we, he wanted to know, produce what he wanted or would he have to make a trip to secure the services of a theatrical specialist?

His first requirement (*Figure 143*) was a forceful, emphatic profile, enough of a likeness to be recognizable but otherwise showing little of his features, and deliberately harsh in treatment. We seated him at a small table whereupon he placed his elbow thereon and shoved his clenched fist under his chin. That, he explained, was the general idea and, quite obviously, it called for a profile lighting such as we have discussed in Chapter 13, but with one important exception to which we will come in a moment. Our main source (*Figure 144*) was a boom spot at the left rear, sufficiently forward to cast a strong light past the nose on the near cheek bone. Then, so his head, shoulder and collar would not be completely lost with a resulting total lack of balance in the picture, we placed a spot at the right but sufficiently far away to keep its intensity down.

Normally our next step would be to add the fill-in by the camera but—and this caused the exception—he wanted all emphasis on the profile with the rest of his features in deep shadow, not opaque but on the other hand not far from it. Hence no fill-in, and the result as shown. You will remember that in Chapter 13, in connection with *Figures 111* and *112*, we suggested you try a couple of experiments, one of them being almost this identical lighting, omitting the fill-in, and we remarked that the result would be dramatic although probably not saleable. In this case, the demand existing, the print was saleable—in fact he wanted quite a number. All of which goes to show that it pays to keep experimenting with your lights because you never know when the most *outré* effect may be exactly what you need to fill a particular assignment. Referring again to Chapter 13, remember what we said about the importance of learning to "read" light because, having attained that ability and knowing as a consequence what you can accomplish with light or the lack of it, the answer to a problem such as this will come to you automatically.

Our dramatic coach, in addition to the profile, also specified a full face (*Figure 145*) but one strongly lighted and heavily shadowed, the sort of thing that, accompanied with an attractive smile, would be the harsh type of portrait which, as we have explained before, is often thought of as glamour but is in reality striking and spectacular although in no sense glamourous. For this we swung him and the table around to face the camera and had him drop his head more to a level, resting his cheek against his clenched fist which still had to be included. Our main source

Figure **146**

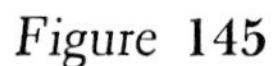

Figure **145**

(*Figure 146*) is now hardly recognizable as such because it is off to the right, high up and shooting down on the features to throw, purposely, sharply defined and angular shadows across the face. For proper balance a spot is required at the left rear and because this time we do need enough illumination in the shadows to bring out his features and personality we make use of our fill-in, to left of the camera, but feather it off the face and well up, the latter to keep light off the forearm in the lower left corner. Attention is thus concentrated on the face and upper portion of the fist, while the white shirt and collar are well subdued. For additional emphasis and to give the portrait stopping power we place a background light behind him, using a spot which is directed on the area around the shoulders and lower part of the head. It doesn't make him handsome but it does present him as a thoughtful, competent, forceful individual who can direct others.

Figure 147 is more on the illustrative order, but conceptions like this have many applications. Entitled "It's Religious," this was originally used as a divider page for a year book. It could, by allowing more space at the right and the bottom, do equally well for a Christmas or Easter greeting card. Or, at Easter, the editor of almost any small town newspaper would be only too happy to feature such an illustration in large space on his front page, with a handsome credit line for the maker. Many other holidays during the year can be similarly featured, merely by varying the composition, the costume and accessories of the subject and substituting a suitable prop for the cross: a heart for Valentine's Day, a pumpkin for Hallowe'en, appropriate silhouettes or busts for Washington's Birthday, Lincoln's Birthday or the like Some professional photographers have become noted in their communities for such timely pictorial contributions, and it is excellent publicity because it is proof of their originality and ability to produce the unusual. A picture like this is far from

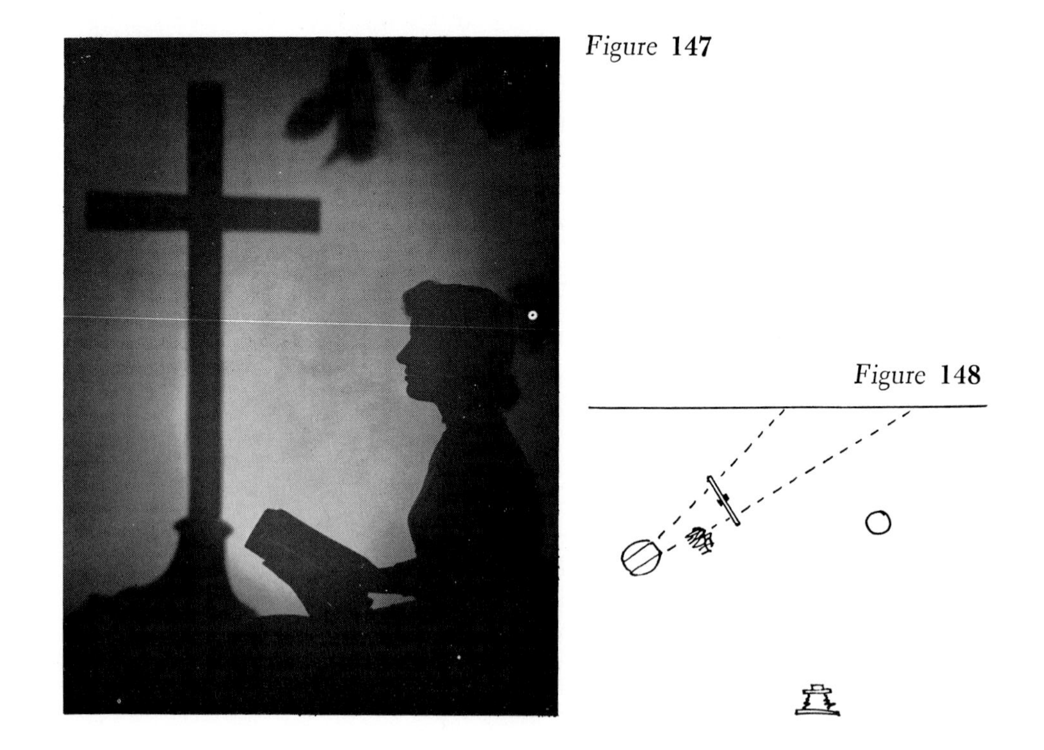

Figure **147**

Figure **148**

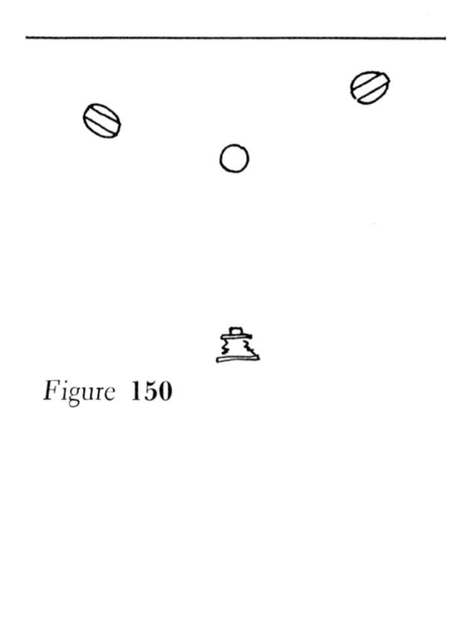

Figure **150**

Figure **149**

difficult—actually, except for securing the necessary props, it could hardly be simpler, as seen in *Figure 148*. The subject, off to the right, appears only in silhouette and, placing the entire setup against a light background, the whole illumination comes from a strong spot at the left which throws, on the background, the shadows of the cross and the leaves. For a suitable pictorial effect, all corners are burned in when printing.

Speaking of Christmas cards, the one shown in *Figure 149* is a treatment one sees used occasionally for groups of two when the "something different" demand arises. For such use the two heads would be more appropriately placed in the picture space—here they are deliberately high and somewhat to the left to allow ample space for the greeting at lower right. This is no mystery—nothing more than a double exposure, an outline shot of the man's profile and then, carefully registered,

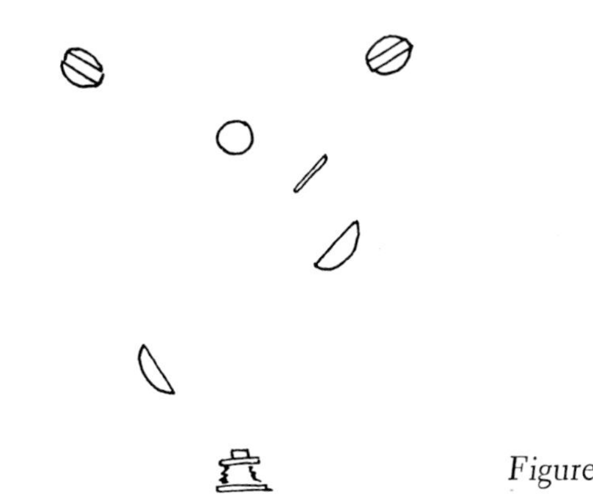

Figure **151**

a full face of the woman. To assure proper registry of the two images, once the profile (which would be the larger of the two) is focused on your groundglass and before you make the exposure, outline it lightly on the glass *with a grease* or *china marking pencil*. Then, when you focus later on the woman, you pull the camera farther back for a smaller image and are careful that it registers entirely within the markings on the glass. Replacing the holder, you make your second exposure and there you are.

The profile of the man (*Figure 150*) must be an edge lighting because you want no detail whatever of the face. This, and the second exposure, are both made against a black background from which all light should be kept away. All you need for this first exposure are two spots, at right and left rear, both of them directed high because you want no light to strike the profile below the chin while as for the back of the head you only want to illuminate the upper part of the hair, and that rather faintly. The portrait of the woman is a rather standard lighting in this case (*Figure 151*) and, in fact, can be any lighting or pose you may think fit, even another profile although probably not a second edge lighting. Spots are used at right and left rear to illuminate the hair, the edges of which must be emphasized to avoid confusion with the man's profile, the main source and fill-in are in approximately normal positions, and our favorite head screen returns to its usual place.

We have made no pretension in this Chapter of covering the tremendous range of variegated lightings and poses that are possible once you become expert with your camera and equipment. If we have offered a few usable ideas we shall consider these few pages more than justified. We do advise, however, that you give serious thought to the production of special illustrations for holiday use, and to the promotion of photographic Christmas and other greeting cards. Granting that much of this field has already been taken over by the wholesale photofinishers and the quantity print specialists, both of them ready to furnish duplicates from amateur prints, mounted and ready in stock greeting card mounts, with envelopes to match, there are still a surprising number of the well-to-do who are only too happy if they can find "something different" for their Christmas cards. It may take some time to create a demand but once that is done you will find the orders can be taken months in advance and finished in what would normally be your slack summer season. Thus you can add materially to your holiday season income because deliveries of the cards—and collections—are completed before the normal holiday rush commences.

CHAPTER 17

What to Do With Hands

If the eyes are, as an old saying has it, "the windows of the soul," certainly the hands are an equal reflection of a person's capacity and character. Even the photographer who limits himself (as we hope none of our readers plan to do) largely to head and shoulder poses will find that one or both hands must occasionally be included. It goes without saying that hands are an essential part of three quarter and full length portraits. So many photographers seem to be seriously perplexed when faced with the problem of posing hands that we wonder if this is not another reason why they hesitate to depart from the standard "bust" portrait. Portraiture as such would be vastly enhanced in its appreciation by the public if hands were more often included; and so, in the accompanying illustrations we are offering a number of poses, none of them difficult. They are not for you to copy "as is," but to serve as points of departure. There can be no such things as standard poses of hands, because hands and fingers are even more expressive than facial features and often, if you will study them carefully, far more diverse.

As in all phases of portraiture, the cameraman must use good judgment, because there are instances when the hands are better omitted. Some subjects are so awkward or nervous that no amount of effort will succeed in arranging their hands and fingers presentably, while others have hands that are ill kept, and even plain ugly. In such cases, be smart and leave them alone. None of this applies to certain salon pictures, or studies, in which even ugly hands must sometimes appear in order to complete a characterization. We have in mind average subjects, and would like to emphasize that our illustrations picture the hands of just such persons—there is not a professional model in the lot. It will pay you to experiment with friends or studio employees until you have, through experience, achieved two skills. First is the ability to recognize on sight a compositionally good pose of hands adopted naturally by a subject. Second is the ability to visualize a desired arrangement of hands and fingers and complete it in the

Figure **152** *Figure* **153**

least time and with the least "handling" of the subject. Studying the arrangements shown here, all of which are basically pleasing and compositionally satisfactory, will help in both respects.

It is important that you do your experimenting before trying out your ideas on actual subjects, because if you are to be thought of as a professional, you will be expected to know what effects you want and to secure them without fumbling around. You must at all times give your subjects the impression that you thoroughly understand what you are doing. You cannot afford to give them any contrary feeling, due to the necessity of returning time and again to move a hand or adjust a finger. The less you have to touch your subjects, the better, because people on the average dislike being "pawed over" or "pushed around."

You will have seen innumerable portraits showing the hands resting in the lap, folded around the knees, or clasped under the chin. Almost invariably such placements are automatically adopted by the subject, and being natural and therefore characteristic, can normally be accepted as they are. It may be necessary to ask that the hands be turned slightly so that the edge, rather than the broad back of a hand, faces the camera. Usually, a word of suggestion is all that is necessary plus, perhaps, a gentle touch to correct a finger or thumb which protrudes unpleasantly. Whenever a subject, even if you are planning only a head and shoulder portrait, adopts a pose of the hands into which they seem to fall with no thought or effort on the subject's part, by all means make your first exposure and then ask the subject to hold the pose. Then include that pose of the hands in a three quarter position, which often will mean nothing more than pulling the camera back. Those often are the proofs which the subject's family and friends will recognize as "Oh, so natural" and which will increase the order.

Because such arrangements of hands are more or less spontaneous—and can almost be thought of as standard—we are not showing them here. Instead we are offering different treatments, which you may find helpful, when you have a subject whose hands and fingers are truly graceful and lovely, or so obviously indicate the subject's age, activities, or characteristics that they literally demand attention. And let us preface what follows with one caution: hands always look better when they are "doing something" or appear active, instead of seeming as if they had been passively dropped like lumps of flesh.

Figure 152 is purely an experimental exercise, not to be attempted with a client, but with someone who is willing to cooperate so that you may, at your leisure, try out some finger arrangements. All you need for this is any kind of stick; a broom handle, if nothing better is available, will suffice perfectly. Here you have a basis for any number of similar arrangements. Note first that none of the fingers are wrapped around the stick in a "death grip," and that both hands, although they do hold the stick, appear relaxed. Note too—and we shall remark on this again—that the hand nearest you has been purposely turned, so that not too much of the back of the hands shows. In the case of the other hand, its size has been reduced because it curves gently around the stick. The palm is not only thus made smaller, but is in addition concealed by the stick. Seldom do either the back or the palm of a hand look attractive in a portrait. Finally, you will realize that the hands merge into each other, although details are not lost, and the entire composition tapers, as do the fingers themselves. These hands look feminine and dainty, as they should.

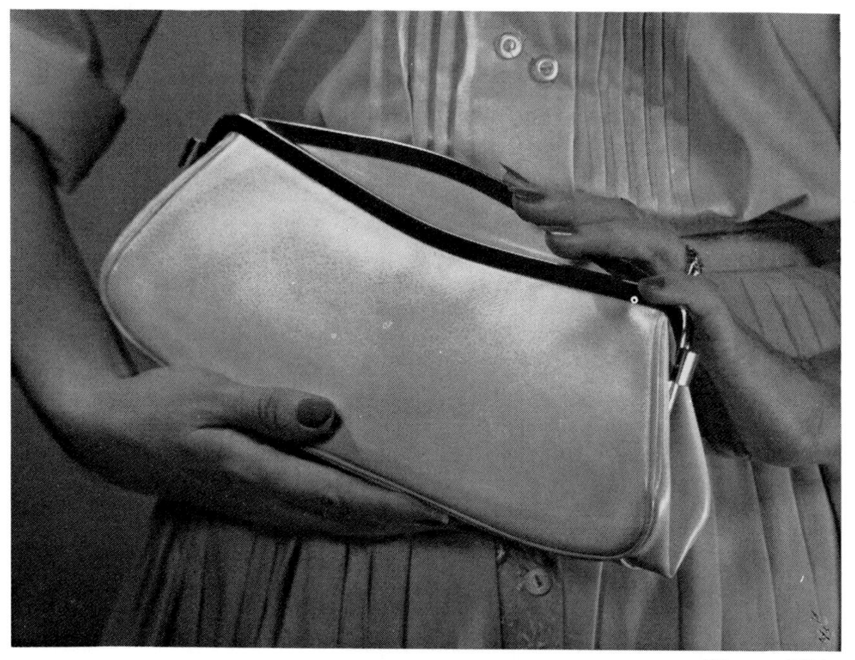

Figure 154

Figure **155**

An easy—and logical—way to include the hands in a head and shoulder portrait appears in *Figure 153.* When hands are included in such a portrait, some method like this must be found to subdue their size in relation to the face (due to the fact that less picture area is available), and their presence should have some purpose. In this case we asked the young lady to take hold of the lapel of her coat with her right hand, and just slightly turn it away from the camera, not only to avoid showing too much of the back of the hand but to add a feeling of action, of movement. The hand is not "bunched up," and the fingers are not clenched, but relaxed. Then the fingers of the other hand were brought up to rest lightly against the bottom of the same coat lapel. Even for a three quarter pose such an arrangement is preferable to the stereotyped one hand in a pocket and the other on a hip.

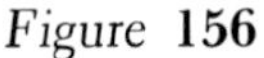

Figure **156**

A very logical position for a woman's hands is to show them holding her handbag, an accessory that every woman carries, and which, on such an occasion as visiting the photographer, is almost sure to be one in which she has pride. Disregard the background in *Figure 154*, because all that interests us is the arrangement of the two hands. The one below the bag shows no strain or effort—the bag is merely resting on it, so that fingers and thumb are relaxed. After all, a handbag is an inanimate object, so there is no need to clutch it tightly. Again, too, we show only the edge of the hand. The hand above the bag rests on it gently and yet the fingers are not static—they give the impression of action, that the bag is about to be opened. This arrangement can be adapted to any number of hand-held items and will be particularly helpful for full length and three quarter poses.

In *Figure 155*, we have tried to give a new look to a standard pose, in which the arms are crossed, with both hands visible, usually one in the crook of each elbow. Instead, we have allowed one hand to slide up the coat sleeve, while the other rests easily on the opposite sleeve or cuff. The result is very natural, relaxed, and feminine. Please note the arrangement of the fingers. Were the hand turned only a little bit more toward the body, the knuckles of the third finger would protrude in silhouette against the coat, giving the effect of an unpleasant bump. Little things like this are what you must watch constantly when you work with hands, if you seek perfection. Only too often, the slightest movement on the part of your subject will spoil what you had planned as a graceful effect. This is why you must work as quickly as possible, having the rest of your pose already completed and arranging the fingers last, being ready to shoot with a minimum of delay.

Figure **157**

Figure **158**

The arrangement shown in *Figure 156* is suitable for many kinds of glamour poses, especially when a subject has smooth, well manicured, graceful hands that show little if any signs of hard work. When a subject is wearing a low cut gown and has good looking shoulders and arms which you want to display, just how to arrange the hands is sometimes a problem. In this case, one arm is thrown over the back of a piece of furniture and the hand is left hanging, which, by itself, would be most awkward and in addition would display too much

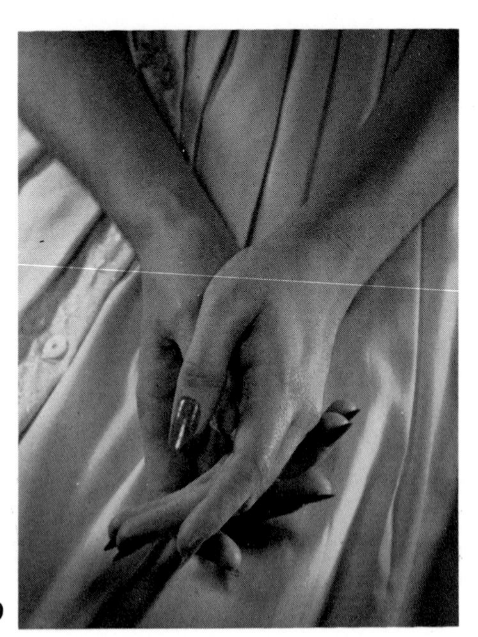

Figure **159**

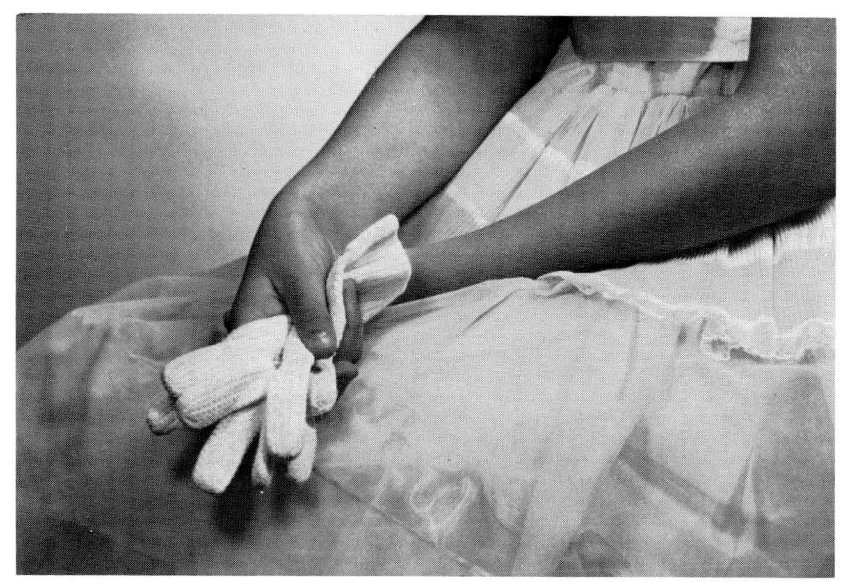

Figure **160**

of the back of the hand. To correct all this, we bring up the other arm, rest that hand on the other wrist, and in a quite logical manner, include in our picture all of our subject's natural charms—shoulders, arms, and hands. The fingers of the first hand will fall into place by themselves, and if those of the second do not, very little rearranging will be necessary.

Let us deal now with a pair of much older hands, those shown in *Figure 157*. These hands, of many years existence, are busy at something which is almost second nature to their owner. They are naturally placed—definitely not posed—in her lap, and despite their age, they are as graceful as any other hands we are illustrating. Hands like these should be held back somewhat in printing so as not to overemphasize the wrinkles, but under no circumstances should they be retouched. By all means give your older subjects something to do with their hands, something to which they are accustomed, and you will seldom find it necessary to do more than watch a moment or two, and then trip your shutter when the composition is most pleasing.

We warned earlier against including hands in ordinary head and shoulder poses without an obvious or logical reason; for an example of their use, look at *Figure 158*. Here is a man in his forties, a big wheat farmer, a hard worker, and an individual of considerable personality and forcefulness. We wanted to picture his determination and "drive," and this was not easy to do with the head and shoulders alone. Yet, to present him in the customary finger-along-the-cheek pose, which is so much overdone, would have been most unsuitable; it would almost make him appear effeminate. Therefore (and frankly we would not recommend this in many cases), we instead doubled his hand into the form of a fist, with the result that all who saw it felt the portrait to be a true likeness. The point here is that when you do include one or both hands in a head and shoulder pose the arrangement of the hands must in some way indicate or emphasize the subject's character or occupation. Which reminds us that there are occasionally women whose occupations or professions are such that a dainty, feminine arrange-

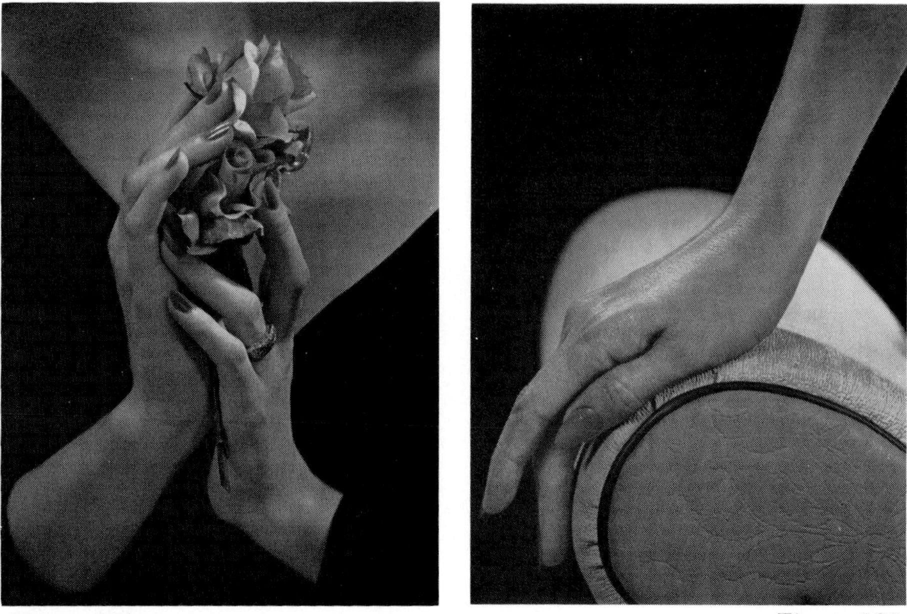

Figure **161**

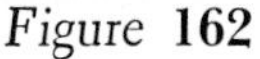

Figure **162**

ment of hands and fingers might be quite inappropriate.

There will be times when, in a three quarter pose, hands must be left in the lap with nothing to occupy them. The subject may have no suitable handbag, gloves, or other accessory, and, perhaps because of her costume, you yourself may have nothing to offer which appears to be just right. Even holding a book or magazine may be inadvisable if in conversation you have discovered that she does little or no reading, and therefore a prop would be obviously unsuitable. Try an arrangement such as that in *Figure 159*, with the hands not centered, but slightly off to one side of the lap. Here, to achieve the desired effect, careful placement of both hands and fingers is definitely your responsibility. Let the upper hand rest in the palm of the lower, and keep the fingers of the lower hand cupped rather than extended. Be careful to show only the edge of the upper hand. In this way you include both hands, but without making them seem bulky. This same arrangement can be used, of course, to hold something small and flexible like a flower or pair of gloves, but as it appears here, completely uncluttered with props or accessories, it is sufficiently graceful, with no appearance of artificiality.

While we are on the subject of hands in the lap, *Figure 160* shows another way to use a pair of gloves. These happen to be the hands and arms of a ten-year-old girl, holding what is probably her first pair of "dress up" gloves, and because at that age girls are often awkward and self-conscious, one hand is practically concealed. Bear this arrangement, or variations of it, in mind; occasions will arise when, although it is necessary to give the impression of including both hands, one must be concealed because of a blemish or even a deformity. Your reputation as a photographer will be enhanced merely because of your thoughtfulness and tact.

In formal portraits, when a gown is considerably *decolleté*, and also sometimes when drapes are used and the same problem arises, an excellent solution—very acceptable when the subject's hands are truly graceful—is to bring both of them up to the V of the *decolletage*. To make the purpose of the pose less obvious, or to disguise the fact that the subject does wish to display her hands, it is well to have them holding a flower or two, as in *Figure 161*. This is also a very good way of displaying a ring, and without being too obvious about it. The smart photographer watches for such details, and when a subject is proud of a ring, which she will often indicate by playing with it or moving her hands in such a manner as to show it prominently, will unfailingly plan one pose to display that ring. Hand the flower to the subject, have her raise her hands to the bottom of the V, and if she knows her hands are good looking, she will probably take it from there. If not, you may have to do a bit of rearranging, bearing in mind that hands and fingers must appear relaxed. If you will refer to *Figure 152*, our comments in that connection will help you here.

Our last illustration (*Figure 162*) may clarify for you a situation you will frequently encounter when working with three quarter or standing poses. Often, to steady your subject, to display the lines of an attractive arm and wrist, or perhaps solely because it is essential to the composition you have in mind, one hand must rest against an object such as a chair arm or back, a table, a desk, or what have you. Once again, and we cannot emphasize this too greatly, be sure to show the edge of the hand and not too much of the back. Be careful also to place it so that there is no sharp, angular break between the hand and the wrist, or at the knuckles. Avoid any appearance of strain, or a clutching or gripping of the support, whatever it may be. And do not let the thumb extend away from the fingers, or down over one edge or side of the support. Arm, wrist, hand, and fingers should flow in a series of graceful curves.

An entire book could be written on this subject, but it would only be able to show and discuss a greater variety of hand poses, and it is not our purpose here to provide you with a set of poses to be copied. Instead we have selected a number which are more or less basic, natural to, and readily adopted by, most subjects, and once you have become familiar with them, easy to vary or alter until you arrive at a style which will become your own. Hands are an integral part of us, and the older we become, the more they disclose about us. Included properly in portraits, they can lift your work above the commonplace and add materially to your reputation as an artist.

CHAPTER 18

Let's Not Forget the Feet

In Chapter 17 it was necessary to talk about and illustrate the posing of hands in rather exhaustive detail because one or both of the hands will appear in every three quarter pose and, now and then, will find their way into head and shoulder portraits. The feet appear much more rarely, occasionally in a seated pose but almost certainly when a subject is photographed at full length. The chief exceptions are bridal portraits, extremely formal full length gowns, and judges, clerics and others in their distinctive robes. In such cases the feet are concealed or there is just a glimpse of the toes of the shoes.

If the reader has already stolen a glimpse at the illustrations chosen for this Chapter, he will have noted that they deal with women only, and for good reason. The cameraman ordinarily does not "pose" a man's feet. If the feet are included in a seated pose and the subject, slouching as so often happens in order to make himself comfortable, stretches out his legs so that his feet—too close to the camera—will be out of drawing or too prominent, a simple request that he sit up a bit straighter will automatically cause him to draw up his legs and the feet with them. Beyond that, a man's feet, whether he is seated or standing, should be firmly planted on the floor. That is where they belong if his portrait is to present him in a suitably dignified manner.

Thus your principal problem when including the feet of male subjects will arise when you are photographing the formalized type of rather large group in which a number of men appear, some seated, some standing. Those who are standing will adopt natural, normal positions in any event and with respect to the others the same solution applies: ask them to sit up straighter. It is well, in such a group and if all those seated are in identically stiff positions, to pick out a man here and there and suggest that he place one foot in front of the other, if only for the sake of variety.

Never, when working with a man, attempt to pose or arrange his feet by touching them. While a woman may well be flattered by such careful attention, a man will only be annoyed and his attitude, if not his expression, will show it. We take it for granted that, unless you are making a character study of some special subject, you will be careful never to include the feet if the shoes are scuffed, badly worn, or down at heel, and that of course goes for women as well as men. The photographer must always use good judgment.

Nor will you find any illustrations of children's feet here, either, even though perhaps as many portraits of children include the full figure as only the head and shoulders. For one thing it is preferable to avoid posing and arranging children because the chief charm in portraits of youngsters lies in their naturalness and spontaneity. If they are seated, let their feet hang naturally. What you must avoid, when photographing children (and babies especially) is the type of pose where the subject is seated on a table or bench with the legs not hanging over the edge but sticking straight out toward the camera. Even if distortion does not result, nothing adds less charm to a child's portrait than two flat shoe soles (or even one) smack in the foreground. If a pair of chubby legs and feet must be included to make the parents happy, at least place them to one side or the other. Never photograph the soles of a child's feet full on.

And now to those subjects to whom, when their feet are included in a portrait, posing and arrangement are important, so much so that, if neglected, an otherwise thoroughly satisfactory and even beautiful proof may be promptly discarded. Like everything else in a woman's portrait, her feet must "do something for her" and that is definitely your responsibility if your subject is to be pleased. How to accomplish that is our purpose here and in that connection let us emphasize that these illustrations are in no sense to be compared with the effects of the commercial illustrator whose aim is to sell fashions, and particularly hose and shoes. We have made no attempt, in preparing these, to show anything more than the posing

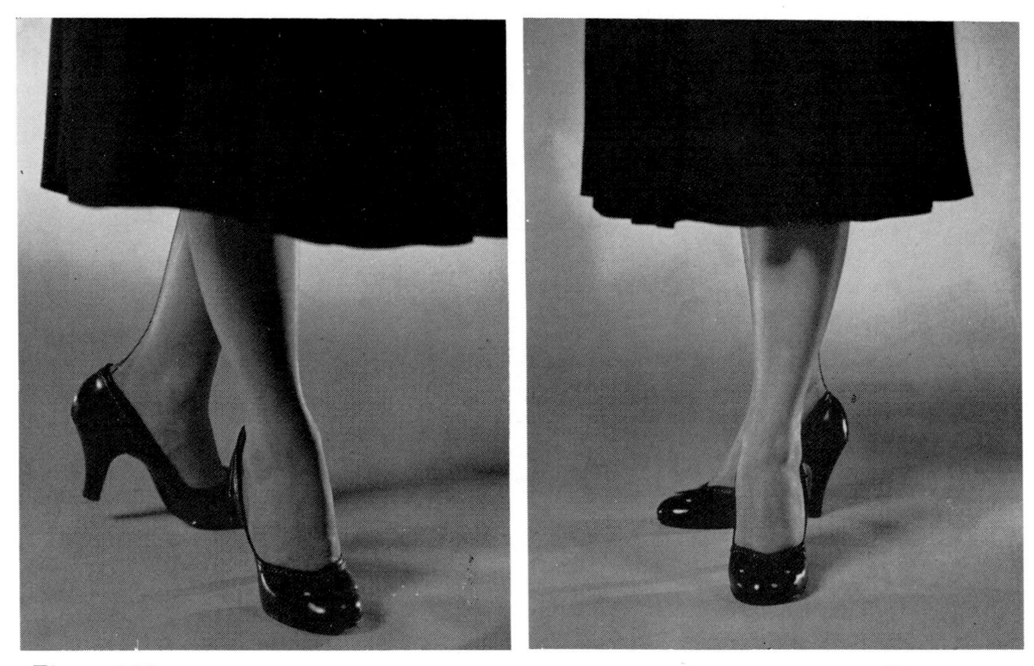

Figure **163**

Figure **164**

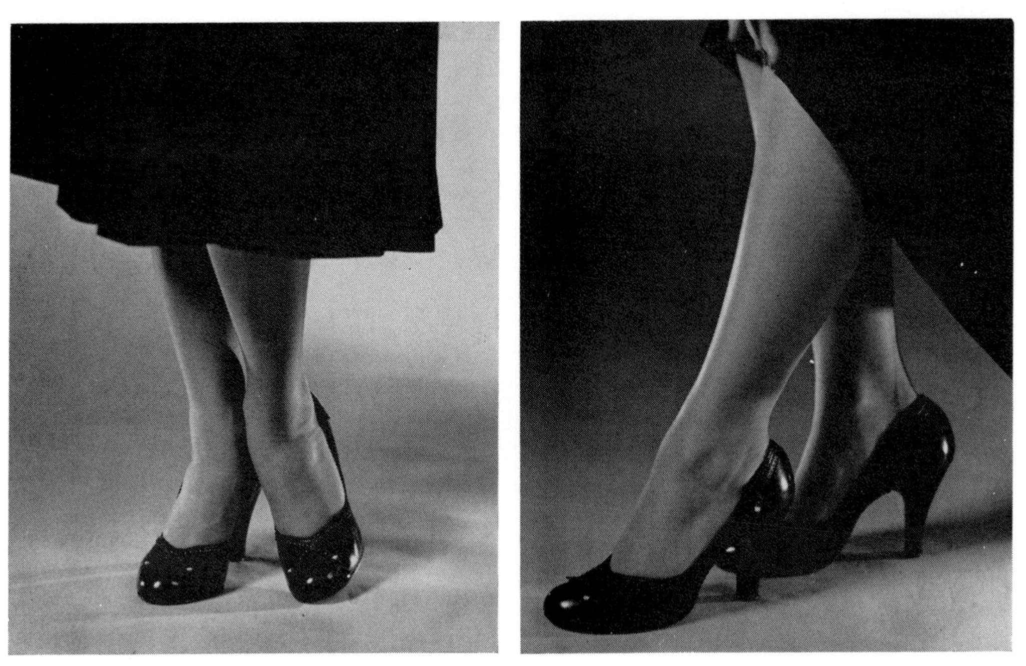

Figure **165** *Figure* **166**

and arrangement of the feet and for that reason asked our subject to wear a simple plain skirt, not too long, so we could direct our efforts and attention to the lower part of the legs and the feet, excluding all else. No lighting diagrams, consequently, are required.

Take a look, then, at *Figure 163*. The weight of the body is carried by the foot which is in front while the position of the one in the rear helps to stabilize the pose—to steady the subject—yet both feet, considered as a unit, convey the illusion of movement. The viewer has the feeling that the subject is in the act of taking a step. There is nothing static about this placement of the feet; it is attractive and graceful and above all it is perfectly natural. Such a positioning of the feet is appropriate for any pose suggesting activity, for example a full length of a subject in any type of sports wear outfit. Many girls and young women have fine clothes that classify in the sports wear bracket and would be happy to be photographed in just such costumes. Remember too that your younger subjects should be made to "look their age" and this is much simpler to do with a full figure pose than by means of the customary head and shoulders. True, the teen agers and younger girls often want to appear older than they are but almost invariably those who want (and probably are paying for) the portraits are the parents, and they prefer to remember their children as they know them best.

In *Figure 164* we have placed the weight of the body on the rear foot and leg, with the foot turned slightly to provide stability, while the toe of the forward foot points to the front and not to the side, a pose that model schools and other authorities on the human figure recommend as indicating poise. Such a position is easily associated with a more formal pose of a young woman, while being at the same time quite correct for the woman of almost any age. It is particularly suitable for any formal costume or if the subject is wearing a shorter style of wedding gown.

Dignified, graceful and correct, this placement of the feet has almost unlimited possibilities and in addition has a slenderizing effect when—as is often—that is desirable. It has the additional advantage that where your subject happens to have heavy legs which, due to a short skirt, cannot be concealed, necessary corrective retouching can be done very easily.

Because this placement of the feet can be useful in so many ways it is important that you be able to "talk" your subjects into it as effortlessly as possible. Try a bit of experimentation with some of those subjects with whom we hope you have been working as you have followed these chapters. Tell your subject you are going to try a full length and ask her to stand at some point which you indicate, facing almost to the right instead of toward the camera. Now ask her to turn and face the camera, moving her left foot in front of the right. To balance herself she will quite naturally assume the desired position and if not, with a light touch of your hand, you can quickly make any needed adjustment.

At other times, and remember that you must always offer your subjects variety, you may want to show your subject at full length beside a column, panel or screen, or perhaps with one hand resting on the back of a chair in what might be called an "at ease" position. For such a pose an appropriate placement of the feet is shown in *Figure 165*, where the weight of the body is carried by the rear foot and leg, with the front leg bent at the knee and the front foot in a relaxed position. This is a useful arrangement whenever you need a more informal placement of the feet.

Perhaps the situation that causes photographers more trouble than any other in this connection is the one of making the feet look graceful when the subject is seated. A simple solution is the placement shown in *Figure 166*, which combines two advantages. It puts the subject at ease because it is comfortable; it looks well and is graceful. We are all familiar with the arrangement in which the toe of one foot is hooked around the ankle or heel of the other, but for many seated positions that is far too informal and, often, looks somewhat awkward. It is most frequently seen in large groups in which, if not adopted by too many of those in the group, it is not too objectionable and does help to add variety. The placement shown here, however, is usually more flattering and is always in perfectly good taste.

Now take another look at these four illustrations because, though the fact does not appear, they have really been carefully planned. Notice that none of the feet look *large* and, when your subject is a woman—young or old—that is a point you must watch if you are to avoid resittings. This was quite easily accomplished by very definitely having some part of one or the other foot concealed—or in one case (*Figure 164*) almost bisected—by its companion. Truly attractive feet are really somewhat of a rarity and yet almost every woman likes to think of hers as tiny and *chic*. Make your women subjects feel proud of their feet and they will feel proud of your photographs. And, in cases where you are asked in advance to make suggestions concerning costumes, urge your subject to wear shoes of graceful lines and without ornamentation. The simpler the shoes, the smaller the feet will look. That very statement, made by you with an air of authority, will do wonders in preventing subjects from arriving for a sitting in shoes that are so elaborate as to be photogenically impossible. Also if, for any reason, you make a photograph which shows the backs of a woman's legs, make sure that if her stockings have seams they are properly centered and straight. If not, ask her to straighten them—don't attempt to do this yourself.

CHAPTER 19

Backgrounds for the Camera Room

Portraiture by whatever medium, with the exception of sculpture and bas-relief, consists of the delineation of a three dimensional live subject on a two dimensional plane. If, however, a portrait is to be a success the image must not appear to the viewer to be as two dimensional (in other words, as flat) as it actually is. There must be a feeling of depth, of roundness, a definite separation of the head and the figure from the background, even if the latter consists of nothing more than a flat tone which may range anywhere from pure white to jet black. What the painter or other type of artist accomplishes through the use of color or, if he is working in monochrome, the heaviness or shading of his pigments or lines, the photographer secures by the manipulation of his lights both on his subject and on whatever he may have selected as a background, or surround, for his subject.

One principal purpose of a background, which is essentially nothing more than a flat vertical surface behind the subject, is to eliminate any extraneous details or objects which might detract from that subject. A background may be nothing more than a white sheet or blank white paper, or at the other extreme, a wide length of black felt or black paper, if we reduce the idea of backgrounds to pure fundamentals. If a pure white background is used it is possible, by means of lighting and as explained in earlier chapters, to "wash it out" entirely. Practically the same thing is done in the case of a vignette. Nevertheless, whether the resulting portrait is a high key lighting on a pure white surface or a low key lighting on a dead black surface, what surrounds the subject is still, as we understand it in photography, a background. If the lighting on the subject is correct the necessary three dimensional feeling of relief will still exist because, no matter how high or low in key the lighting, there will still remain an appreciable difference between the tonal quality of the image of the subject and the surrounding white or black as the case may be.

The second, and for the experienced professional, more accepted purpose of a background is its use as the base against which any portrait is created and this applies whether the background is to become an integral part of the finished portrait or not. Without some definite surface in the rear against which to visualize the subject it is extremely difficult for the photographer to plan his pose and lighting and to estimate the effect of his final result. It is this very lack of flat background that explains why so many amateur portraits, especially those taken out of doors, will disclose a small tree or some other object "growing" out of the subject's head. The same thing often happens in the case of home portraits—even occasionally those taken by professionals—when, upon development, a vase, table lamp or something similar unexpectedly appears in a most undesirable spot. Lacking the customary background the cameraman concentrates upon his subject and fails to notice extraneous objects, often because they are so much to the rear that he does not realize they will register on the negative.

Consequently a background, of whatever nature, is one of the first things you will need in addition to your camera and lights, if it serves no other purpose than to give you some general idea of where to place your subject. We are talking here about your camera room, large or small, and without reference to home portraiture which we shall discuss later. The photographer who is working with a normal range of subjects will need at least one background, preferably fairly large, of smooth surface and in a medium tone of gray or a light photogenic brown. If yours is a long narrow camera room this background, to be most serviceable, might well be within a couple of feet of sufficient size to cover the narrow width at one end of the room. It should not be the full width because there will be occasions when you will want it out of the way, and you must have room enough to get around either end and manipulate it. This ground should be nine or ten feet high, on a frame of two by four lumber, mounted on a base of the same material and the whole on casters so it may easily be moved when necessary.

If you decide to construct such a ground—and it is a simple matter for the most amateur carpenter—it will be wise to build it so that there is no right angle break at the floor line. This can be done by having the background carried down on the floor with a curved surface of at least an eighteen inch radius, this being covered with whatever material you are using for the background. You can then paint that part of the floor, which is normally in front of the background, the same color and thus avoid having any disturbing break when you are taking full length or group portraits. It is of course quite possible to have the background material itself extend over the curved surface and continue on the floor but this, due to wear and tear on that portion of the background material, is far from economical.

You may prefer to build this as a standard movable background with no extension on the floor—and most professionals have one or more such grounds, often with a white or light tone on one side and black or dark on the other—but we advise the floor extension because you will find it extremely helpful and well worth the small amount of extra trouble and cost. Without such a floor extension you will find it necessary to install from the ceiling at one wall of your camera room a holder on which to hang one or more rolls of the wide seamless background paper, now available in widths of nine feet and more and in many colors, which we have already mentioned frequently. This will solve the "floor cloth" problem for you, and this elimination of the abrupt break between background and floor is a matter you will have to consider if you expect to work successfully with full lengths and groups.

So far as your painted background is concerned it is not necessary to limit yourself to white, gray and black. Your camera room need not, in fact should not be, drab, dull and unattractive. You can of course buy backgrounds but it is easy to paint one for yourself and thus make an immediate start at individualizing your camera room. Soft, warm grays and browns are always suitable and in the case of browns the addition of a very slight amount of red to the paint can make them most attractive. You will of course be using flat paints in any event but one way to be sure of securing the effects you want is to mix your proposed color, paint a sample card of fair size with it, and then photograph it with your customary lighting setup and the film you use most frequently. Process the negative, make a print and then if the result is not what you want, dilute, or add more color.

Years ago many firms advertised and sold painted backgrounds. Many of these were most elaborate and would be quite out of place in a modern camera room, but some can still be had in various types of gently shaded effects, graded from bottom to top or from the sides to the center, which are in good taste for certain types of portraiture, usually the head and shoulders. Whether you decide to use such backgrounds will depend largely upon the type of persons with whom you are going to deal, and one way of discovering what their tastes are will be to make a careful study of the samples being shown by established studios in your vicinity. In arriving at any decision with respect to backgrounds, take your time. One, along the general lines of what we have suggested, you cannot do without. Almost certainly you will need the wide seamless paper as well. What else you accumulate must depend on the amount of space you have available and what, as your experience grows, you find to be in most demand.

For ordinary head and shoulder work, assuming your camera room is of fair size and you do not want to keep moving the large background back and forth, you will find what is called a "flat" to be very handy. This is a small background on a light frame, about five by six feet in size, painted in a light tone on one side and darker tone on the other, mounted on a standard with a caster base. For a touch of variety we have found frequent use for two larger flats each about four feet wide and nine feet high, painted differently on both sides and also mounted on casters. These can be placed, separately or together, in front of a standard larger background in such a manner as to imply doorways or openings.

If your camera room is large enough so that you have several walls which can themselves be used as backgrounds—implying sufficient background to camera distance in several directions—it may be well to consider finishing one wall in wood paneling. This is not as expensive as it sounds because there are numerous materials on the market, wallboards and the like, and even some wallpapers, which simulate such paneling perfectly from a photogenic standpoint at least, and which are neither costly nor hard to install. Finishing one wall in a rough plaster or stucco effect is another possibility, and the texture thus obtained makes a handsome background for many types of portraits. If you photograph many men, some bookshelves on one wall, either filled with books or with fake backs such as used in stage sets, would be appropriate. In this connection we are reminded that, if your camera room is large enough to allow you reasonable space behind your normal background, you can offer your subjects an unlimited variety of background effects. First, in your home and those of your friends, make 2 x 2 color slides of interesting wall treatments, library shelves or whatever strikes your fancy—even attractive scenics are suitable at times. Substitute a translucent screen for your background and project your slides on this from the *back*. If your space is limited, place a mirror against the back wall, project the slides on that so they will reflect from it to the screen, and the results will amaze you.

There is no limit, as you can see, to what you can do with backgrounds in giving a touch of your own personality not only to your camera room but to the portraits you produce there. And, as you progress, your success in creating a demand for your work will depend largely on your ability to give the subject not only poses and lightings, but background treatments, that are not to be found in every other show window up and down the street. We could continue indefinitely describing what has been done along these lines not only by photographers of the present day, against whose portraiture your own work will have to be judged, but by many famous workers of the past, but too many suggestions would be more likely to confuse you than to help. You have here a suitable foundation on which to build.

CHAPTER 20

Props and Accessories

Props and accessories, in the parlance of the professional photographer, are those items of studio furniture and miscellaneous equipment which are either necessary or helpful in posing a subject. There is considerable overlapping between the two terms but for our purposes and to simplify this discussion of them, we shall classify camera room furniture of whatever type, moveable or fixed, as "props," and small items whether added to a subject's attire or held in his or her hand, as "accessories." Toys and playthings, used in the photography of children, may be either props or accessories but have already been treated adequately in Chapters 7 and 8. Drapes, certainly, are accessories of a kind but are in our opinion so important that we shall devote Chapter 21 to them exclusively. And let us take this opportunity to emphasize that the judicious selection and use of an appropriate prop or accessory can at times be as important in the proper rendition of a subject's character or mannerisms—referring to older persons in general and men in particular—as the pose and lighting you may plan for that same purpose.

The basic prop, and the one no professional can do without, is something on which to seat the subject, usually referred to as the "posing chair" although it may not be a chair at all and is quite often a stool or bench. One of these you must have, and preferably several of different types. For head and shoulder work an old time piano stool, especially if you can find one with a back, is about as all purpose and utilitarian as anything you can secure. Even if the legs are ornate in the style of years gone by, they will not appear in a standard head and shoulders pose and the adjustable height of such a stool is a never ending convenience. In a studio of modern *decor* such a stool is an anachronism and any decorator will want to throw it out but this the experienced professional fortunate enough to own one will valiantly resist. There are modern stools to be had which are adjustable in height from around eighteen to twenty four inches and, if you expect to photograph many family groups, you will find need for at least two or three. As a substitute for group purposes, if your budget is limited, folding canvas camp stools will serve. These, light in weight and occupying little space when not in use because they fold up so easily, will also be invaluable—in addition to the stools already mentioned—for the occasional larger groups and weddings.

You must have, in addition to at least one adjustable stool, one or more chairs. In buying these, look for simple lines and avoid florid details, protruding knobs, legs the ends of which rise above the seats as in the case of cane seated chairs—in fact, anything which is likely to draw attention to itself and away from your subject. Bulky, upholstered chairs are unsuitable as well as too heavy to move easily, and beware of sloping backs and over soft cushions which, due to their very comfort, promptly cause the subject to slump. Barrel back or socalled Captain's chairs are good posing pieces. One very popular item which may be bought in many photo supply stores is a three legged posing chair with a triangular seat with, at the apex, a vertical rod to which is affixed a horizontal arm rest. The rod is adjustable in height and swings in a horizontal plane so it serves as a back rest, an arm rest or, with the chair turned around so the rod is in front of the sitter, something on which to lean one or both arms. The frame is aluminum, seat and rod are covered in a choice of plastic artificial leathers and, having been designed by a practical professional of many years' experience, this comes as close to an ideal all purpose posing chair as anything we remember.

By all means consider, as a third essential prop, a small table (on casters) about thirty inches high, adjustable in height if at all possible, with a top about eighteen by thirty six inches. We have mentioned such a table in earlier chapters and you will find many uses for it. Assuming, then, that your space is very limited you can "get by" for almost any average sitting, including modest groups, with a minimum of one adjustable posing stool, one general purpose posing chair, several folding canvas camp stools, and the small table. Even the table, in an emergency and when placed in the rear, will do as a perch for some member of a group. If you have a little more room, and we hope you have, an old fashioned roll end parlor couch—what your grandparents used to call a sofa—is a real find although you may have to search some family attics or used furniture stores for it. Failing one of these a more modern "love seat" will do, or any type of bench with a high roll end and, for full length poses, a ladder back chair such as described in Chapters 12 and 16.

Before we leave the subject of props we have a few additional suggestions to make. We are not offering any specific recommendations because, beyond what we have already suggested, additional items must depend first upon the general type or class of subjects with whom you expect to deal and, second, on your own ability to visualize pictorial treatments and surroundings that will, when your portraits are compared with those made by your competitors, cause yours to merit attention. For children a set of several small chairs and a table, all white, is not only a useful posing prop but will help to keep them occupied while you talk to their parents. These sets take up little space and can be shoved inconspicuously into some corner when not in use. For the little tyke who is not only constantly on the move himself but shoves his chair around with him, buy from a restaurant supply house a small chair with vacuum cups on the feet. That, once set firmly on the floor, cannot be moved and once you have focused on it, you know you have your quarry whenever you can get the youngster back in it. If you plan to follow our advice, so often repeated, and intend to include at least one three quarter or full length in every set of proofs, you will need some props to add variety to your background effects, such as columns, pedestals, railings or even simulated windows. Many of these you can make yourself, or they can be had from almost any firm dealing in window display supplies. And referring once again to backgrounds, remember our remarks concerning the use of glam'e cloth for that purpose, and that any fabric, hung and properly draped from a support, can be used to vary your background treatments.

Digressing for a moment before we turn to accessories, let us urge that you always have a sufficient supply of ashtrays in easy reach and in plain view, and not little dinky affairs but of ample size. This applies to your camera room as well as your reception room or any other rooms that your subjects may have occasion to visit. With ashtrays visible those who feel themselves compelled to smoke, and many do, are relieved of the embarrassment of asking if they may. Men especially, usually nervous upon entering a camera room, will light up without thinking and then their tension is increased when, with no ashtray in sight, they commence wondering what to do with the ashes or the cigar stump. Nor does it help the situation if the cameraman has to interrupt the sitting and scurry around for the missing ash depository. This is far from the small matter that it may seem. It is difficult enough in any event to get a man before your camera; once you have accomplished that, do everything possible to make him comfortable and set him at ease. Smokers, do not forget, are far in the majority today.

Accessories, helpful though they may be to you in completing the composition of a portrait or aiding in your characterization of a subject, are also an important part of the service that you render to your sitters. Within reason, therefore, you should consider them as much a part of your necessary studio investment as your photographic equipment. Perhaps the most standard accessory in any studio is a bridal bouquet. These, made of artificial flowers, can be secured from numerous sources and it is wise to have more than one. It is well to supplement these with one or two corsages or small sprays and a *boutonniere*, the latter for men who come in with their wives for anniversary portraits and the like. These artificial flowers will last almost indefinitely if you are careful to keep them in boxes where they are protected from dust. But be sure that these, and all other accessories with which a subject is likely to come in contact, are at all times scrupulously clean. Discard immediately any that show signs of soil or wear.

Very helpful are fans of the folding type, one light and one dark, a couple of *mantillas*, one white and one black, as well as a couple of decorative high back combs of the Spanish type, again one light and one dark, a string of pearl beads of the choker type and another of dark glass or plastic, as well as one or two longer strings. The choker, or short single string which hugs the neck closely, can be tremendously helpful in breaking a long neckline when a subject—perhaps in summer—comes to the studio with a low neck dress. Just as it seems to be true that most women who wear slacks are the ones who shouldn't, frequently those who wear low dresses display bones and hollows at the base of the neck. A choker not only hides these but saves a lot of retouching time.

Items like these, if you want to secure a pleased reaction from your subject, should always be taken out of a clean, good looking case and not be hastily dragged from a pigeon hole or half open drawer. Gloves, too, are often useful—not to be worn but to be held by the subject. Two pairs for women, one light and one dark, and one of cape or pigskin for the men. Several books, of different sizes and thicknesses and in good bindings, will find frequent use. In selecting these try to find books whose

Figure **167**

contents are printed on antique rather then slick white paper so that their open pages will not appear as brilliant highlights when you use them in a portrait. One book should by all means be a Bible, and preferably showing some signs of use. You should also have another Bible, small, bound in white and spotlessly new, for bridal portraits. Other accessories will suggest themselves to you as time goes on but these will give you the general idea.

Because books are as inexpensive and handy accessories as you can possibly have, and do not even need to be specially purchased because you can always pick up a couple in your home, we want to show you a few easy ways of using them in portraiture. Not only does a book add interest to a composition but it provides something purposeful to occupy your subject's hands. Take the case of the older man whose hands appear in *Figure 167*. He happens to be a cigar smoker of the confirmed type and therefore if we did not include his cigar in at least one pose of his set of proofs we would be failing to characterize him properly, to say nothing of overlooking an almost certain sale of extra prints. Yet a cigar, whether burning or not, is not a good looking object when held in the hand alone. A pipe is something else again because it can be positioned in many different ways, frequently so that the stem becomes part of the composition. A cigarette, because of its color, and especially if in a holder, can add a highlight in a wanted spot. On the other hand a fresh cigar is pointless as an accessory while one that is burning should not be too obvious.

So we resort to that small table once again, lay an opened book on it and ask our subject to lean forward and place his hands on the book. Thus we add verisimilitude by including the cigar in an entirely logical manner and give our subject something better to do with his hands than the stereotyped hand-with-cigar-in-the-air pose which always looks just that—posed. And, before we leave *Figure 167*, notice (as we mentioned before) that the pages of the book are not a brilliant white. The book is only an accessory, an aid to our composition, and is not intended to draw attention to itself. The moment any accessory becomes too obviously a part of the picture it becomes a detriment instead of an asset. Correctly positioned and lighted, any accessory appears—to the viewer—as something which acceptably "belongs" in the picture.

Still on the subject of books as accessories, you will find them very helpful when you are dealing with older people. The subject of *Figure 168* is an older lady and in such a case your Bible will be most appropriate. In this example we treat the hands differently, one underneath the Bible, supporting it and out of sight, and the other pointing directly to a particular line on the page which also gives us an excellent opportunity to display both the wedding ring and the watch. We do not stress the fact that she is holding a Bible, although what is visible of the typography would indicate the fact, and again the pages are not white but in a subdued tone. And why a Bible? You can hand a man a book and the chances are he will accept it almost without looking at it, or will pay little attention to it if he does. A woman will look at the title and if, by any chance, you have picked up a volume that is controversial, her attitude may tense immediately. Your taste in books may not be that of your subjects, but the Bible is always safe.

There will be times when a subject, usually a man, insists on being photographed with a certain book—he may even be the author—or for some reason of your own you consider a book unusually suitable. This calls for a different treatment because now the book is no longer a mere accessory but an integral part of the portrait. The subject of *Figure 169* is a college president who is photographed every year for the institution's annual, which means that he is seldom shown in a static head and shoulder pose. Knowing him well, when we made the appointment we suggested that he bring a book of his own choice with him. He selected the previous year's annual and because it was so appropriate, we placed it on our small table to take full advantage of the cover, had him rest his hands on it, and that was that. The point is that a book need not always lie flat on a table or even be opened to add interest and purpose to a composition. Rarely is a book unsuitable as an accessory for an older person, and few items are handier in the camera room. Many's the time you will use books which will never show in a picture at all—to prop up the feet

Figure **168**

Figure **169**

of a very short subject, to raise an elbow to get a hand in just the right position, to lift up the legs of the table (or even the camera stand itself) when you are seeking a slightly bizarre effect. Don't underestimate the book!

A subject who wears glasses constantly is not going to look natural without them. Glasses are therefore a debatable accessory and yet there are many people who, compelled to wear them a good part of the time, nevertheless dislike and remove them at every opportunity. There are also those whose glasses are as often in their hands as on their noses. All of us are familiar with the platform speaker who is constantly put-

Figure **170**

ting them on and taking them off, the latter often to brandish them while making a point. Under such conditions your characterization will be better if the glasses are not worn and yet are included in the portrait and the trick then is to have them held in a manner which is not only graceful but adds to the composition. This applies chiefly to the temples, the lines of which must not protrude from your composition in such a manner as to attract too much attention or pull the viewer's eye away from the face. We include *Figure 170* as one answer to just such a situation. This is a matter of watching your subject closely from the time he or she enters the camera room, and noting mentally the poses that are both characteristic and appealing.

We have no intention of confusing the issue with a wide variety of accessory pictures if only because there would be so little chance of our being to duplicate either your subjects or the particular props and accessories you may finally select for yourself. We make no excuse for showing several book suggestions because we know they will be helpful on many occasions and whether you are dealing with either sex. Fans, flowers and such other items as we have suggested do not have such general application and so we do not illustrate them here. But study the women who come to your studio, young or old, and the items of apparel they have with them. Most of the time their own belongings will be all you require. And, as one very live accessory, never overlook the pet that is brought to the studio. Whether or not requested, be sure to make at least one pose with that pet. It will be a sure fire sale and may very probably bring you considerable added business.

In closing this chapter we do want to emphasize, in spite of all we have written about accessories, that the really skilled cameraman will use them in limited number and, by the use of imagination in posing and lighting, will secure more varied and interesting effects than an imitator could achieve with an unlimited supply. Accessories are helpful and, at times, necessary to give your poses variety, but never make the mistake of using the same accessory in the same way constantly. Nothing will more surely "date" your portraits or indicate to every one that you are taking "the easy way out."

CHAPTER 21

Drapes and How to Use Them

"Drapes" and "draping," as the professional photographer uses those terms, have nothing in common with the draperies and other materials which are dealt with by the interior decorator. A drape, as arranged by a decorator, and hanging in a public room, or even in a residence, might well be selected for use as a background by a photographer. And a photographer might hang or throw a length of fabric over a support for use, but neither of these instances would be what is meant here by "drape." Simply stated, a drape is a length of material used to enhance the appearance of a portrait subject. Usually, it is some type of fabric (tulle, lace, silk, satin, or velvet—sometimes ornamented with sequins or beads,); furs are also often used, and feathers such as marabou.

Most commonly, a drape is comparatively short, not too wide, and is placed over a subject's shoulders in such a manner as to form a V *decolletage*. In longer lengths and larger widths, and in the hands of those who have devoted some study to the art of draping, material can be so arranged as to simulate the latest fashions in necklines, or, when necessity demands, can be manipulated in such a manner as to make it appear that the subject is wearing quite an elaborate formal gown. Obviously, such effects take time to prepare. The photographer who has an assistant with the necessary artistic *flair* (or who possesses it himself) has no small edge over his competitors, and can command a premium for portraits so created.

There are many established photographers who claim they see no need for such a service; the truth is, that having failed to analyze thoroughly the needs and desires of their sitters, they are overlooking an excellent source of both word of mouth advertising and added profits. Even they will occasionally be asked outright for a draped effect, and in such cases they have only two alternatives: to try and talk the subject out of the idea, or to admit frankly that they do not make draped portraits. In either event not only is a prospective customer permanently lost, but she will tell her friends of her experience. Because simple

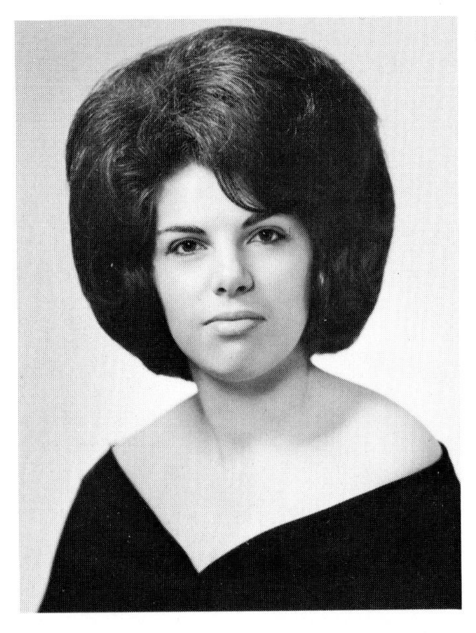

Figure **171**

draping has no terrors for any competent photographer, as we propose to explain, and requires only a small investment in a few pieces of material, we hope none of our readers will ever find themselves in such a situation.

Ordinarily draping is a service that is requested by the subject, and one way to assure yourself of calls for it is to show samples of draped portraits in your window and showcase displays. Under such conditions, the way is left open for you to explain that because draping takes time, there is a higher charge for such portraits; if your charge is reasonable an objection will seldom be raised. On other occasions, a dress or neckline may be unsuitable or—and more frequently—may expose an unattractive neck and shoulders. You may then suggest a drape, in order to avoid dissatisfaction when the proofs are shown, and also to reduce retouching costs. An extra charge under such circumstances is inadvisable, if not actually uncalled for, because then the use of a drape is as much a part of your responsibility as is the careful posing needed to make a stout subject look slim, or to disguise other defects. That, of course, is something you must decide for yourself; the point to remember at all times is that your subject must not only be satisfied but pleased to the point of enthusiasm when she sees the proofs.

Suppose we consider first why a girl or young woman will ask for a drape when she appears before your camera. Almost surely, the request is made because she realizes she lacks a garment with a suitable neckline, and having seen examples of what you can do, is convinced that you can portray her pleasingly. Your ability to create an appropriate neckline through draping means that she can have her portraits without the delay and expense of shopping for a new dress, which means less money to spend for her portraits. It also eliminates the danger that in the meantime she may see samples she prefers in a competitor's window display. The time to clinch a sitting is when the prospect is in the mood, and your response

Figure **172**

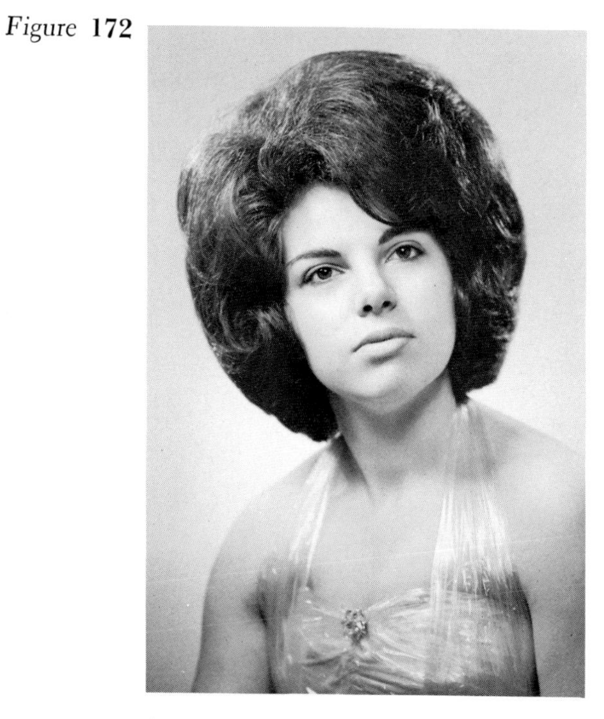

should be: "Certainly we can create a lovely neckline for you—let's step into the camera room."

Before we go seriously into this subject of draping, just for the record take a look at *Figure 171*, which illustrates the simplest and most standard form of drape. It is frequently called for in school portraits, when it is desired that there shall be no competition between students in the matter of clothing. An additional advantage is that time is saved in scheduling sittings, because the students can

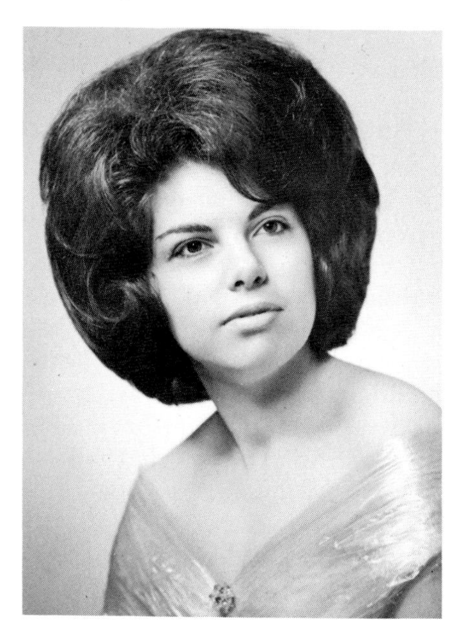

Figure **173**

Figure **174**

Figure **175**

come straight from school, without the necessity of changing clothes. The drape consists of nothing more than a length of black velvet placed across the shoulders, brought to a V of suitable depth in front and temporarily secured with a simple concealed pin. Yet, there are many times when this is more appropriate than some complicated creation. For a subject who is dark, with a good neck and shoulders, it is sufficiently dignified and formal for many purposes. It requires almost no time, and is not something for which you can justifiably make an extra charge. It should be considered, when you find it appropriate, as your own contribution to the success of a sitting.

Let us take up next the case of the young lady who, during a visit in person, or during the making of an appointment over the telephone, says quite frankly that what she wants is the effect of a formal gown, but at the moment she has nothing suitable. Items of clothing that were once considered as "unmentionables" are so extensively publicized today that they are no longer embarrassing as subjects of conversation, and so, do not fail to mention that she should wear a strapless brassiere when she comes for her sitting. Though a drape can be applied directly over the brassiere, it is well for you to have available a light foundation garment, which she can don in the dressing room. This way, upon entering the camera room, she will have no feeling of undue exposure.

We are going to produce the effect shown in *Figure 172*, for which a rather ample length of plastic is required. One end of this is held at the back, brought around the body, under the arms, and secured at the back, with one or more ordinary pins. Next, the remainder of the cloth is folded and brought up from under one arm, around the back of the neck, and then down under the other arm. A couple of graceful folds are arranged in front and held in place with a small costume jewelry brooch, not too ornamental. This creates a halter neckline, and we defy anyone who sees this portrait to think of the results as anything but a handsome, and probably expensive, formal evening gown. We should add that when a sitting involves the special creation of drapes of this kind, a mirror of fair size (but not full length) should be provided in the camera room, so that the subject may at least have a general idea of the effect that is being worked out. Also it is well, before completing the drape and finally pinning it into place, to check the effect on the groundglass.

Strictly speaking, this is not a man's job, and as we mentioned in *Chapter 15*, on glamour portraiture, you should select some member of your staff—probably your receptionist, if yours is the average small studio—and insist that she devote some time to the subject. Here, however, we have to assume that you are working alone; we can allay any hesitation on your part by assuring you that many professionals not only do their own draping but actually prefer doing so. After all, as a professional photographer, you are supposed to be an artist, and most women will accept from you without hesitation such instructions as may be necessary, and even a limited amount of personal contact, which, under other circumstances, would be totally unpermissible. Women today have become quite accustomed to appearing *deshabillé* before costume designers and other men to whom this sort of thing is all in the day's work. Act first of all with complete confidence and assurance, touch your subject no more than is absolutely necessary, offer a slight, smiling apology when you have to do so, and under no conditions show any sign of embarrassment.

A halter effect is preferable when a formal is specified, and the subject is perhaps not as well proportioned as she might be. Our next drape (*Figure 173*) is particularly suitable when the subject is blessed with a graceful neck and fine

Figure **176**

shoulders. This, an off-the-shoulder formal, is even simpler to prepare and uses the same length of plastic. This time, just below the shoulders, it is wrapped around the figure, arms and all, and again pinned at the back. The material is then carefully pleated, drawn down into a very shallow V at the front, and fastened with a brooch. More may be used if desired, but in any event such jewelry should never be conspicuous.

We would like to remind you to keep all materials that you use for draping spotlessly clean. Do not have them hanging in your camera or dressing room. Long lengths of material may be kept on hangers, at all times properly covered, while shorter pieces should be in clean boxes, wrapped in tissue paper. Transparent plastic boxes, inexpensive and obtainable in many sizes and shapes, are particularly appropriate for such purposes. Such items should stay in place until you are ready to use them, and then you should remove them in full view of the subject, always handling them carefully and making sure they do not trail on the floor. Your subjects will then have no hesitancy in coming in contact with them. In cases where you are working with very long lengths of material, parts of which must necessarily remain on the floor while you are working, always spread a sheet, or other clean cloth, on the floor first.

So far as the average man is concerned, there is not much he can do in creating formals beyond the two styles we have explained, although these do lend themselves to considerable variation by the use of different materials and slight changes of angles, folding, and pleating. You really do need a member of the opposite sex to help you, or substitute for you entirely, when it comes to draping. Give a woman a few pieces of material and enough pins, ribbons, and other notions, plus the latest fashion magazines, and there will be no limit to what she can devise and even duplicate. Once the fact becomes known that such a service is available, you will have plenty of calls for it. At the moment, though, and considering that you are just beginning, it is time we turned to some more simple drapes, which you can handle easily.

Figure **177**

Figure **178**

For example, it is not necessarily true that once you have selected a suitable material, posed your subject, and tripped the shutter, you have exhausted the possibilities. Perhaps the same girl, with another drape, and a change in pose, may look every bit as attractive, but in a quite different way. Confronted with two proofs which are not just changes in pose but also in material and style, your subject will be almost compelled to select both, and your objective is always to increase the final order, by any legitimate means. Compare then, *Figures 174 and 175*, where we show a young lady who is "loaded" with personality; we have presented two completely contrasting facets of her character.

For *Figure 174* we selected a length of plastic material, to give a touch of glitter, placed it around her shoulders, and had her look over one of them directly at the camera, with a charming smile. Then (*Figure 175*), having her face the camera, we substituted a length of black lace, which we placed horizontally, and to glamourize the result, posed her with one shoulder lower than the other. A pose like this is very suitable when the subject does not have a wide face but does have good shoulders. However, to secure the desired upward gaze of the eyes, it is necessary to hold the head down, concealing the neck and resulting in a lack of separation between head and shoulders. To correct this, we chose from our stock of accessories a short string of beads. In *Figure 174*, the drape is hardly noticeable, providing nothing more than a touch of sparkle and balance at the bottom of the picture area. In *Figure 175*, the drape is much more a part of the total composition.

The subject of *Figure 176* had been selected by her sorority to be their candidate for "Homecoming Queen," and they needed a portrait to use in connection with the campaign. It had to be somewhat off the beaten track to secure attention—and the needed votes. The pose speaks for itself, but it was the drape that helped to combine a "come hither" look with the necessary appearance of dignity. Apparently, she is wearing a formal with a rather high shoulder treatment; in fact, this is a drape, and one that was rather largely created on the spur of the moment, because little time was available. It consists of nothing more than a length of metallic cloth, tucked in over her brassiere, with one end carried over each shoulder and allowed to hang loose in the back. She won the contest, too.

Our next two illustrations are both over-the-shoulder poses. *Figure 177* shows how helpful marabou—the feather material which we mentioned earlier—can be for draping. An ordinary "boa" of marabou, which is the form in which it is commonly purchased, is not wide enough, and does not have enough body, for photographic purposes. Buy several strands—they are not costly—and have them sewn side by side on a cloth base, to whatever width you think advisable. In *Figure 177*, we wanted to show the line of the back, and consequently used the drape only over the near shoulder, to break up that line which otherwise would have resulted in an unpleasantly triangular effect. The marabou is very easy to handle and produces a pleasing, soft result. If you will have marabou made up in the shape of a stole about six feet long, you will be able to use it in many ways, even as a complete wrap around the shoulders for three quarter poses. It photographs well, and its soft texture is especially useful for breaking up areas that might otherwise be uninteresting.

The purpose of *Figure 178* is to show how effective a very simple piece of net material can be. We had no desire to conceal a beautiful shoulder, but we did want to give the lower part of the back a change of tone, and without having to extend the near arm too far, which might have seemed awkward, we wanted to give the composition a more suitable base. Drawing the net forward a bit from the figure took care of that, and also added a variation of light tone without drawing attention away from the face.

Whether you decide that a drape is necessary, or your subject requests one, do not forget that the drape must never "steal" the picture. A drape is an accessory, and must always be treated as such. "Fussy" arrangements of folds and pleats, brooches or other jewelry that is too large or shiny, so that it reflects light, will defeat your purpose. The drape must appear to be an essential part of the picture, in order to be accepted by the viewer as a conventional item of clothing. And, as we remarked when discussing glamour, always keep your drapes conservative and in good taste.

CHAPTER 22

The Camera Vignette

No book on portraiture would be complete without a discussion of vignettes. It is a style of portraiture normally limited, in so far as adults are concerned, to head and shoulders, in which the lower part of the figure, and often the sides as well, fade into the background, be it white, gray, or black. From the standpoint of pure photography, an artist or a jury will turn thumbs down on sight of a vignette, for the sole reason that the subject of the picture has no base, and is apparently floating in air, thereby violating a fundamental rule of accepted pictorial composition. Nevertheless, vignettes of babies and children, against white backgrounds especially, can be very lovely indeed, and can be equally attractive as treatments of older subjects. There are times, too, when physical deformities, or clothing that is photographically objectionable, make resort to the vignette almost essential.

There is no question but that, for some years, vignetted photographs have been in disrepute among photographers as well as their more knowledgeable subjects. This is chiefly due to a deliberate misuse of the process by studios devoted largely to cheap quantity production. A cheaply produced vignette, rendering much of the lower portion of a portrait totally black, can cover a multitude of sins, and enable even a comparatively inexperienced cameraman to produce prints which, thanks to high pressure methods, are at least saleable. That the subject will almost surely never return is of no consequence to studios of this type. They exist for the moment, not for the future, and once the immediate market is exhausted, it is a simple matter to find a new location and start over. Such vignettes are made on the negative in the darkroom, by means of a cutting reducer, and the results are necessarily crude. It is hardly surprising that vignettes fell into disfavor.

Totally different is the camera vignette, the effect of which is a pleasing blending of the subject into the background, with no abrupt transition of dark to light or vice versa. Because the negative itself has the vignette, no darkroom work is

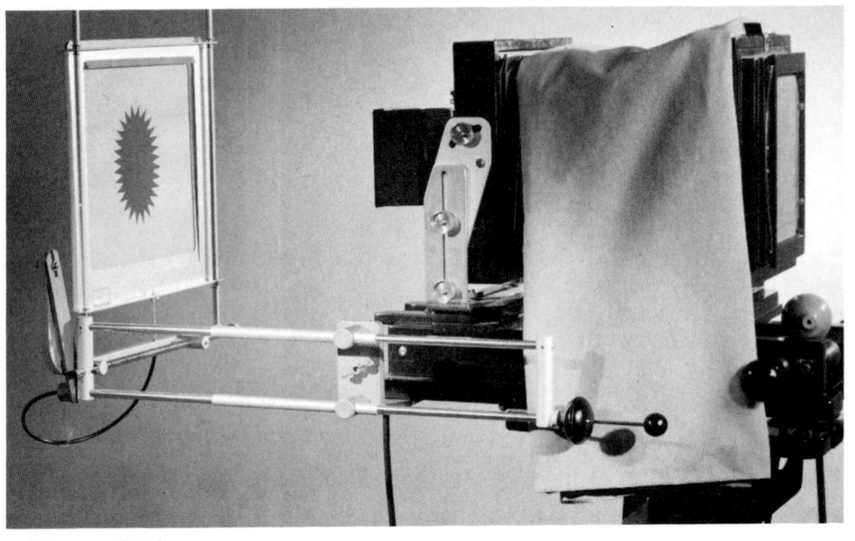

Figure **178A**

necessary, and all prints are uniform. To duplicate a vignette made by the customary darkroom process is far from easy, if not quite impossible. Once you have learned to make a camera vignette you will find it to be less trouble than the darkroom method. It will simply mean a little more care in your lighting and posing, and the addition of two items to your equipment.

It is necessary to have, for attachment to the front of your camera, a device to hold the masks or cards (these are of several types) which actually produce the vignette effect. You will also need one more light, either a small spot or a bulb in a reflector. Any competent amateur or gadget-minded professional can easily make the vignetting attachment, although we do not recommend home-made equipment. No matter how well it works, it seldom, if ever, looks "professional," and it will not leave a favorable impression on your subjects. We ourselves happen to be familiar with only one camera vignetter that is on the market, and, because it is an efficient and good looking device, we show it in *Figure 178–A*. There may be others, but this one can be purchased from any dealer in photographic equipment.

Its important advantage lies in the fact that with it you can easily control the placement of the vignette mask, moving it up, down, to one side or the other, and closer or farther away from the lens. At the same time, you can watch the image on your groundglass, without having to move your camera. Furthermore, the whole thing can be attached to, or removed from, the camera in a moment or two. Three masks accompany the equipment, two of them being complete elliptical cutouts, one of black material and the other translucent with a ground surface, while the other is a half mask (also translucent), used when you only wish to vignette the lower portion of the negative.

The purpose of the mask, or cutout, is to conceal from the lens all extraneous detail surrounding the subject (or only that at the bottom when you are using the half mask). The soft blending effect is due to the fact that the edges of the cutout are serrated, instead of being left smooth. You have a choice of several possible vignette effects, depending on your selection of the black mask or one of the translucent ones, plus the manner in which you use the auxiliary light.

Look now at ***Figure 179,*** the picture of the couple, and you will see that the lower part of the figures is blended away into a tone which closely approximates the overall background tone, yet there is no sharp cutting off or breaking away into a solid black. This portrait is in itself a graphic example of how the standard placement of main source and fill-in can be applied, whether you are photographing one person or two. A small light has been used behind the couple (*see* ***Figure 180***) to throw a low illumination on the background, for separation. The only difference between this and an everyday picture is that the vignette holder has been affixed to the camera, and holds the transparent half mask, which cuts off the lower part of the image; also, there is the use of the small light we mentioned earlier. This (see ***Figure 180***) is placed to the left of the camera, and somewhat behind it, to strike the mask only.

Perhaps we should explain here that the theory of the camera vignette consists in a carefully controlled fogging of the area to be subdued or vignetted. This can be accomplished in two ways, by allowing a small amount of the fill-in light to strike the mask, or by the use of the small auxiliary light. The latter is what we suggest, and therefore indicate in the accompanying diagrams, because it is far simpler to direct onto the mask in this manner exactly the desired amount of light. Even a slight movement of your fill-in to include the mask, especially after it has been positioned, may nullify all of your previous effort. The added light, combined with the translucent mask, enables you to match the illumination on the background to that of the light reflected into the lens by the mask. You will readily

Figure **180**

Figure **179**

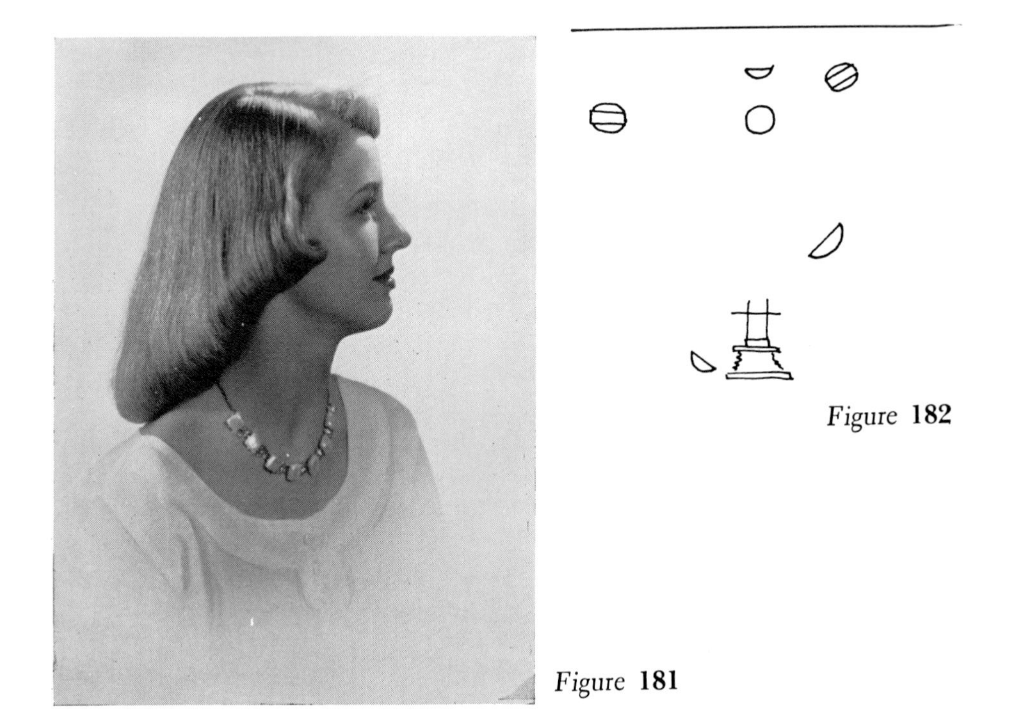

Figure **182**

Figure **181**

understand what we mean if, while studying the groundglass of your camera, you move the auxiliary light toward or away from the mask, and watch the resulting effect.

Using the half mask for the bottom, as in the case of *Figure 179*, is very helpful when you photograph small groups in which the knees and feet are a problem to handle. You will also find it is a valuable method of concealing much of an overly buxom figure, when making a head and shoulder portrait. Used skillfully, the half mask will solve a multitude of problems, and by carefully controlling the illumination on the mask itself, you will find you can make some very beautiful portraits, without resorting to the full masks for complete image vignetting. The half mask is the simpler way to use the camera vignetter, but you should not limit yourself to it, because the full effect of the camera vignette only discloses itself when you vignette completely, as in the following illustrations.

In *Figure 181*, we have a profile of a young lady who happens to be endowed with a considerable mass of blonde hair, a type of subject for whom a light or high key vignette is always suitable. For this, the subject is placed before a white background, which is given an overall illumination by means of a small light behind the subject. Because we are making a profile, our main source is really the spot at right rear, and of course we need another spot at left of the subject, though farther away, to lighten up the hair. What was our main source now becomes the fill-in—the light at center right. We place the full transparent mask in the vignette holder before the lens, and by means of the auxiliary light to left of the camera (this time rather close to the lens), we throw enough light on the vignette so that, upon looking in the groundglass, it becomes the same tone as the background. A glance at the diagram (*Figure 182*) will make this all quite clear. Notice that the background of this portrait—everything surrounding

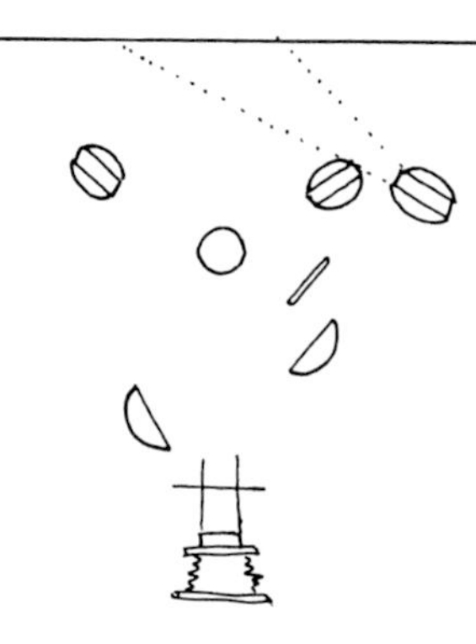

Figure **185**

Figure **183**

the image—is the same in tone, but that it is not pure white. Had this been done by projection printing, it would have been pure white; instead, we have a soft all over tone value. When a vignette is largely blank white paper, it loses all of its charm.

While light background vignettes, such as *Figure 181*, are very appealing and

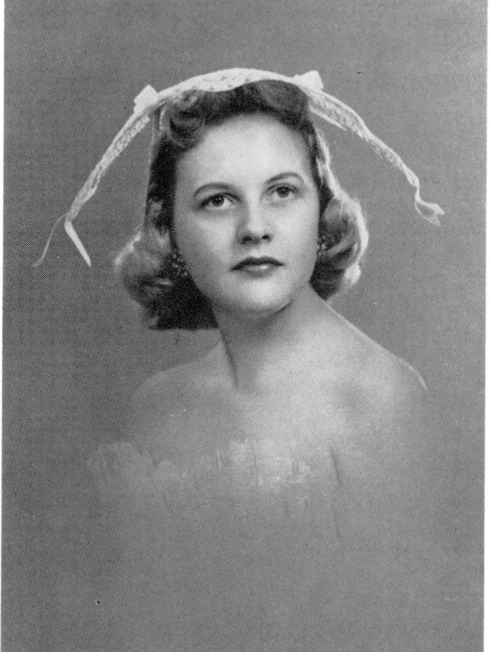

Figure **184**

readily saleable, we do not consider them quite as effective as the gray vignettes shown in *Figures 183* and *184*. You must realize that—as we remarked earlier—many people will have already seen so many made-in-the-darkroom vignettes, harsh, cold, and cheap in appearance, that they fail to appreciate the skill required to produce a well executed light background camera vignette. Not having one of the other type at hand, so the two may be compared, they may not realize the difference. While making the gray vignette is a little more difficult, the result is uncommon, and cannot be duplicated by any sort of darkroom manipulation. Remember, however, that these require great care both in your processing and print handling. Our subject for these vignettes (*Figures 183* and *184*) is a blonde, wearing a light colored formal. Having decided on gray vignettes, quite a few changes in our steps will be necessary.

First, we hang over our standard background a sufficient length of wide background paper in a pink shade. Against this (*Figure 185*); we direct a 500-watt spot—in this case from right rear—using a soft beam, instead of a more concentrated one with sharp edges, to bring the entire background up to our desired light level. We place our subject considerably farther away from the background than before, and prepare a standard lighting, with our main source and fill-in in approximately their customary positions. At left and right rear, we add spots to outline the head and shoulders, not only to assure separation from the background, but to add emphasis and interest. Finally, we place the full translucent mask in the vignette holder, but we use no illumination on the mask at all. Shoulders, arms, and gown all blend gently and gradually into the background tone. The result is *Figure 183*; the only change necessary to make the next portrait (*Figure 184*) was to adjust the vignette so the sides of the hat would not be

Figure **187**

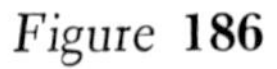

Figure **186**

cut off, plus, in the retouching, a bit of highlighting on the top edge of the gown to bring it out a little more distinctly.

One other type—the black vignette—remains to be explained, and this we see in *Figure 186* and its accompanying lighting diagram, *Figure 187*. For an effect like this, you need first of all a black background. Black felt, which is what we used, is very satisfactory. The standard placement of main source and fill-in works out perfectly for this, supplemented by two spots, at right and left rear, to outline the head and shoulders, so they will stand out properly from the black background. In the vignette holder you use the full black mask, and, of course, throw no light on it at all. No light is used on the background, and care must be taken that no illumination reaches it from either the main source or fill-in. The light from the spots, we might add, should be somewhat stronger than normal, especially when the subject has brown or black hair. Be careful, also, not to overdevelop.

As is the case with so many photographic procedures and techniques, no amount of explanation can properly substitute for actual practice. In cold type, and without the vignetting device and a set of masks before you, what you read here unavoidably sounds like a cumbersome and tedious process, instead of the very simple matter that it really is. At this stage in our text, and your own experimenting, as you have followed our instructions, the placement of your camera and lights for almost any type of lighting should be almost second nature. You now add to your equipment a vignetter and a set of masks. You have a subject before you, and decide you want to make a vignetted portrait. You set up your lights and camera accordingly, attach the vignetter to the camera, insert the appropriate mask, and there you are. Whether you need to use the small auxiliary light or not—consult the illustrations and the diagrams—depends on the kind of vignette you have in mind. That's all there is to it.

CHAPTER 23

Portraiture in the Home

Professional portraiture in the home of the customer is nothing new, in fact it was practiced by some photographers as far back as the days of the open flash, with magnesium powder spread on a small tray and fired by means of a spark. This was inconvenient to say the least and portraits were seldom made in the home under such conditions unless, a subject being incapacitated in some manner, a photograph could be made in no other way. The invention of the flash bag simplified the problem greatly and home portraiture as such really came into being at that time.

Today there are many professionals who operate exclusively in the homes of their customers, using their own residences as their headquarters. Their darkrooms and processing facilities—and sometimes these are more complete and modern than anything to be found in a formal studio—are thus right at hand and, not having to maintain two establishments, their overhead expenses are greatly reduced. They do not save time by eliminating transportation between home and studio, however, because of course they are constantly on the move back and forth to the homes of their customers.

Also to be considered is the professional who conducts what is generally called a "residence studio." He may or may not be a home portraitist. If, to reduce overhead costs, he has merely bought or built a home and remodeled or planned it for photographic purposes, the result will very probably be as much a formal studio as if it were located in a store or office building in the business district. On the other hand, and we know many professionals who have been highly successful with such operations, his actual photographic requirements may involve only that part of the home which is reserved for processing, finishing, filing negatives and the like and in such cases he will almost surely be a home portrait specialist. Such a photographer will make sittings in his home, using the living room, dining room, hall and stairway or any other portions which offer suitable background effects. He will rarely use a formal background, if indeed he owns one at all, and whether or not he is visiting the homes of his customers he is definitely producing home portraits.

Usually he does do much of his work in the homes of others but he has one advantage over the exclusive home portraitist in that, when a customer's home is too small (as in the case of many modern apartments) or otherwise unsuitable, he can always make the sitting at his own residence and thus maintain the intimate atmosphere that accompanies true home portraiture.

There are still others—and while a limited few are top rank craftsmen this is not true of the great majority—who do not even bother to develop and finish their own work, thus reducing their costs still more. They do little more than expose the negatives and then deliver or mail those to one of a number of specialists in what is called "finishing for the trade," who complete the processing, do the necessary proof retouching and return a set of proofs. The cameraman—or, more often, a "proof passer"—shows the proofs, takes the order, and then returns the negatives to the finisher who completes the work even to the mounting of the finished prints. This is the usual method of operation of the itinerant and for many reasons we advise against it. Of these the most important as we see it is the complete loss of personal touch with his work on the part of the photographer who, having made his exposure, has no control thereafter over the results.

Quite aside from that the itinerant, lacking a permanent base for his operations, has no standing in the community. He is here today and gone tomorrow. Such guarantees as he may make concerning the permanence of his prints, the maintenance of negative files, the fairness or honesty of his prices, mean nothing whatever should a customer wish to contact him again, because by then he is miles away. This is not professional photography as we like to think of it nor, as we hope, the readers of this book plan to enter into it. Certainly such methods are not conducive to good craftsmanship, pride in one's profession or the building of a permanent reputation and business.

Home portraiture, when practiced by a professional who takes pride in his work and his reputation, has much to recommend it. We have no intention of entering here into the pros and cons of home versus studio portraiture and devote this and following chapters to the subject of portraits in the home chiefly because no book on practical portrait photography would be complete without them. It cannot be gainsaid that many subjects, and children especially, are more relaxed and at ease at home than in any studio and because this makes for better character rendition and more natural results due to the inclusion of the subject's accustomed surroundings the home portraitist has at least one argument in his favor which is not easily overthrown.

The main charm of—and reason for—home portraits being the fact that they have greater appeal to family and friends due to the inclusion of furnishings and surroundings with which all are familiar, there is little if any necessity for what might be called the studio type of background. Nevertheless most experienced home portraitists find it advisable to add to their paraphernalia one or two roll backgrounds which can quickly be affixed to hang from a light metal stand. Such a background will usually be white or cream on one side and black or a very dark shade on the other and one may be sufficiently long to reach the floor while the other is more the size of a studio flat, such as we mentioned in Chapter 19. Now and then one finds a home so profusely furnished that an overabundance of accessories makes it impossible to select a setting which will not compete too greatly with the subject. On other occasions drapes, hangings and even wallpaper are so strident in pattern that it becomes necessary to block them out of the picture. There will be times when the only suitable spot on which to photograph a baby or small child is a davenport or large chair adorned with an impossibly loud pattern. A simple way to solve this problem is to keep in your car an olive drab army blanket which can be used to cover the offending piece of furniture.

You will have to train yourself to become observant so that almost immediately upon entering a home, be it a house or an apartment, you begin to select or discard those areas or furniture groupings which may or may not be suitable as background material and, having done so, it is well to commence setting up your equipment as rapidly as you can, keeping a light conversation going while you do. With your camera and a light or two already in place it becomes more difficult for your subject—or the mother if children are to be photographed—to urge that you work in some favorite corner or include certain cherished possessions which, nine times out of ten, are probably not merely unsuitable but likely to be photogenically disastrous. Diplomatic you must be, at all times, but what you must gently emphasize is that while of course you do plan to include as much of the environment as you can, what your customer really wants is a good portrait. If nothing else will do, waste an exposure or two, or even simulate a couple while failing to open the shutter or pull the slide, and then return to the setting you have selected.

Avoid ornate furniture at all times, and overstuffed and wing chairs in particular, unless your subject is an adult and one whose size and bulk is sufficient not to be "lost" in the chair. Occasionally even a small woman can be satisfactorily portrayed in such a chair provided she is wearing a gown with a sufficiently voluminous skirt, but usually heavy furniture should be reserved for men, and large men at that. If you are planning a group, and once in a home you should always try to sell that idea before you leave, a fireplace or mantel will be your most obvious basis for it. If a home is of the older type, with the windows recessed so there are deep ledges in front of them, few locations are better for at least some poses of children, or even adults if the ledges are sufficiently large. When you are using a mantel as a background do not let the unaccustomed color of home furnishings—as compared with your camera room interior—confuse you. Make certain, as you study your groundglass, that objects on the mantel itself are not "growing out" of your subject's heads or sticking out of their ears, and raise or lower your camera to avoid having the heads apparently cut in half by the horizontal line of the mantel.

Beware of mirrors, not just because your camera or lights may be reflected in them, but especially when working with flash because the extra volume of light reflected from a mirror which you had not taken into your calculations may destroy your carefully planned balance of light and shade. When you must, as you frequently will find necessary, move furniture, lamps or bric-a-brac, do not hesitate to do so but always offer a word of apology. "I'm sorry I have to move this, but I'll put it right back where it was," will be sufficiently reassuring to the anxious housewife. And if, by any chance, your lights are above normal wattage do not fail to check the fuse box first. Nothing, especially in these days of home freezers, will make you less popular than blowing out the house lights.

Home freezers remind us of that even more modern development, the ranch type or split level home, with its patio or other outdoor family area and, increasingly, a swimming pool. Whenever the weather is propitious or if you are fortunate enough to live in a section of the country where outdoor living is more or less accepted the year around, take advantage of the extra settings you are thus afforded and make as many exposures as you can of your subjects, children or adults, engaged in their normal outdoor activities. Those are the pictures that will increase the order and help to make each trip more profitable. Failing that possibility, and if yours is to be a residence studio, plan a sufficiently attractive garden area for outdoor portraiture and make use of it at every opportunity when you are making "home" sittings at your own place. This is even more advisable if the interior of your residence studio has been equipped for formal portraiture because it will enable you to offer your customers that "something different" which gives you that all important "edge" over your competitors.

Whether or not home portraiture is your eventual goal, you will find many occasions in the operation of whatever type of formal studio you plan to establish when a working knowledge of basic home portrait procedure will prove to be a valuable asset. You may be highly averse to leaving your studio to make a sitting but a flat refusal on your part to depart from your accustomed procedure to accommodate older persons, or those who are incapacitated, by portraying them in their homes only leaves a wide opening for the first itinerant who comes along, and in addition will lessen the reputation you must build for yourself as the person on whom to depend for all photographic needs. The chances are, also, that you will make an occasional commercial photograph and, while on such assignments, may be asked to make a portrait of a plant foreman or some other employee who cannot readily visit the studio, whereupon an understanding of home portraiture techniques will come in handy.

It should not be necessary to remind you that you are a guest in the home and should conduct yourself accordingly, and yet there are home portraitists who seem to lack even such minor essentialities in the creation of good will. You are, like it or not, an intruder upon the normal peace and quiet of the household, so let your visit be as speedy as possible, return to its place anything you may have had to move, make sure you pick up any spent flashbulbs and, rather than have your customers heave a sigh of relief when you go, leave them with the feeling that it has been a pleasant experience and they have a desire to welcome you again.

The illustrations accompanying the three following chapters have been carefully selected as being well within the possibilities of the reader who has diligently followed our earlier suggestions. In producing them, we have worked with a minimum of equipment, no more than anyone intending to take up portraiture seriously should already have in his possession, or should be able to acquire with a comparatively small investment. For example, most of the illustrations were taken with a 4 x 5 camera equipped with a six inch F/4.5 lens, the same camera that you might well have used in all of your work up to this point. For the first illustration we used an 8 x 10 camera with an old sixteen and half inch F/3.8 portrait lens, while the second and third were taken with a fourteen inch F/5.6 lens on a 5 x 7 view camera. All of which goes to show, as we have remarked before, that it isn't the camera, or the lens, but how you use them. The film used in all instances was not one of the ultra speed types—nothing of the sort is necessary for home portraiture—but carried an A.S.A. rating of daylight 160 and tungsten 125, which by modern standards is not considered fast. Processing throughout was done by tank according to recommended procedures.

We also kept the lighting equipment to a minimum, using neither a large number of lights nor any that were expensive to buy. For work in the home the main thing to bear in mind is portability and small size, because you cannot afford to burden yourself with a lot of weight. The second point to remember is that your equipment should be such that you can rapidly set it up and, the sitting over, as quickly put it away. In actual fact, all the lighting equipment we used to make the illustrations for the chapters on incandescent and flash could be duplicated for less than fifty dollars, a point worth mentioning only to prove to you that from the cost standpoint home portraiture is within the reach of anyone who already owns a suitable camera. By all means, do not decide to immure yourself in a studio and ignore the possibilities of working with your subjects in their own familiar surroundings.

CHAPTER 24

Home Portraiture by Daylight

"By daylight?" the reader will probably say to himself a bit doubtfully as he reads the above title, and we reply: "By daylight, certainly, and why not?" For many years after the Daguerreotype became the first accepted "photographic" process, and even for a long time after it was succeeded by hand sensitized glass plates, daylight was the only form of illumination available. The most important feature of every Daguerreotype "gallery" was a carefully constructed north skylight, and such a skylight was still an essential part of every camera room into the first decade of this century. Although Daguerreotype exposures ran into many minutes (requiring the use of head clamps for portraiture) and the early photographs on plates took as many seconds, many of the portraits that were produced in those days are among the finest ever made. In truth, no finer source of photographic illumination exists even today and the real reason why artificial light has almost completely supplanted daylight is the matter of convenience, the ability to make photographs regardless of existing light conditions.

Natural light—daylight—is not at all difficult to use and is—just like artificial light—purely a matter of proper control. With modern fast lenses and the many films that are now available—notable not only for their great speed but their wide latitude—making portraits in the home or elsewhere by daylight offers few complexities. The more you understand about daylight the better you can appreciate its modern successors such as the incandescent lamps (customarily spoken of nowadays as photofloods even though ordinary house type bulbs will serve as well in emergency), fluorescent tubes, photoflash bulbs and the more recent strobes or speedlights. So accustomed to artificial light are all of us nowadays that the newcomer to professional portraiture is more than likely to have little if any appreciation or understanding of the beautiful results that can be obtained by daylight. He is so familiar with the harsh lightings evident in the outdoor snaps of his amateur friends, from which he tends to judge daylight results exclusively, that the thought of making professional portraits indoors with daylight just does not occur to him. A

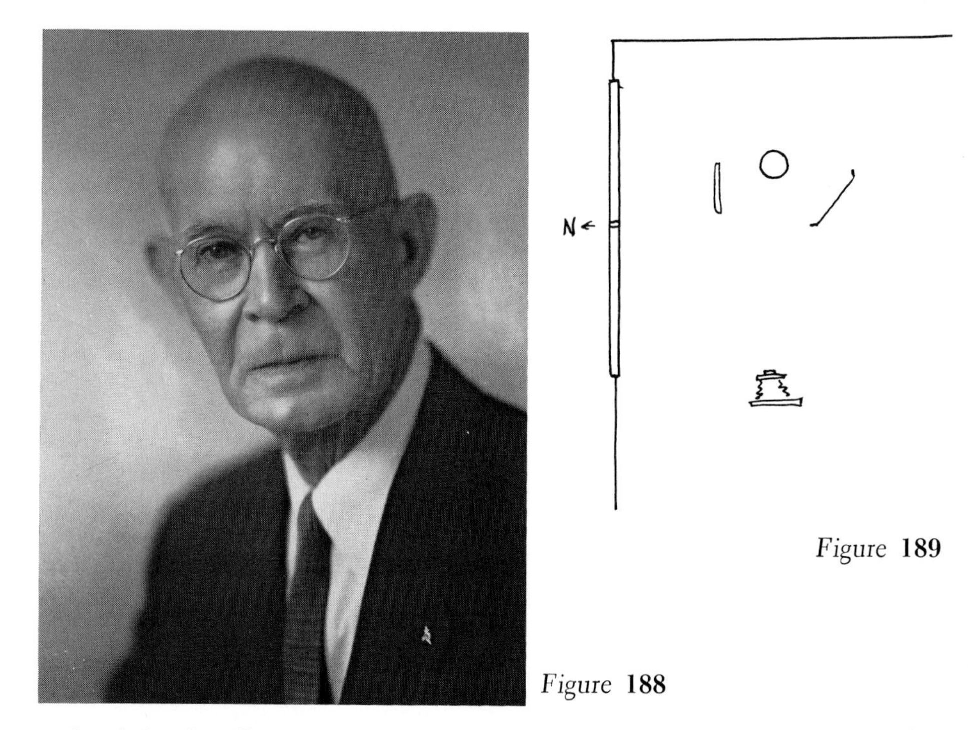

Figure **189**

Figure **188**

study of the five illustrations accompanying this chapter should quickly disabuse you if you have been suffering from that same misunderstanding.

The only requisites for daylight portraiture are first of all an adequate source of illumination, which means a large enough window or windows to admit the light, preferably with drapes, hangings or blinds by means of which the amount of light can be controlled to some extent (although these are not imperative), a head screen and a suitable reflector. This last is extremely important because without it you cannot balance the light on the shadow side. This reflector acts in the same manner as your fill-in when you are using artificial light. What we really should say is that your fill-in serves the same purpose as the reflector does when you are working with daylight because daylight came first. Your main source, no matter what type of artificial light it may be, substitutes for the daylight coming through a window or other opening, and that light must be balanced. When working with artificial light it can be balanced with a fill-in or with a reflector. When working with daylight alone, obviously a reflector is the only answer.

What should that reflector be; is the next question. Any suitably sized white or light surface will do. For the average head and shoulder portrait a reflector about twenty two inches wide by thirty high (which is what we used in making *Figures 188, 190* and *191*) will be quite adequate. Those are not required dimensions, anything in the neighborhood of two feet wide by two and a half high will do. For full lengths and groups, and even for three quarter poses, a much larger reflector and perhaps more than one may be needed if the lower portions of the figure or figures are not to be lost in darkness. For this a portable white full length background such as we mentioned in Chapter 23 will serve very well. What we used for these three illustrations was nothing more than a sheet of white, dull coated cardboard.

Some professionals, when they do use reflectors, prefer a heavier card or even a small flat of wallboard covered with crinkled tinfoil, the purpose of the crinkling being to soften, break up or diffuse the reflected light. In some cases mirrors or stands are used, but we do not advise the use of a mirror because the light it reflects is likely to be much too strong so that instead of softly illuminating the shadows it burns them out entirely.

Although made in the home, all of our first three illustrations have been produced deliberately to simulate studio portraiture. Not only did we want to show you the beautiful possibilities of daylight, but there will be times when, despite being unable to visit your camera room, a subject wants a formal rather than a home portrait. We doubt if the most experienced professional, not being forewarned, would not assume offhand that these three portraits had been made in a studio camera room under the most favorable photographic conditions and with a standard placement of the lights. All were taken, as *Figure 189* shows, in an average sized room that happened to have a fairly large north window which, thanks to being unobstructed by any other building close enough to cut off the light, afforded ample illumination. Because it happened to be a very bright, sunny day it was necessary to pull the drapes across part of the window area to cut down some of the volume of light.

The subject of *Figure 188* is a gentleman you have seen before and we chose him purposely to prove that even without all the controls you might have on hand in your own camera room, it is still possible, with daylight only, to photograph a considerable expanse of bald head without burning it up with light or trying to conceal it by merging it into the background. We were aiming for a studio effect and so it would normally have been necessary to block out everything behind him with a portable background, white or light gray, but here this was unnecessary inasmuch as we were working against the plainly painted wall of the room, and were able to throw even that out of focus because, as mentioned in Chapter 23, we were using that old F/3.8 portrait lens at full aperture, giving us little depth of focus. Our subject is wearing glasses, to make the problem, as you might think, even more complex, yet complete detail appears through the lenses and there are no disturbing reflections. Glasses will not bother you when working with daylight if you remember not to turn the face too much toward the light and not to get your reflector too far forward so it reflects light into the lenses. Note also that there is only one catch-light in the eyes, which is correct because there is only one light source, the window.

As we said, this was a fairly large north window but no larger than you will find in many homes nowadays and actually by no means as wide in expanse as many of the socalled picture windows you see in recently built houses. The lighting setup (*Figure 189*) could hardly be simpler. The subject was five feet away from the wall, with enough daylight behind to provide ample relief from the background. The reflector speaks for itself and—of course—a head screen was used on the highlight side of the face, high enough to give us control of the light on top of the head and to subdue the ear on that side. For much daylight portraiture a head screen is essential and one should always be ready at hand. For a final touch, to relieve the severity of the plain ground, we worked in a little sketch effect on a sheet of groundglass taped to the negative, as explained in an earlier chapter. We have photographed this gentleman several times with different types of light and it is his opinion (and he knows what a good portrait should be) as well as ours that this simple study by daylight is by far the best of the lot.

Figure **190**

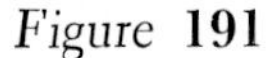

Figure **191**

The lighting diagram shown in *Figure 189* will also apply to *Figures 190* and *191*, which were made in the same place in the same home, the only change being that for these we dispensed with the head screen and moved the reflector farther away from the subjects to assure an even balance of lighting. These were taken with the F/5.6 lens, stopped to F/8, and the exposure was a fast bulb, perhaps a half second. Again the ample daylight gave us fine separation from the background and, because of the larger head sizes, we felt there was no need to work in any background effects. In printing both of these we burned in the lower portions slightly when printing. This was necessary to counteract what would otherwise have been over illumination in that area, which resulted from the fact that we were working in a very narrow room, and thus lacked sufficient space to manipulate one or more screens to control that part of the light from the window. In a large room and in earlier days, before the idea of burning in part of a negative had been thought of, undesirable daylight had to be controlled and screens of various sizes—similar to though larger than head screens—were used for the purpose. Studio skylights were a different matter. They were covered with numerous small squares of cloth, any or all of which could be shoved aside, thus permitting control of any desired area. Given more space we could easily have used screens but under the circumstances burning in is a more than acceptable substitute—and a lot simpler and quicker. Could these two portraits, we might ask, be made any more acceptable if taken in a camera room with any amount of artificial lighting equipment?

There will be occasions when you will have to make home portraits (and we use the term now as including any interior portrait not taken in a camera room) with harsher light such as direct sunlight or "snappier" light not coming from a north window. This situation will often obtain when your subject is a man in his office, as in *Figure 192* of a college president at his desk. We had intended to make this with incandescents and were all ready to set up our equipment when we entered the office. Immediately, though, noticing the fine lighting on his face resulting from the sun streaming through the windows—on the south side, incidentally—we discarded the idea temporarily because we felt we must make at least one portrait taking advantage of this wonderfully snappy light, and with as little alteration as possible. Actually there was not much we could do to alter it because, expecting to use photofloods, we had failed to bring our head screen. Worse than that, we did not even have a reflector but that only goes to show how nearly anything can be used for that purpose in an emergency, even a sheet of newspaper if there are not too many dark areas on it.

The desk was about five feet from the rear wall (*Figure 193*) and another small window and, this being an office picture and not intended to simulate a studio portrait, we made no endeavor to conceal what was behind the subject beyond throwing it somewhat out of focus. Looking over the office we discovered a roll of large plans which our "girl Friday" was able to spread out to a sufficient size, about three by four feet, to serve as a reflector and which, lacking any kind of suitable stand, she perforce had to hold in her hands at the place shown in the diagram. We managed to control the volume of light reasonably well by adjusting the blinds and, with our assistant spotted, used a meter to make a very careful exposure calculation. This portrait has all the life, sparkle and punch that could be expected from any made by artificial light, but the light was daylight only and of a harder quality than what would have resulted from a north window. Separation from the background is ample. Collar, cuffs, handkerchief and even the pages of the open folder have fine tone value and detail; there is no harsh contrast anywhere, all of which once again goes to show that just as it isn't the camera and lens but how you use them, it isn't the light either, but your ability to take full advantage of its possibilities.

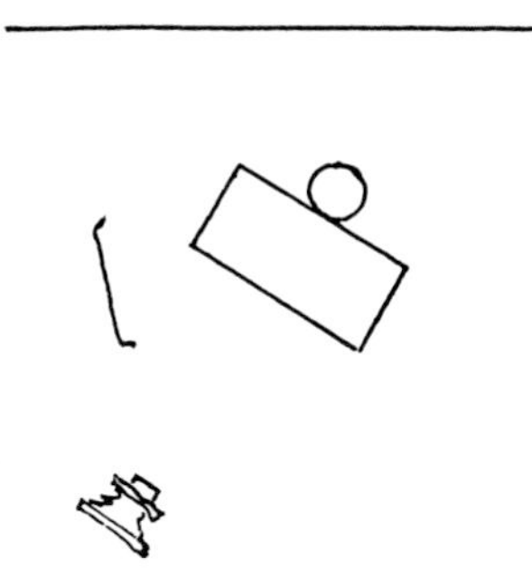

Figure **193**

Figure **192**

Now let us show you, and still by daylight, a group that anyone will recognize as taken in a home. We have photographed this family of three in a corner of their dining room, which also doubles as a family room and discloses through the windows a nicely landscaped back yard. They are proud of the home and its surroundings and so, while concentrating interest on them, why not include as much of the rest as we can, even what appears through the windows? As for light, we have more than enough, coming from windows on the north, east and west. No competent cameraman could ask for more, and with a room of ample size it is only a matter of judiciously selecting that area which will provide the most attractive result. Reflectors and screens are useless because of the profusion of light from all directions. So we select the north east corner (*Figure 195*) and decide on an informal grouping—*Figure 194*.

We want our subjects to look just as natural as they might appear had the mother and daughter unexpectedly interrupted the father's reading to ask his advice on some minor family problem, so we explain what we have in mind, ask them to take their places and see what happens. The light—remember we cannot control it at all—is what we must watch carefully, what we must "read" as we study the groundglass, on the figures, the clothes, the faces. Satisfied with the general effect we consult the exposure meter because for a photograph like this the exposure is everything, particularly because we want to show the exterior through the windows instead of blank glares of glass. The exposure decided, we propose a few final

Figure **194**

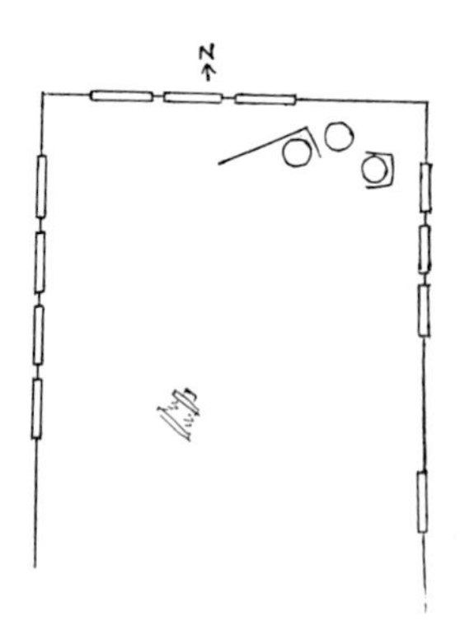

Figure **195**

changes in posture, make one remark to secure the suggestion of a smile on faces of father and daughter, and there we are. We ask again, could this have been done any better with a room full of artificial lights?

But don't misunderstand us. We are not advocating daylight for home portraiture or any other purposes if for no other reason than that no modern professional can base his business or his appointments on whether or not the sun will be shining at the appointed time. We do want to show you that if you have refrained from—or are likely to avoid—attempting portraiture in the home, office or factory merely because you think you lack the proper lighting equipment, you confine yourself to a very narrow field. With God given light, modern lenses and emulsions, all you need is incentive and you can produce some remarkable results. What is so new about "available" or "existing" light, concerning which you read so much in photographic periodicals? Light has always been available; it is only up to you to use it properly.

CHAPTER 25

The Electronic Flash

As long as there have been photographers making portraits for their livelihood, there has been a constant quest for faster exposures, to the end that countless brands of high speed film and plates have come forth over the years, as well as new ideas and types of lighting equipment. One of the most remarkable of these items is the electronic flash, commonly referred to as "speedlight," with which we are to deal in this chapter. I am not going into a lot of theory about these lights—theory has never yet made a picture. I have learned a great deal about these lights since I first worked with them in 1940, and I want to tell you some of the more pertinent things to look for in buying your lights, or in using the lights you may now have. I am assuming you intend to make portraits that are really pleasing, and to do this consistently. This being the case, one of the first things to consider is the type of unit that has a "modeling light" that is positioned at the same point that the flash will come from. To accomplish this, provision is made for mounting the modeling light bulb inside the flash tube, as you will see by referring to *Figure 196*. This eliminates guess work as to what your light is doing to the subject.

The lights I use are known as Studiomasters, and are all equipped with modeling lights. These modeling lights have two filaments, a 35-watt and a 25-watt filament; with both burning you have 60 watts of incandescent light to focus your camera by. This is adequate, as these bulbs are very efficient. I use them all, burning at their full brilliance (there is an adjustment that dims or brightens them as you change the watt-second settings on your power pack on each lighting unit). I use all lights at the same watt-second setting, and leave all modeling lights burning at full brilliance, depending on my light reading of the subject, just as I would with other types of lighting.

If you are just starting to use electronic flash, I would suggest that you very carefully measure your light distances from your subject, keep accurate track of the lens stop used, and make a series of negatives carrying them through development and even to the point of making test proofs on your favorite paper. By keeping track of what you did, you will have negatives to use as a standard, and then you can easily fasten a length of cord to each lighting unit and place knots in this cord at the distances which tests found to give you the most pleasing negative. Yes, there are meters, and if you have one sensitive enough, you can take your readings with the modeling lights on and arrive at a good idea of your lighting ratio. However, the string is much quicker to use, and to my mind it makes a better impression on the subject. I may be biased; I have three of the best meters on the market, BUT, I never use them on a customer. I make my calculations on someone else beforehand. You can never tell today, your sitter might own a much better meter than you are using!

Good lighting equipment will pay you rich rewards over the years, and even though these lights are not cheap, they will give you a uniformity of negative that is hard to achieve with other types of lights. Also, you very seldom get any movement in your subject, as the flash is of extremely short duration. The light is easy on your subject's eyes, and cool to sit under. There are many kinds of electronic flash on the market. I would not suggest any that did not have good, well placed modeling lights, and I prefer each lamp to have its own power pack rather than to work from a central power pack. Do not try to mix different makes of lights—pick the units that suit you best, and use them for all your lights. If you will be using a camera that has a ground glass focusing panel, dab a small bit of Vaseline on the ground side of this ground glass, at the place where the image of the face usually falls. Rub the Vaseline down well, and wipe off the excess (DO NOT put it all over the ground glass, as this will defeat the purpose). Your image will then look much brighter, as the Vaseline has made the ground glass more translucent in this spot.

Much has been written about development, reciprocity failure, etc., in connection with electronic flash. To get into discussions of this would fill a book. Just let me say this: if you use common sense in placing your lights, so as to get something of a balanced lighting, and give adequate exposure, you have little to worry about. Each of the makers of film has emulsions for sale that work beautifully with speedlight, and some of them have films that are built especially for speedlight.

In today's fast-changing photographic materials market, it is somewhat foolish to offer a list of all films; I will say that of the films on today's market, the films listed below give fine results:

Kodak: Super Panchro Press Type B. Super XX, Portrait Pan

Ansco: Super Pan Press

Du Pont: High Speed Pan, Superior Press

Gevaert: Gevapan 33

Ilford: HP 3

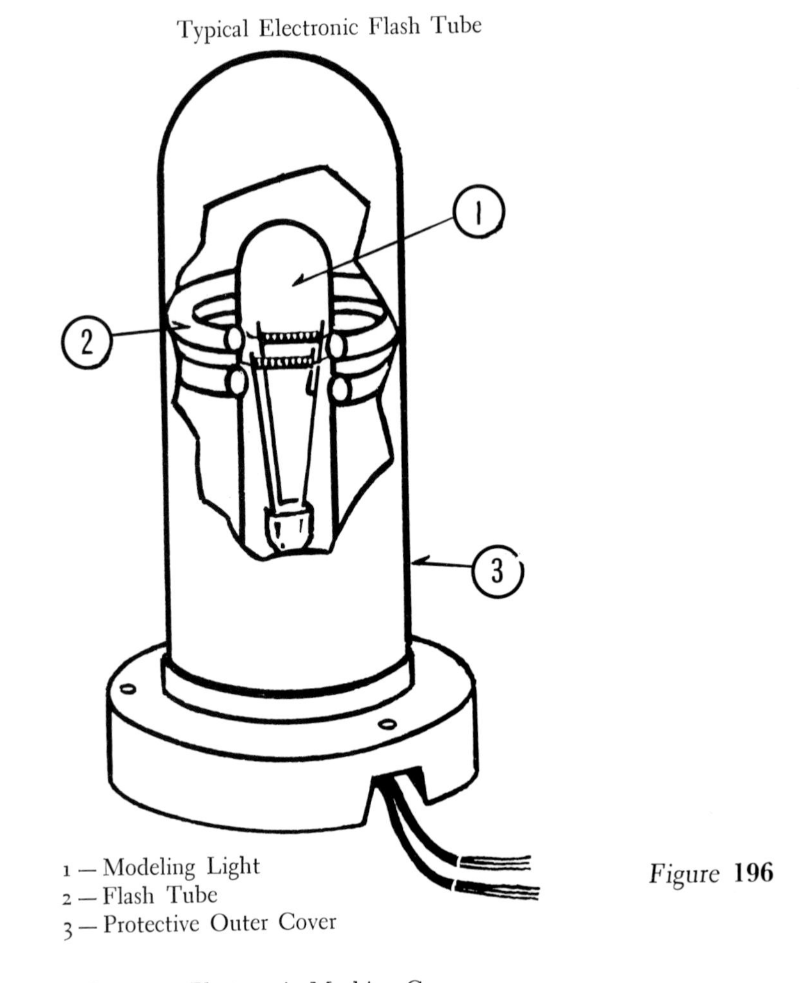

Figure **196**

None of these films requires special attention in developing, if given adequate exposure.

For those wanting to use larger lens openings, or a soft focus lens, the recently introduced Kodak LS Pan film is a wonderful choice—this film is really built with electronic flash in mind, and was used in making *Figures 200, 202,* and *204*. I do not want to give the impression that speedlights will not make bad negatives; they have to be handled with judgment to get good results, just as any other light source does. I do feel that there is a tendency for most photographers to try to work their lights too far from their subjects. This results in underexposure and consequent forcing in development, which results in inferior negative quality. Regardless of any advances in materials, it is still a basic fact that *you cannot develop onto a negative what you haven't put there by exposure,* and this is true with speedlight as well as any other light for photography.

Now, lest I dwell too long on the virtues of speedlight, let us consider some of the portraits made with these lights. Children's pictures are a natural with speedlight; you can capture the most fleeting expression, the most charming pose. If you are working with the faster type films, you can be stopped down enough so that your subject can move considerably in or out of the exact plane of focus, and you will still have a presentable negative. I do feel that it is good to conceal the bulb that triggers your exposure—some children figure out what you are doing, when you get hold of the bulb, and will be "posing" too much. The picture of the baby in *Figure 197* is typical of the pleasing portraits that can be made with a very simple lighting set-up. A boom light is placed above and behind the child's head, so as not to hit the face. The point light and fill are placed as indicated in *Figure 199*, the overhead light about four feet high, and the point light about three and a half feet high and about that distance away from the subject. The fill light was placed about three and a half to four feet high and about six feet from subject. All lights contained 100 watt-seconds, and the lens was stopped between *f*/11 and *f*/16.

The little lady in *Figure 198* was made with practically the same placing of lights. The roundness in this subject's face was brought out by the lighting, and not by any trickery in retouching or printing. I don't believe any type of light could do it better. When first introduced, speedlight was considered as only suitable for children's pictures by many studios. I have never subscribed to this thought, as the first negatives I ever saw made with speedlight were of an older man, and they were beautiful. We will forego men's portraits for a bit, and consider the fair sex. *Figure 200* is an example of today's young woman, presented in an over-the-shoulder pose, which is so popular today. Referring to *Figure 201*, you will see that I have used two boom lights to the back of the subject, and high up, to illuminate the hair. A background light is used to keep the

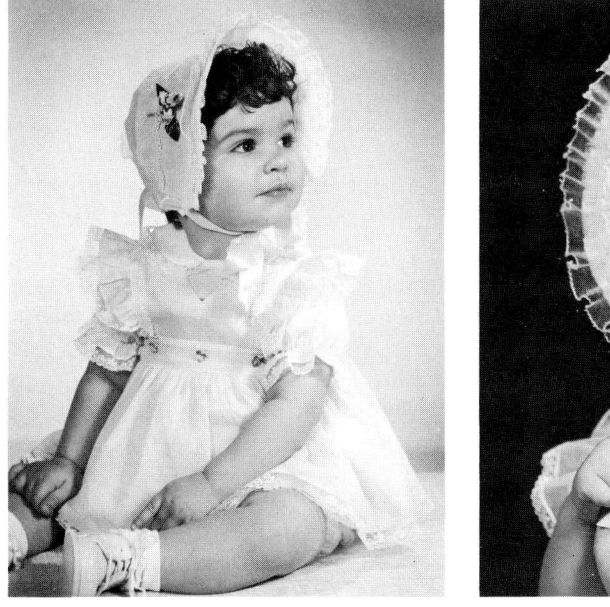

Figure **197**

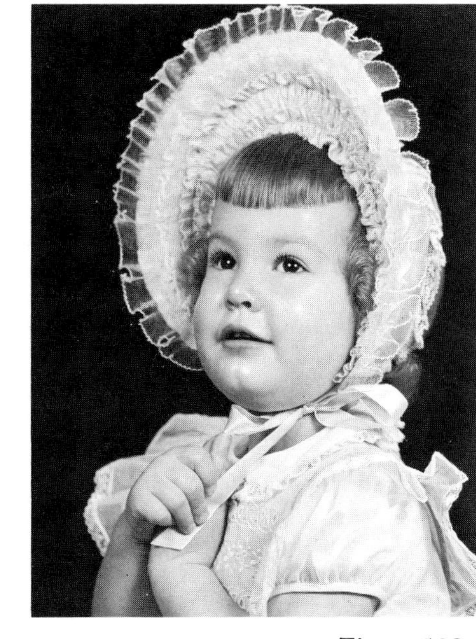

Figure **198**

Figure **199**

Figure **200**

background in a lighter tone, and the point and fill lights are used as indicated. This portrait was made with an Imagon lens, used without too much diffusion, and was made on Kodak LS Pan film. The medium was used on the Imagon, which is about *f*/11, and 100 watt-seconds were used on all lighting units. In *Figure 202*, we have another over-the-shoulder pose, using a plastic drape and the camera vignette. This was made with the same lighting arrangement as in *Figure 200* with the same lens, film, and exposure time. In both of these portraits, I ask that you consider the detail in the hair, the detail in the shadows, and the over-all roundness. I would find this difficult to excel with any other kind of light, and certainly speedlight was very easy on the subjects. In *Figure 203*, we have a very gracious lady of greater maturity. This is with a drape and a camera vignette. If you will refer to the lighting diagram (*Figure 203A*), you will see we have used a different placement of our lights. We have used only one boom hair light, high and to the subject's back; we have used a background unit with a smaller aperature over the light to keep it from spreading too much. Our point light was used well around to the subject's left, to keep the light from spreading too wide across the face; the shadow side of the face was illuminated with our fill light, back toward the camera position, and feathered to keep from overlighting the shadow side of the face. This type of lighting is very good for older people, or subjects who have very broad faces. Personally, I feel that this has made a very charming portrait of a beautiful subject. This portrait was made on the faster type of film, and because we were using a sharp lens (Heliar) and did not want to stop down too far, we used 50 watt-seconds on each lighting unit, with a stop between *f*/8 and *f*/11.

While it is desirable to keep a consistent standard in your portrait work, it is not always a good idea to carry this to the point that you never try anything different. Our subject in *Figure 204* called, to my mind, for something off the beaten track. He is a friend of mine, and a very likeable fellow, and I wanted to show him in a typical expression with no polishing up; this is a straight print from an unretouched negative. While I am sure the reproduction will lose a lot of the texture in the original print, there is every pore of his skin showing. True, we could do a lot of retouching on this negative, and make him a lot "smoother" looking; but it would not be "Sarge" as I wanted him. If you will refer to *Figure 204A*, you will see that I used only one light on the front of the face, at the left side of the camera and lighting the right side of face. The "barn-door" on the light was folded over, to tone down the light on the left side of the face and the left ear. If you will look at the shadow under the nose and the catchlights in the eyes, you will see that this light was not up too high, thus getting the light under the hat brim. The boom lights were used well back, and screened carefully, to control the amount of light hitting the face. If the reproduction of this print is good, I feel sure that you will see a lot of roundness in this portrait, a lot of skin texture, and the soft-sharpness that is possible with an Imagon lens. This portrait was made on LS Pan film, using 100 watt-seconds and a stop of *f*/11.

While is it fun to make a picture now and then for the pure pleasure of doing something different, good business dictates that you keep pretty well on a level keel most of the time. We have found that men as a whole are about as

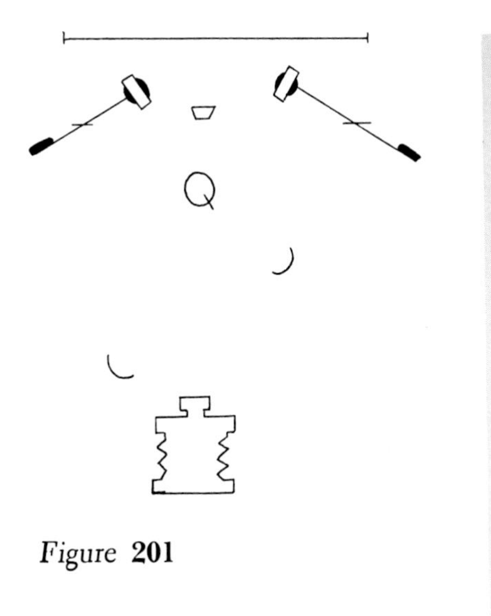

Figure **201**

Figure **202**

vain as women, and generally don't want to be shown as sourdoughs or roughnecks. In *Figure 205*, we have another friend of mine whom we are showing in the style that we have found to be very acceptable to men in many walks of life. It is a truly good portrait that can be used for any purpose, business or personal. This lighting was made with light placement so similar to that shown in *Figure 201* that I am asking you to look back at that diagram. About the only difference in the lighting is that the point light, which was used on the subject's left side, was moved a bit more around to the side of his face than is indicated in the diagram. To digress here a bit: lighting diagrams are intended only to give a general indication of light placement; they guide you, but you must learn to "see" the light on the face, before you will be an accomplished person in handling lights.

It may be well to mention that you will not have too much trouble with eyeglasses; just keep your lights up high enough to be out of the eyeglass lens. Generally, your fill light, which is more out in front of the subject, will be the light you will have to watch most carefully.

You will notice that we have a fairly strong highlight on the left side of the man's forehead, and that some of this backlight is hitting the left ear. This is because he has a good head of hair and ears that do not stand out from his head. However, if your subject is bald, or has standout ears, you will do well to be very conservative in your use of backlighting if at all. This negative has been beautifully retouched, not overdone. It is a very good portrait of a man in

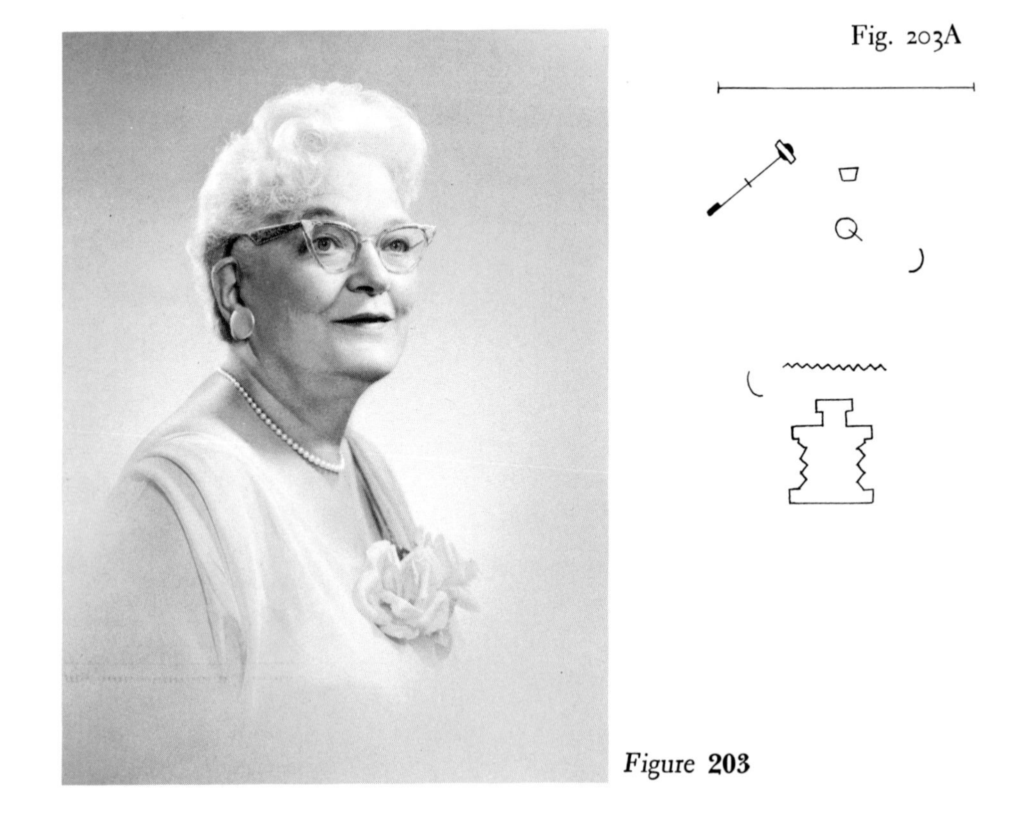

Fig. 203A

Figure **203**

Fig. 204A

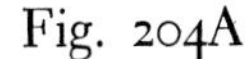

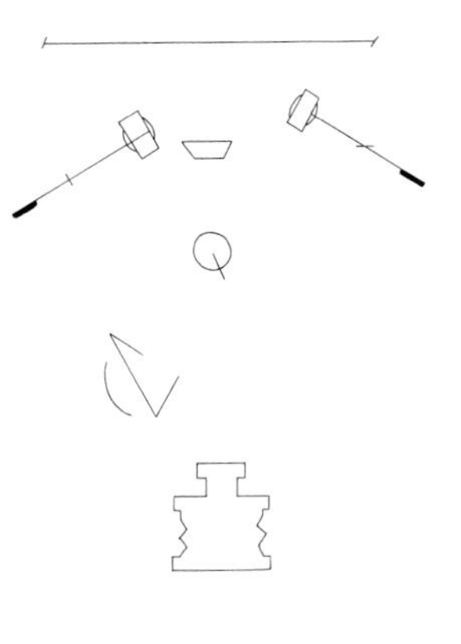

Figure **204**

middle age, one that he, his family, and his friends will accept.

I am often asked about full lengths with speedlight. Really, they are no different than those done with any other type of light. Good lighting equipment is always provided, with means of tilting the lamp heads up or down, and lamps without barn-doors can be feathered up or down, to control the intensity of light on the upper or lower parts of the figures. Studiomaster speedlights are equipped with barn-doors that revolve a full 360°. By closing or opening these barn-doors you have a fine and delicate control over figure, costume, hands, or any part you wish to subdue or lighten. In *Figure 206*, we are showing a full length, posed with the minimum of "props", and very simple accessories. This girl had her sun glasses and the beach towel with her; all we supplied was an inexpensive stool for her to sit on. Not being a dry-land swimming suit model, this girl was pretty well tanned, especially the lower part of her legs. Referring to *Figure 207*, you will see that this is not an elaborate lighting set-up. It follows pretty much a standard approach to lighting, except that we had to use our background light more on her left side, to keep it out of the picture. Because of the greater distance away from the background, for this light, it was used at 200 watt-seconds, while the other lighting units were all working at 100 watt-seconds.

Up to this point, nothing has been said about speedlight for home use. Many makers of studio speedlights offer smaller units, equipped with good modeling

Figure **205**

lights. They are of sufficient strength to allow fine black and white, as well as direct color work, away from the studio. Among these lights is an outfit called "Flashmaster," and in the units just mentioned, you will find them much less

Figure **207**

Figure **206**

costly than the larger "Studiomaster" units, and highly capable of producing beautiful results.

As to small portable units for hand held camera use, I cannot honestly make other than general recommendations. If you have been using flash bulbs, and are making an average of less than a hundred flashes per month, I would stay with flash bulbs. If your volume is greater than this, I would most certainly go to a good *powerful* electronic flash outfit. There are many good lines on the market, and it is not my purpose to "plug" equipment. DON'T let price influence you too much; spend a bit more at the outset, and get a unit (or units) that will really give you an adequate volume of light. I see too much work that is far from acceptable, produced with small, inadequate, portable speedlights. Portable units without modeling lights will have to be used much the same as flash bulbs, in regard to estimating where your light is falling upon your subjects.

Summing up, it has been our experience that those who work with well made studio type speedlights can get much better lighting effects than they do with the conventional incandescent lights. They have greater assurance of uniformity, and the sitter has greater comfort. Don't feel that we are saying that speedlight is foolproof—it definitely is NOT—but if you will give some thought to your light balance and ratio of highlights to shadows, you will make fine negatives, which will please your most particular customers. Personally, our studio has used speedlights for almost all of our production, over the past twenty years. You therefore have our sincerest assurance that, given reasonable consideration in use, you will be working with the ultimate in lighting equipment when you start using well designed speedlight units.

CHAPTER 26

Home Portraiture with Incandescent Light

All artificial photographic lighting resulting from the use of an electrical current falls into five general classifications; the arc lamp, the incandescent bulb; the fluorescent lamp, the flashbulb; the strobe or speedlight. Of these the arc lamp has all but passed from the picture except in photo engraving plants, where it still remains supreme, and for rare technical photographic uses. The fluorescent lamp, in the camera room at least, can be used almost interchangeably with the incandescent. The flash and the strobe we have already discussed. Now we propose to take up the use of incandescent light in home portraiture and perhaps should explain to the uninitiated that in photography today the words incandescent and photoflood have become almost synonymous because of the tremendous advantage of the photoflood, for photographic purposes, over the standard incandescent of whatever size. Therefore while in the title of this chapter we have used the word incandescent in order to be strictly correct, let it be understood that we are concerning ourselves exclusively with photofloods.

The value of the photoflood, as every reader surely knows, is its ability to produce a far greater light output than an incandescent of equivalent or even considerably larger size, thus making possible the use of smaller and more portable reflectors and stands. Home portraiture, so far as incandescent light is concerned, did not really come into its own until the photoflood lamp was developed, promptly followed by the introduction of a wide variety of light weight equipment enabling the home portraitist to carry with him the equivalent of a volume of light theretofore quite unheard of. And in that connection we should not go too far into our subject without offering this warning: don't let the appearance of a photoflood lamp fool you because it draws, at the moment of exposure, far more current than a standard bulb of equivalent size. Do not, therefore, in any home or office, connect too many photofloods to any single lighting circuit or blown fuses will result. In the modern home you will be safe in connecting three #1 photofloods to one circuit, or one #2 and two of the #1, but a greater load than this we would not recommend. In

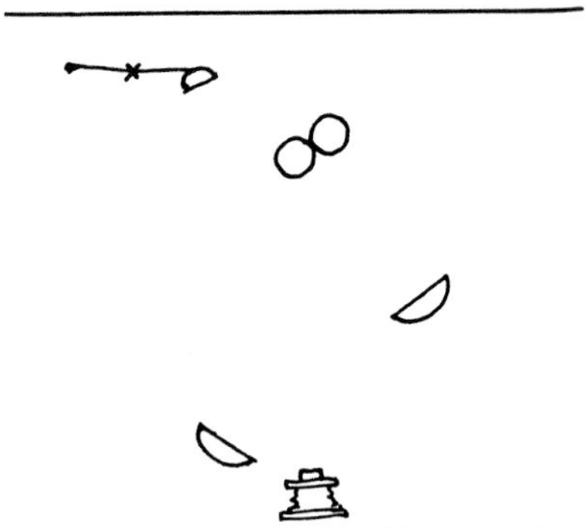

Figure 209

Figure 208

older homes you will be wise to limit your connections to not more than three #1 lamps to any circuit. And always make sure that whatever circuit you select does not at the same time happen to have an electric heater or something similar, which draws an abnormal amount of current, plugged in.

For some years there have been available reflector type photoflood bulbs which, the reflector being integral with the bulb, do not require the usual professional type of separate reflector. Excellent though these are for amateur use, home movies and certain types of commercial work, we do not advocate them for professional home portraiture because, in our experience—and we believe all practicing professionals will agree—they cannot satisfactorily substitute for standard photoflood bulbs, in suitable reflectors preferably equipped with some means whereby diffusing screens of one type or another or light reducing devices such as "barn doors" may be attached. Photoflood light is extremely intense and some means of diffusion is advisable on most occasions. We have found architects' tracing cloth to be quite satisfactory although other materials such as spun glass and the like are on the market. In any event do not place tracing cloth or any other fabric in contact with photoflood bulbs or you will be inviting the danger of fire because they generate considerable heat. As for reflectors you will find that one of sixteen inch diameter will be sufficient for your main source, plus a couple of twelve inchers for your fill-in and other supplementary lights. All should be mounted on suitable light weight collapsible stands.

Photoflood bulbs, due to the considerable amount of light they generate in comparison to their rather small size, tend to darken rather rapidly and this fact, as your lamps become older, must be taken into consideration when estimating exposures.

Like all professionals who have been behind the camera for many years, we pride ourselves on our ability to estimate exposure by looking at the groundglass but, while that is our customary practice in the camera room, we have never felt ourselves above the use of an exposure meter when out on a home portrait assignment and particularly when working with photofloods. We consequently advise that a good photoelectric exposure meter be considered as an essential part of your home portrait outfit.

In this chapter we present six illustrations, three of them which might be considered as studio type portraits though taken in the home, two rather typical home portrait groups, and one office portrait. In *Figure 208* we have a group of two young girls photographed in a living room the walls of which are painted in a rather flat dark blue gray, serving as an excellent background. Having noticed, on entering, a small end table of the step or two-level type, it struck us immediately as a handy accessory for a group of two so, asking permission, we moved it to a suitable place and posed the young ladies accordingly. For this as the diagram (*Figure 209*) indicates, we used three photofloods. Our main source was a #1 at right center, at about a 45° angle from the group. The fill-in was the #2 at the camera, feathered up. For a hair light, and to provide adequate separation from the background, another #1, on a boom, was placed to the rear and a bit to the left. None were diffused. Upon studying the proof we felt the composition was especially appropriate for an elliptical mask and printed it accordingly, doing a little working in on the background to avoid monotony. It is always well, in home portraiture, to show some proofs which vary from the standard rectangular form provided, of course, that you have poses and surroundings which lend themselves to such treatment. They will be an appreciated surprise because so seldom does anything of that sort result from a home sitting.

When working in the home your main objective must always be the best possible

Figure **211**

Figure **210**

presentation of your subject so, when the latter is attractive, suitably gowned and hatted, concentrate on the subject and forget that you are working in a home. In other words, if a studio portrait seems called for, proceed on that basis and disregard the environment, which brings us to *Figure 210* where the subject wears a dress which would almost certainly clash with any surrounding furniture and a hat which would be lost against anything but a plain background. This young lady is seated on the arm of a very handsome antique chair, of which we carefully eliminated all but the back on which her right arm rests. Seating her on the arm instead of the chair seat also, incidentally, adds an effect of height and dignity, lengthening the figure in a manner not possible had she been normally seated and enabling us to keep the camera at approximately normal height instead of shooting down and losing the lines of neck and shoulders.

Again the background (*Figure 211*) is a plain wall from against which we have removed one or two items of furniture which would only have been distracting. Our two chief lights, the main source and the fill-in, remain almost exactly where they were before but we have made one important alteration. Our boom light—the second #1 photoflood—is now directed upward against the wall behind the sitter, our purpose being to hold the filmy hat in soft relief, almost like a halo around the head. For this portrait the main source, the first #1 photoflood, has been raised from its former position and well feathered up, while the fill-in, the #2 at the camera, has been feathered up also; in neither case do we want too much light on the lower part of the figure. The background which, due to the light thrown upon it, would have been an all over lighter tone, has been given variety, centering interest on head and figure, by a slight burning in of the edges of the negative during print-

Figure **212**

Figure 214

Figure 213

ing. Once again, no diffusers were used.

The obvious step to follow was a portrait of the other girl, and let us interpolate here that when you are photographing several members of a family, and sisters or brothers in particular, do not make the mistake of seeming to favor one over the other. Certainly you are not going to picture them in identical positions but be tactful in planning poses that, while they are different, emphasize the character and best features of each so that your subjects are not likely to exclaim later: "He certainly made a lovely picture of you but he didn't take any pains with me!" In this case, having made a three quarter seated pose of one, a three quarter standing pose of the other (*Figure 212*) was a ready, and fortunately quite appropriate solution. Using the same chair we merely turned it around and had her rest her hands on it. The main source and fill-in remained exactly as they were but we returned the boom light to its original position so that the diagram shown in *Figure 209* applies. Again, not only for variety but because it seemed called for, we used an elliptical mask.

So here we have a group of three home portraits which have taken up very little of the family's—or our own—time, having involved a minimum of moving around and rearranging furniture and even less moving and adjustment of lighting equipment with its consequent searching for outlets and trailing of electrical cords around the room. It is fast, efficient action like this—combined of course with the later showing of proofs even better than were anticipated—that will endear you to the family and cause them to recommend you to their friends as a photographer who really knows what he is about.

Returning to our illustrations, consider the group of a couple, taken in their not too large living room, which appears as *Figure 213*. Because these people are flower lovers—note the still life on the wall and the gardening guide he holds in his hand—we thought it well to include a bit of greenery in the setting and moved

Figure 215

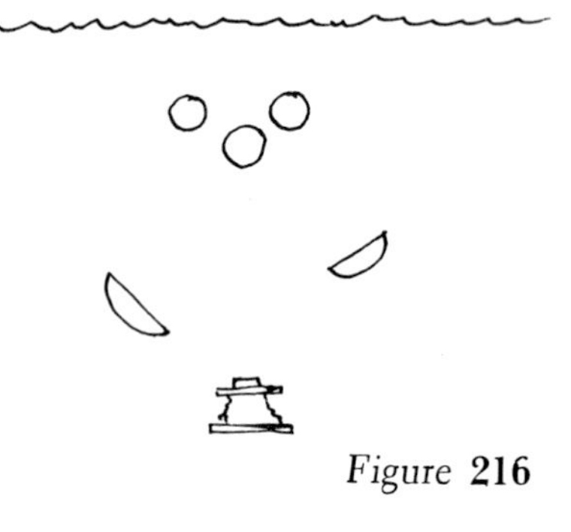

Figure 216

the potted plant from another part of the room to the table. We selected a corner of the living room for several reasons: to avoid shooting into any windows for one, and so we might use a diagonal "camera throw" to take advantage of a bit more distance. We had to work quite closely into the corner at that and, while some may object to the lamp shade jutting into the picture area, we felt that to show less of it would have been even more jarring to the composition while, after all, it was their lamp shade and part of the room, quite aside from the fact that it would have been difficult to move and there would have been almost no other place to put it. This is another example of those necessary compromises with which the home portraitist is so frequently faced.

For this we used two #1 photofloods as shown by *Figure 214*, with the main source, that at the left, in a twelve inch reflector and the one at the camera in a sixteen inch. Because the subjects were so close to the corner, and some illumination behind them was necessary to insure separation and depth, we took advantage of a small goose neck desk lamp we found in another room, put an ordinary 75-watt bulb in it, and placed it behind the lady. Due to the conditions some shadows were unavoidable and you will find that, in the average home, you will seldom if ever be able to place your lights as high as you would like in order to eliminate such shadows. The best you can do is move the lights until a placement is found that renders the shadows least objectionable. In any event, given a natural pose, good expression and likeness, shadows—while you and other professionals may object to them—will be the last thing your subjects will notice or complain about.

In many farming communities Saturday night is about the only opportunity the farmer and his family have of driving into town and what with his buying supplies while the others do their shopping, plus a natural desire to spend what spare time is left on taking in the latest movie, a visit to a photographic studio is about the last thing to be considered. The photographer who is willing and able to portray his farm customers in their homes has a distinct advantage and will often be a busy individual while his competitors are idly sitting back waiting for sitters to drop in. *Figure 215* is a group taken in just such a farm home using, as *Figure 216* indicates, only two #1 photofloods. This is a simple group and a simple lighting because our intention is not to show you what can be produced in the way of elaborate lighting setups in a home but, to the contrary, how with the simplest of equipment you can produce good, saleable home portraits.

Once you have attained competence with such basic lightings you can advance to more complicated setups as rapidly as you wish and because of the knowledge you will have gained, you will have to do very little further experimenting. With modern films and lenses and under almost any conditions you will not find it at all difficult to prepare, with only two #1 bulbs, a lighting for a single subject or a group like this, and feel confident of securing with an exposure of one twenty fifth second at F/8 negatives that will be uniformly printable with no darkroom complications. This was another case where, with not too much space available, we had to place our young subjects rather closely against the curtains behind them. While the lighting placement is rather similar to a standard studio lighting, lack of height has left shadows which we would prefer to have avoided, as in *Figure 213*. Nevertheless we have an acceptable group, with good flesh tones, good modeling and excellent detail in even the white garments. All this, accomplished quickly and effectively with only two photofloods.

You will remember that, in Chapter 24, we told of photographing a college president at his desk, by daylight. We remarked that it had been our intention to use artificial light and that we merely seized the opportunity to make a daylight ex-

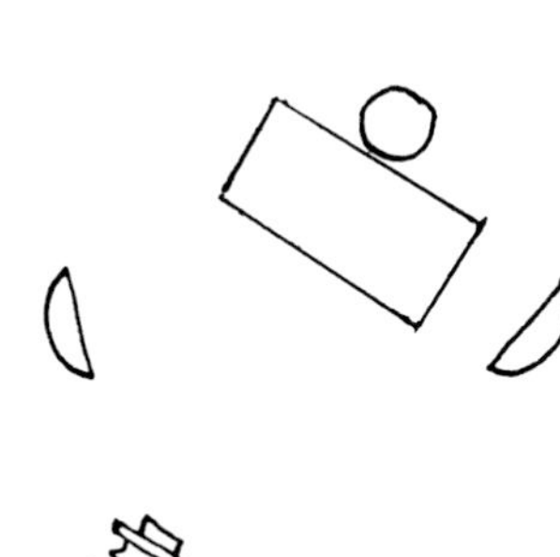

Figure **218**

Figure **217**

posure. In *Figure 217* he appears again, photographed during our same visit to his office, but this time with two photofloods. Before some reader objects to the hands, let us explain that the college is in process of an expansion program involving several million dollars for new construction, practically all of it the president's direct responsibility. Nothing seemed more appropriate, under the circumstances, than to show him studying one of the many plans almost constantly to be found on his desk, and particularly because an event of such magnitude does not happen to the average college president during his working lifetime.

Inasmuch as one of the portraits made during this sitting was to be a feature of the college year book, we felt that one of the plans had to be included, not just as a sheet of paper on the desk, but in sufficient detail to make obvious what it is. So again we compromised, sacrificing correct composition and permitting even a bit of distortion of the one hand, in order to put over a point that the president himself, the faculty, the student body and the alumni would all understand at a glance. This is no apology but a practical lesson on how to make a portrait "tell a story." When faced with similar situations you, too, will have to make a decision concerning which photographic rule you will have to break. In this case we sacrifice the composition, to emphasize the theme that "he has the whole problem in his hands."

As we remarked, only two #1 photofloods were needed as in *Figure 218*, the main source at the right in a sixteen inch reflector being very carefully feathered to assure good modeling of the face, while the fill-in was another #1 in a twelve inch reflector. We were fortunate in this case because the ceiling was high, enabling us to elevate both lights sufficiently to carry well over the head and onto the wall, affording us excellent separation. The only darkroom manipulation required was to burn in slightly the edge of the plan in the extreme foreground.

While we have not attempted to cover every imaginable situation with our illustrations in these chapters on home portraiture, we have tried to emphasize the most salient features of this type of photography, bearing in mind that every home portrait is a problem in itself but that, like all other portraits, lightings and posings never diverge too greatly from the fundamentals which we have detailed in such length in our earlier pages. Learn those fundamentals thoroughly and portrait photography, in the studio or in the home, will present no situation beyond your mastery.

CHAPTER 27

Beware of Blank Paper

Few elements are as disturbing in a portrait as flat white areas which, upon inspection, one realizes are nothing more than blank paper from which the last vestige of silver has been washed away. These are all too often overlooked by even the most competent professionals while still others deliberately ignore them or refuse to consider them as objectionable. White is white, argue these latter, and so why not photograph it as such? Disregarding for the moment that, in nature, white is very rarely pure white, let us remember that in portraiture our primary purpose is to produce an acceptable rendition or characterization of our subject. Admitting that, and we cannot do otherwise, it is the subject's face that must at all times be the center of interest. The moment we include in the picture area any strong highlight, other than those on the face itself, we draw attention away from the face and features.

Your strongest highlights therefore should be among those which, on the nose, forehead, cheek bones and chin, cause those elements of the face to appear as if they were projected from the otherwise flat surface of the photograph. It is this use of the highlights, plus of course the suitable separation of the head and figure from the background, which combines to present in a portrait the desired feeling of roundness, or solidity, of actually being in three dimensions rather than the two to which your flat surface limits you. In any truly good portrait all but a very slight fraction of those highlights will have some definite tone value and only that comparatively small portion of the highlight where the light strikes with its fullest intensity will appear in the print, after final processing, as blank white paper. It should be obvious, therefore, that all other brilliant areas in the picture space will to some extent defeat your purpose and, if they are large and unduly noticeable, will ruin it completely.

This fault, and we consider it serious enough to devote this entire Chapter—even though brief—to the subject, is most consistently found in portraits of men, business men as a rule, wearing the customary white shirt, collar and cuffs and with the ubiquitous carefully folded handkerchief in the breast pocket. In too many portraits these come out as blank white paper and, to make the situation worse, they appear as three or four completely unrelated highlights in as many different parts of the picture area with the result that the interest of the picture is scattered instead of concentrated, while the viewer's eye bounces from one to the other and almost overlooks the face entirely. In the case of a woman or child wearing a white blouse or dress there is at least the saving grace that there is only one large white area and the viewer's eye tiring of that, it will settle with relief on the face and features.

What the photographer fails to realize is that, as we said before, white in nature is very seldom truly white. As the painter knows, and as he takes pains to render it with his brush, there is always a certain amount of color in any white area because that white both absorbs and reflects part of the color which surrounds it. (A lighting technologist will question that statement, but we are speaking solely from the layman's observation.) The photographer, and we are necessarily speaking of the worker in monochrome, lacks the painter's advantage but certainly should not lack the painter's seeing eye, and thus it becomes the photographer's responsibility to render those colors as tones in monochrome. Take a careful look at the men you meet or contact during the next few hours—the white collar workers. Granting that their collars, shirts and other haberdashery are white, do your eyes go first to those white areas or first to their faces? To the faces, without question, and why? Because those white areas are by no means as glaring and noticeable as they are rendered in the average portrait.

Take a ride on a trolley or bus, which will give you an opportunity to study those seated opposite you a bit more closely without making yourself objectionable. Even if they happen to be bathed in harsh sunlight, those collars and shirts will still not be so white that you see them before you see the faces. Look again at the collars and shirts. The man in the blue serge—his collar reflects definite tones of blue; the man wearing black—his collar appears gray; the little girl in the red jumper—her white blouse and collar reflect pinkish shades. And so it goes everywhere you gaze. As a matter of fact, even the old time celluloid collars (and your memory probably will not run back so far) were not flat white surfaces because, aside from reflecting other colors just as we have described, they were also treated to resemble the texture of linen. In addition, like a linen collar, they were flexible.

Which brings us, though perhaps in a roundabout manner, to the answer to what should really not be a problem at all. All these items of clothing to which we have been referring have texture, and all of them are flexible. Even a stiff, starched collar—which one seldom sees nowadays unless worn with full evening dress (white tie)—is flexible although the gloss of the starch may have made its texture almost invisible. First of all it curves around the neck, if nothing more, so that there is a play of light and shade around that curve. Because ninety nine out of a hundred men's collars today are soft, they are seldom flat even at the very points so there is light and shadow there, as well. White cuffs also are rarely starched; they curve far more than do collars and often form an interesting S curve if cuff links are worn. If a man's arm and hand are included in a portrait, if he is to be portrayed correctly and dressily half an inch of cuff should be drawn out to show, and again there is a play of light and shade. A shirt seldom if ever lies flat and even when a collar is attached, the latter is certainly not all one white area with the shirt, yet how often does one see a man's portrait without as much as a distinguishing line to show where the collar ends and the shirt begins? The handkerchief, too, even though it is often carefully patted to lie flatly, curves at the top and has texture.

There is, then, tone value in all of these areas we have been discussing. Actually there is, visible to the eye, both color and light and shade, but it is the light and shade—the tone value—which are all that concern us due to the limitations of our monochrome emulsion. The secret is all in proper lighting and exposure, followed by correct development. Granted, these are light and delicate tone values and you can easily burn them out by over exposing. You can also lose them, even though you capture them on the negative, by over development and, finally, by printing from a good negative on a paper which is too hard or contrasty. But, although you have perhaps both over exposed and over developed, you can still save the situation —although it will mean a lot more trouble—by some judicious dodging when you make the prints, or by local reduction on the negative.

There is no excuse, in our opinion, for a professional portrait which renders white areas of clothing as blank white paper. Your subject is not wearing stiff, unbending cardboard, but soft, yielding fabric of one kind or another. One specific way of making certain that your portraits, especially those of men, will be above the average, is to keep this one point—the proper rendition of whites—so constantly in mind that it becomes automatic. Even if you have no intention of becoming a conservative portraitist so far as your poses and lightings are concerned your purpose in a portrait is still to feature your subject. Even though your subjects may prefer bizarre poses, harsh lightings on the faces, "blowups" that show every pore of the skin, your main object in any portrait remains the face. Keep it that way by subduing those unrelated white areas.

CHAPTER 28

The Importance of Retouching

It is not possible to teach the art of retouching—and that competent retouching is an art any professional will agree—in one or even several chapters of a book like this, nor would we be foolish enough to attempt it. What we do want to emphasize, and cannot permit the reader to overlook, is the almost unfailing necessity for retouching in portraiture and the consequent need for an understanding of retouching, its possibilities and its limitations, on the part of the cameraman. Given an equal facility at lighting and posing, the one element that will immediately set apart the professional portrait from one made by an amateur will be the retouching whereby the professional produces a craftsmanlike, finished result.

No process has yet been devised which totally eliminates the need for retouching which is even necessary in the case of babies and small children because the former, while they do not normally have blemishes or wrinkles like their elders, almost always have discolorations under the skin which show up in the negative and which, if not removed, will appear as unpleasant blotches. Older children frequently show marks of bumps and bruises, and sometimes scratches, which of course must be removed. Soft focus lenses can materially reduce the amount of retouching required on a negative, but many subjects should not be photographed in soft focus while a majority demand that their portraits be sharp and clear. Ways have even been devised of treating negatives in a manner to soften and obscure wrinkles, lines and other defects, in attempts to speed up quantity production, but these have never proved acceptable for anything more than the cheapest type of photography. Like it or not, whether you plan to do your own retouching, employ someone to do it for you, or send your negatives out to a trade retoucher, as thousands of professionals do, retouching remains a service to your subjects (and a cost of doing business) which cannot be avoided.

In other words, retouching can mean the difference between your success and failure as a portrait photographer. Much has been said and written on the subject and there is a trend among some professionals to minimize the need for retouching to an extent with which we cannot agree. While it is quite true that an unqualified retoucher can go too far and destroy a likeness, really competent retouching can add prestige to your reputation. So far as women, young or old, are concerned you have not too much to fear from over retouching, so long as the likeness is retained, because the majority of women expect and want themselves to appear in portraits with smooth faces devoid of blemishes and with lines and wrinkles softened if not removed entirely. Men as well are more vain than is generally realized and while most of them do want their character lines retained, few will be unhappy with a really good job of retouching.

Probably one of the reasons why it has admittedly become much harder to "sell" the idea of portraiture nowadays is the modern drift toward a lackadaisical attitude with respect toward retouching. So much inferior work is being produced today that the public opinion of professional portraiture has fallen seriously, and in great part this inferiority is not nearly so much a matter of lighting and posing, or even securing a satisfactory likeness, as it is a lack of attention to details, retouching in particular. Many studio owners, trying to combat cheap competition and being unable or unwilling to produce portraits obviously above the average and therefore desirable regardless of cost, have lowered their prices. Doing so, assuming that the prices were fair and reasonable in the first place, means that costs must be cut and under such circumstances the retouching bill is among the first to be slashed. Our chief purpose here is to warn you not to fall into that trap. Few if any of those who will come to you for portraits will be blessed with ideal faces and figures and therefore, no matter how competent you become with respect to lighting and posing, you must yourself understand how to correct your negatives to compensate for these irregularities, have someone in your employ who can, or rely on a trade retoucher to do this work for you.

As we have said you yourself in the camera room can do a great deal by means of proper posing and lighting to lessen the need for retouching but despite the most flattering lighting your lens sees what is there, and because you see your subjects in color, even on your groundglass, many minor details cannot help but go virtually without notice except to the lens, which misses nothing. Color disguises—and this is true no matter how well you learn to read light—fine lines around the eyes and pouches below them, softens furrows in the forehead and the always present lines from nose to mouth, to mention only a very few of the characteristics of every face. None of these, in life, are actual defects or blemishes; if they were most of us would dislike looking at our closest friends and our own families. But when they appear in a photograph, they are defects as the subject sees the picture and it is the subject who must be satisfied. There are a few strict realists who claim that because such things exist they should be shown and there are a very few people who agree and will accept such portraits. If all people were like that photography would be simple indeed and there would be no need for retouching.

The world being what it is and people what they are, your purpose in making portraits must be to present your subjects at their best. While they may not quite understand what retouching is, they can and will definitely show a preference between prints from well retouched negatives and others which, while they may be likenesses, show little attempt to "do something" for the subject. What many professionals fail to appreciate is that a good retoucher is fully as much an artist as the person behind the camera. Whether the retoucher uses one of the modern

Figure 219

retouching machines or works solely by hand is immaterial. No machine can tell the retoucher where or how much lead to put on a negative or what areas require the use of the etching knife. Retouching machines do enable the retoucher to work faster, more smoothly and more accurately and, because they lessen the retoucher's physical strain, they reduce the tension under which the retoucher works and thus make possible better quality.

But no machine can think for the retoucher, who must have at least enough anatomical knowledge to understand the muscular structure of the face, neck, shoulders and hands. Given that knowledge as a basis, good eyesight and a steady hand, retouching is not difficult to learn. A course in a good school—and there are several—is the surest way to become expert in the shortest time. The basic essentials can also be learned from one of several books and even from correspondence courses, but the latter—and books as well—lack the necessary practical training which only results from working with an accomplished retoucher beside you, explaining with actual negatives just what is needed and why until you yourself can achieve that faculty. Thus, if you cannot spare the time to attend a course personally, you will at best have to supplement books and correspondence courses with a week or so under the personal tuition of a practicing retoucher.

To show you what ordinary portrait retouching consists of we have selected from our files two portraits which are so nearly identical, except for a slight change of expression on the one, that they will do quite well for our purposes. These happen to be a bit more on the order of a glamour lighting, with the result that the lines below the eyes are overly accented. This is all the better because it helps to show what competent retouching can accomplish. *Figure 219* is of course a print from an unretouched negative. Pose and lighting are all satisfactory from our standpoint as photographers but as professionals we would not dream of delivering this fin-

Figure 220

ished print. In fact no really smart professional would even show this as a proof because of the disappointment it would engender in the mind of the subject and the vast amount of explanation it would require to convince the subject that the heavy shadows and lines could and would be corrected. We grant you that many successful professionals do show proofs like this, even of the red, untoned type, and succeed in making a living. But every sale from such a proof requires untold explanation, if not argument, so why, when proof retouching (the correction and elimination of the most obvious defeats) is something you should be able to do yourself and quite quickly, have to be on the defense every time you show a set of proofs? It just doesn't make sense.

Now compare *Figure 219* with *Figure 220,* the result of a competent job of retouching. The heavy lines—almost bags—below the eyes have been changed to soft shadows; the lines—almost furrows—from nose to mouth have been softened so that while they necessarily remain as part of the muscular structure they are no longer objectionable; the dent below the lip resulting in a heavy shadow accompanied by a white highlight has been corrected with a combination of pencil and etching knife; the harsh lights and shadows around the base of the neck and collar bones have been smoothed away; a bit of over lighting on the forehead has been corrected and a touch of highlight added where it was needed. Even the edges of the triangular highlight on the cheekbone have been harmoniously blended into the shadow on the check. None of this was the fault of the cameraman who was lighting and posing his subject for a specific effect—and succeeded. These were actual parts of the image that the lens saw and registered on the emulsion and the only thing the cameraman could have done to eliminate them, and then only partially, would have been to use a soft focus lens whereupon the desired sharpness of the entire portrait would have been destroyed. Perhaps all this sounds like a lot of work, and in a way it is, but what has been accomplished here is in no sense an abnormal amount of retouching for any one negative, and everything we have enumerated was necessary if the finished portrait was to satisfy the subject. Hence the need of, the necessity for, and the importance of retouching.

So far we have limited ourselves to every day portrait retouching, but you will be confronted now and again with the occasional subject who requires a great deal more in the way of facial correction. The term for this type of work is "corrective" retouching and we discuss it here only so that you may appreciate its possibilities. Few photographers and, for that matter, very few retouchers are capable of doing this type of work. It is taught in a very few schools and here and there, around the country, are trade retouchers who, sufficiently qualified in this specialty, advertise their availability. When it is required it is badly needed indeed and it will help you materially in building a reputation for yourself if you make it a point to find out where such service can be secured when necessary.

The corrective retoucher employs the pencil and the knife, while a thorough working knowledge of the use of the airbrush as well as retouching dyes can be a big help, but beyond all these he or she must fully understand the anatomy of the face, head and shoulders because the competent corrective retoucher must be the equivalent, photographically, of the plastic surgeon. Wens, goiters and other excrescences can be removed by corrective retouching, while missing parts of features and even eyes can be added with complete fidelity to reality. What such a worker can accomplish will often seem almost unbelievable to your grateful subjects and you can accordingly well appreciate why you should at least know what it can mean.

Figure **221**

For our next two illustrations we are greatly indebted to the kindly lady who has permitted us to make use of them in this book. She has children who wanted her picture, not as a young woman, but as she is today. She was at one time involved in an accident that required surgery which left her with scars that do not alter her kindness and graciousness, but are definitely and—distressingly to her—noticeable in her portraits. Some will say, upon looking at *Figure 221*, that a soft focus lens was called for but that had been tried before and neither she nor her family approved of the results. Quite aside from that, we do not believe in resorting to the subterfuge of a diffused image when the difficulty can be corrected by other means. Being ourselves specialists in corrective retouching, we know what is and is not possible and, had we not been able to do this work ourselves, we also know of others who can.

When this lady entered the camera room she explained that, due to the surgery, she could not smile naturally because the muscles would pull her mouth to one side. We therefore decided on a standard head and shoulder pose, with a very conservative lighting, working only for a pleasant, sweet expression and making no effort whatever to subdue any of the irregularities from which she suffered. Thus, in *Figure 221*, you will note the very obvious scar on her left cheek. When she is talking this is not nearly as noticeable as she imagines but, to please her, we softened it to where in *Figure 222* it is not much more than a large dimple. Now, in *Figure 221*, look at the line from nose to mouth on the same side as the scar. This we accented slightly and, in so doing lessened, apparently, the width of the cheek and created a more rounded effect, all as shown in *Figure 222*. Next compare the mouth in both illustrations. By carefully retaining the essential lines and softening or eliminating

Figure 222

the others we have removed the strained appearance of the lips and, if anything, accentuated the pleasant expression.

Her next concern was the lines in and the heaviness of the neck. This is not too uncommon a condition with persons of middle age and, while in her case a little more obvious in a photograph, should not present too great a problem to a competent retoucher. The thing to watch, however, is the use of judgment in how much to eliminate. We were careful not to smooth the lines or the fullness completely away because, had we done so, the effect would not have been in keeping with the lines and texture of the face, necessarily those of an older person. Many a retoucher, too anxious to please, will carry such work too far. For a very minor point, in *Figure 221* there are some strands of hair below the right earring which certainly do not help the portrait. It was a simple matter to remove those, and little bits of attention like that can make a great deal of difference between a really good portrait and one that "just gets by."

From a purely corrective standpoint this is far from a complicated piece of retouching but at the same time it is more than can be expected from any ordinarily competent retoucher. You may seldom if ever be confronted with a subject who has to wear a dark lens in one of his spectacles to conceal a defective eye and who would welcome a portrait showing him with two good eyes (although this is entirely possible) but you will certainly meet many subjects who have been disfigured as a result of automobile and similar accidents. It is therefore important for you to know that if you can produce a portrait in the camera room which would be pleasing were it not for the defects, those defects can be eliminated or corrected by retouching and you can make such a subject not only happy but a permanent and highly vocal announcer of your ability as a portraitist. Nor, of course, need the subject ever know—if you are careful not to show any preliminary proofs or discuss the aspects of what will have to be done—but what through some magical legerdemain you did accomplish the miracle solely with your camera.

CHAPTER 29

Standardize Your Methods

One hears a lot about standardization of operations and methods nowadays and it can be properly applied to the production of good portraits to a larger extent than might at first thought be realized. While standardization, as we shall explain, properly commences in your camera room and should then be carried on clear through to the finished prints, obviously we do not have in mind anything of the sort with reference to the subjects in front of your camera. In the early days of the department store chain studios, when their rapid success was built on the two factors of novelty and low price, even the sittings were standardized. The veriest beginners were trained to become "cameramen" in a matter of a few days, chiefly because every camera room in a chain was identically equipped, camera and lights were in fixed positions (and literally so because often they were fastened to the floor and could not be moved), subjects were seated and told to face first this way and then that, whereupon the sitting was over. For some years the system worked until the novelty wore off and, competition growing apace, even the chains had to produce more presentable portraits.

What you must keep in mind is that you will be judged by the finished product, the final print and that, therefore, if your prints are to be consistent in quality, you must first—in your camera room—produce negatives of consistent quality. It is consequently important that you standardize your lightings, not with respect to your lighting placements or setups—which should vary with every individual subject—but with respect to the density ratio of the highlight and shadow areas in your negatives. To some extent this will come as the result of experience and the extent to which the prints you will make satisfy you and—more importantly—your subjects or customers. All of this is necessarily a matter of proper exposure combined with a correct placement of your lights, but placement of the lights is the primary element. Correct exposure is something you can always check, until it virtually becomes second nature, by the use of a light meter; correct placement of the lights is a matter of experiment until you learn what produces the best results under your own lighting conditions and limitations.

To put it briefly, if your prints appear to be flat and lifeless you are probably making negatives in which the ratio between the highlights and shadow areas is too small. On the other hand if your prints lack sufficient detail in the shadow areas and the highlights are contrasty and hard, your ratio is too great. The answer lies in the placement of your main source and fill-in lights, not with relation to the subject before the camera because first of all they must be so placed that the face and figure are properly illuminated, but with respect to their respective distances from the subject in relation to each other. You may, for example, have secured what appears on the groundglass to be a completely satisfactory portrait, so far as likeness and character rendition are concerned, and yet the whole lacks conviction or "punch." Or, conversely, what your groundglass discloses may be too much on the order of "soot and whitewash." What has gone wrong is simply that the ratio between your main source and fill-in is incorrect. Speaking in averages, and *only* in averages, a ratio of one to two and a half is about right, which would be to say that if your main source is two feet from the subject, the fill-in should be five feet away.

If you really intend to produce quality portraits you will spend considerable time in lighting experiments until you arrive at the ratio which, in your camera room and with your customary equipment, will consistently produce balanced negatives which, correctly printed on the right kind and grade of paper, will render a good amount of shadow detail with proper modeling in the highlight areas. By the right kind of paper we refer only to the purpose the manufacturer, whomever he may be, has in mind—a paper with an emulsion intended for portrait use, whether contact or projection. While the inefficient or careless worker may on occasion try to salvage a poor negative by printing it on a commercial or other grade of paper, and may be successful, how much easier it is to make the negative right in the first place by standardizing in your camera room on a correct lighting ratio.

Before we leave the camera room we advise that, having found the particular make and type of film that is most satisfactory for your purposes, you stick to it exclusively. You may well select two types of film, a panchromatic emulsion for the greater part of your work and an orthochromatic for certain subjects whose coloring is more satisfactorily reproduced by an emulsion less sensitive to red than the panchromatic. Whether both are of the same make or not is immaterial; the thing is to select those which produce the best results for you and stick with them. We do not imply that you should close your eyes completely to new and better emulsions that come on the market from time to time. By all means keep up to date and try out what is new and seems to be worth while, but keep anything of the sort on an experimental basis and handle it separately from your standardized procedure. Not until something new definitely proves to you that it is better than what you are already using should you attempt a substitution but then, when you know you are right, make the substitution complete, discarding the old entirely and proceeding to standardize again on the new.

We now move on to the darkroom where negligence can of course completely nullify all the pains you have taken in properly lighting and exposing your negatives. Here standardization is of the utmost importance if you want to produce negatives that are uniform and of good quality without wasted effort and energy. You have a great advantage over those photographers who entered the profession in the days when all developing was done by inspection—constantly removing negatives from the tray or tank and holding them up to the safelight to judge their progress. Today, following the modern principles of "time and temperature," you develop at one time as many negatives as your tank will accommodate. You fill the tank with a given developer, which you maintain at a specific temperature and, except for proper agitation of the negatives, they remain in the tank for a given number of minutes at the end of which time they are removed and almost without looking at them you know they are going to be right.

We do advise, and emphatically, that to secure the best possible results you use the developer recommended by the manufacturer of the film or films you are using. His reason for recommending it is entirely selfish because, having tested all kinds of developers in his research laboratories and in a manner more accurate than anything you could approach or possibly even imagine, the developer he finally recommends is the one he knows will get the best results from his emulsion. Because results are the only factor that will hold you as a permanent customer for his film, he has a definite interest in making sure you get them. Hence his recommendations and the reason why you should follow them implicitly. Once you have processed a few negatives and have satisfied yourself as to the precise density you want for your own printing purposes you need only standardize from then on with respect to time and temperature, following of course the manufacturer's instructions as to replenishment of the developer when necessary, and your results will be consistently satisfactory. Nearly everything to be found in print on the general subject of negative problems would not have had to be written in the first place if photographers would only be satisfied to follow instructions.

There is one factor in connection with negative development which you must watch because carelessness in this one respect can wreck all the gains you have made through standardization. This is the matter of proper agitation during development. Again it is only a matter of following instructions but to many it seems like such a minor detail that it is ignored. In order to assure uniform action of the developer on all parts of the emulsion, and to avoid stains and streaks caused by concentration of the developer around those portions of the negative which are in contact with the developing hanger, the films must be agitated at specific intervals, and this does not mean merely jiggling the hangers up and down.

Assuming that you will not, at first, invest in the modern nitrogen burst equipment which really does enable you to leave your films in the tank and forget them until the proper time has elapsed, here is the method we advise. At the end of the first minute lift each film hanger (or the entire rack if you are processing several in a rack) from the tank, tilt it and let it drain back into the tank from one corner. A minute later repeat the performance, but drain from the other corner. Alternate thereafter. This operation does not imply that you hold the hanger or rack out of the developer for long because a second or two will suffice. Draining to the corner in this manner breaks up any airbells that may have clung to the surface of the film along the edges of the hanger, in addition to keeping the developer generally in motion. Incidentally it will be wise to set up, adjacent to your developing area, a viewing light by which you can inspect your negatives after they have been fixed. In order to maintain a constant check of uniformity many experienced darkroom workers affix to this light a sample negative which has been brought to the density they prefer, using this as a guide or standard.

The final process, that of printing from the negative, is in some respects the most important of all because, regardless of everything that has gone before, it is the print itself by which your ability as a craftsman will stand or fall. Again, if you have standardized all of your operations up to this point, and then standardize on what follows, you should have little difficulty. To recapitulate, we have progressed from the making of a balanced lighting, correctly exposed on a negative material processed according to instructions in a recommended developer, and we have produced a negative which, except for retouching, is ready for printing. That negative may vary toward the thin side, or toward the dense, depending entirely upon your own preference. The only matter of importance is that all your negatives should be alike in quality because then the question of thinness or density requires only a minor adjustment in the printing exposure. If all are alike your exposure times will be the same, with very minor variations, and again you can standardize, save time and avoid wasted materials. Troubles in printing result more from unbalanced lighting than from negative density. If you make an out of balance lighting you will end with a less than fine print regardless of what the density may be, and no matter how you dodge, burn in, or attempt other types of hocus pocus you will not have as acceptable a portrait as if you had used a little more care in planning your lighting and exposing correctly. While you can correct in printing for a greater than average variation in thinness or density, you will find the process time consuming and wasteful.

Again assuming that you are producing good, printable negatives, the question of standardization in printing is perhaps the simplest of all. You are, almost certainly, going to print by projection because few professionals nowadays work by contact, for an assortment of reasons. You have, from which to choose, a wide variety of excellent projection papers made by several manufacturers. They vary as to relative brilliance even though most are of normal contrast. Select a negative which is typical of what is to be your standard quality and make your own tests, on various papers, until you find the one which, with normal handling, produces the brilliance you desire. Remember that paper surface has considerable bearing on the brilliance of a finished print. Surfaces with lustre will naturally produce a more snappy effect than those of the matte type. Having selected the paper you like the best, by all means use the manufacturer's recommended developer—for the same reason we explained when discussing negatives—and follow his instructions.

Because what we have been trying to sell you throughout this book is the idea of producing the best possible negatives through proper lighting in the camera room—and if we have been successful you will not be faced with the problem of out of balance negatives which require special treatment in the darkroom—we shall not discuss here the innumerable tricks of the trade which can be attempted in an effort to salvage negatives which are unsatisfactory even to the point of being almost unprintable. Such processes are so many and varied that entire books have been written on the subject, and we do not have the space. Nor does the truly competent craftsman, such as we hope you will become, have to resort to them.

One point now remains, while we are on this subject of standardization, which cannot be overlooked, and that is the urgency of proper fixing and washing. You cannot produce permanent prints if your fixing and washing are conducted on a hit or miss basis and few occasions are as embarrassing to a professional photographer as to have brought back to him, or to see in the home of a subject or customer, a faded or stained print bearing his signature. This is something that should never occur and yet, hate to admit it though we do, it happens all the time and in many cases the offending prints bear the names of some of the most famed studios in the country. We say it should never occur because its sole reason is laxity on the part of the photographer, laxity which consists of carelessness in fixing and too much haste in washing.

This directly affects the chief responsibility of the portrait photographer who has, whether he likes to realize it or not, a direct moral obligation to his subjects: that of preserving their likenesses for posterity. When he produces prints that stain or fade, and whether they do so in five years, twenty five or fifty is beside the point, he is evading that obligation which is, basically, his only legitimate reason for entering the profession.

Let us begin by saying that we firmly believe in printing for a full tonal range, not caring greatly for high exposure speed in either contact or projection printing. We might liken a magnified cross section of a print to a piece of meringue topped pie. If you do not dip far enough to get through the meringue, you never get to the genuine flavor of the pie. In other words, if you only make a "surface" print you never get through to all the good silver which is in the emulsion on the paper. Neither does your developer with the result that you leave a considerable amount of silver which, not having been affected by light or developer due to too fast an exposure, will not be affected by the fixing bath either. It therefore remains in the emulsion, eventually to change color and spoil the appearance of the print. Assuming then that we have made a fully exposed print and developed it for at least the maximum recommended time in the proper developer at the right temperature, let us explain just how we handle such a print from the time it leaves the developer to the time it is ready for drying.

Many experienced professionals will grouse at what follows, as involving a quite unnecessary amount of time and trouble. Our only rejoinder—and we think it sufficient—is to suggest (if they have been in business long enough) that they examine some of the prints they produced thirty, forty and fifty years ago and see if they look as fresh and clear as if they had been turned out the day before. We have yet to see a print of ours, no matter how old, for which we have had to apologize. Nor are we being unreasonable in mentioning such long periods of time. More than half a century ago, when photographic periodicals had comparatively small circulations and the halftone process of reproduction had not been invented, it was common practice to bind or tip in actual photographs as illustrations. We do not say that all of those are still perfect but the majority are, and a comparison of those prints with many that have been produced even in the past ten years is truly shameful. If you intend to say—or advertise—truthfully that your photographs are "permanent" what follows is something for you to think about—and standardize on.

First we take that completely developed print and, after draining-off the developer from one corner, place it *face up* in a short stop bath consisting of one and a half ounces of twenty eight percent acetic acid to the quart of water (six ounces to the gallon), leaving it there for fifteen seconds, with agitation. We then drain it and place it in *hypo bath number one* for five minutes. Note—and this is important—that we place the print in the hypo bath face up, as we did in the short stop. There is a reason for both. Both the short stop and the hypo are heavier than water and we want both to soak into the print, the short stop to stop the action of any remaining developer as rapidly as possible, and the hypo so it will penetrate the entire print.

Also we do not let that print lie idly or become stacked up with others in the bath because if prints are to be properly fixed they must become thoroughly saturated with the hypo, which means handling or agitation to keep both surfaces in contact with the solution. If later you have trouble with streaks and stains in prints which you are trying to tone, think back and you will almost certainly remember that, being in a hurry, you allowed them to stack up in the hypo with the result that they were only partially fixed.

After five minutes in fixing bath number one we transfer the print to *fixing bath number two,* where it remains for five minutes with equal agitation. Follow this identical procedure and you may rest assured that your prints are properly fixed, remembering of course that we are speaking of conventional fixing baths, whether of the packaged type or that you mix yourself, and not of the special speed fixers so frequently advertised. These have their purposes for the newspaper and other fields where the securing of a satisfactory image without delay is essential, but their use should not be considered by the portraitist who wants to produce permanent prints.

And then, equally important, the washing to remove the hypo. We drain each print as it is removed from the number two fixing bath and place it, *face down,* in a stainless steel bath which, in our case, is filled and drained by a tray siphon; face down so that the hypo, heavier than water, will settle out. This is only a temporary arrangement until enough prints, twenty five which is all any tray siphon can satisfactorily handle, have accumulated to be transferred to the final washing. For this we use a large tray in the washing sink, with a gentle stream of water running through the tray, and again the prints go in face down. Instead of the siphon, the prints would be quite safe merely soaking in a large tray of water until the final washing. When the day's batch of printing is finished, the entire lot are run through two complete changes of water.

There have been on the market for some time special chemical preparations for the elimination of hypo and we strongly urge their use. The one we favor is called Hypo Clearing Agent and is bought as a dry chemical, from which we prepare our bath for print treatment. After we have run the prints through the two complete changes of water, which removes much of the surface hypo, we then treat them (incidentally we are speaking of double weight prints which you would naturally be using for your finished work) for three to four minutes in the hypo clearing bath, keeping them well separated or agitated. This treatment materially reduces the time required for washing and permits the use of much colder wash water, but still with the assurance of effective washing. If a conventional hypo elimination test (and we advise this no matter what procedure you decide to follow in washing your prints) then indicates that the prints are clear of hypo, they are ready for drying. If not, return them to the trays for more washing, until the test is positive. Granted, all this takes a bit more time, but the satisfaction of knowing that your prints are truly permanent is well worth it.

CHAPTER 30

A Sensible Approach to Pricing

It would seem to be a reasonable assumption that a majority of those who buy and read this book fall into one of two classifications. Either you the reader, for example, are a practicing professional portrait photographer but are not entirely satisfied with the quality of your craftsmanship, or you are one of that large fraternity who, because of your personal liking for and enjoyment of photography, want to produce portraits sufficiently good that others will want to have or even buy them. In either event the question of what you should charge for your work, and how you should arrive at your prices, is a matter of serious importance. It is, incidentally, as important to your competitors as it is to yourself if you propose to conduct or establish a permanent business or studio and want to be respected as a reputable ethical member of the photographic fraternity, not only by the public but by other professionals in your locality.

If you are starting "cold" and perhaps without a formal studio but as a home portrait photographer working from your own home, with a minimum of equipment and very possibly a somewhat makeshift darkroom and finishing area, do not make the initial mistake that ruins so many a beginner. Do not, to put it bluntly, adopt the defeatist attitude that because you are a comparative unknown you must price your work at a minimum. While it is true that there are always people whose object in life seems to be to buy whatever they need at the lowest possible price, regardless of quality, it is also true that those same people will desert you the moment someone comes along whose price is lower, and there is never a limit to the cutting of prices. If yours is a large metropolitan community, you may indeed be able to operate almost indefinitely in that very low priced fringe occupied by those photographers unable or unwilling to produce quality or even average portraiture. In such areas there is always a slice of the public which will at least buy once because of low price, if only because to them any recognizable map of the features is a portrait. But why condemn yourself to the meager subsistence with which you must satisfy yourself, and your family or others dependent upon you, because your low prices leave you no reasonable margin of profit, or—a condition which usually accompanies such a situation—find yourself constantly harassed by creditors?

Neither we nor anyone else can offer you a standardized set of prices nor can we tell or even suggest to you what you should charge. That must be based on several factors which must necessarily depend on your method of operation. These are: a) your cost of doing business, or "overhead;" b) your "material" cost—what you have to spend for supplies of whatever nature: c) an appropriate "salary" for yourself, and, d) a reasonable "profit." Finally, to a certain extent, your prices must take into consideration the general competitive situation because, no matter how good your portraits may be, and unless they are so tremendously outstanding that there is no comparison with the work of others, if your prices are too far out of line with those in general effect in your locality, your work will not sell. We can only analyze these factors briefly for your guidance here because this is not a book on cost accounting and our purpose in this closing chapter is solely to start you off on the right track.

Do not ever fool yourself—and we have known many seemingly intelligent photographers who have made this same error—that you have no "overhead" and for that reason can charge much less than others for apparently the same type of work. If you have, or plan to open, a formal studio you will face and will quickly recognize many of your overhead costs immediately because they will not be disguised and must be paid. But if, like so many, you start to operate from your home, you will only be cheating yourself and will virtually be giving money out of your pocket to your customer every time you deliver a finished order if you fail to take into account and charge as part of your costs a reasonable and sensible percentage of the following: rent, heat and light, telephone, taxes, insurance—to mention the most important; automobile upkeep and depreciation; time (at a reasonable valuation) spent by any members of your family on whom you call at times for odd emergency jobs and, in addition, depreciation on your photographic equipment because if you do not charge depreciation you will have no funds available to replace that equipment when it wears out. All of which will show you how ridiculous it is to say that you have no overhead because you work from your home, be it a house which you own or rent or an apartment.

Your material cost is comparatively easy: figure whatever you spend for films, papers, chemicals, mountings and albums, and the like—not forgetting the quarter here or half dollar there for adhesives, staples and similar small items which are always cropping up and can run into quite a few dollars in the course of a month. You will need stationery and envelopes, billheads, perhaps labels, not to mention wrapping paper, string and postage, most of such items being usually paid for by the beginner in cash with no proper record, and often an important reason why when all bills are paid, every thirty days a financial crisis arrives. All these represent money out of your pocket and unless they are properly estimated and figured as part of your prices they are in fact money that you are donating to your customers. Some of this may sound childish to any established photographer but it is lack of regard for expenses like these that causes many a beginner to quote prices that make no sense to the worker of experience.

Next: unless you charge your portrait business with an adequate salary for yourself you will be making another all too common error, and this is equally true if your photography is a part time activity, in what you fondly think of as your "spare time." If you are an even reasonably competent workman you could be drawing a salary as a photographic employee, or perhaps in some other capacity and, having put in your forty hours or whatever it may be per week, your time would be your own. No one in business for himself can escape a certain amount of mental worry and frustration and the whole point of operating your own business is that you expect to make a better living than you would as an employee, in addition to being own boss. But don't be over ambitious in setting up that salary figure; it should represent what you honestly feel you would be worth to an employer, no more and no less.

We have already emphasized that we are not attempting an all inclusive coverage of this subject but are only trying to give you a general idea of what, in the way of cost and general expense, you should bear in mind when you begin to work out a price list for your portraiture. You still must discover, in one way or another, the prices charged by those studios and individuals with whom you will be in direct competition, and take care that your own are not so high that you are likely to "price yourself out" of the possible field. Nor, if your work is in general equal to what your competitors produce, should your prices be too low or the public will regard you as a "cheap" workman in whose ability not too much confidence can be placed. To some extent, when you first establish yourself, your price list will have to be flexible inasmuch as a permanent price list can only be established once you have made enough sittings to enable you to arrive at a defiinite understanding of your expenses, such as time involved per sitting, material cost per sitting and the like. We do not use the word flexible as implying that you will charge one customer one price and another something different, "all the traffic will bear" as this method is called. That is not only unethical if not even dishonest, but sooner or later customers will compare prices, the word will spread and you will be out of business. The point is that, until you have gained the necessary cost experience, you may have to adjust your prices up or down, in other words make up a new price list. It is always easy to reduce prices but it is extremely difficult to increase them, which is another reason for not setting them too low in the first place. You may also find, if you set up different prices for varying types or styles of finishes, that some must be increased and others reduced until you can finally settle on what may be considered as your permanent price list.

No matter what may be the general income bracket of that section of the public which you plan to consider as your particular objective, you will still find it necessary to offer several styles of work in different price ranges. Whether you deal with the wealthy, the middle class or those who have little spare cash to spend, it will be easier to make sales if you offer a choice of styles and finishes. How you wish to do this is a matter for your own judgment but we have a few suggestions which may be helpful. We see little value in the adoption of high sounding names to describe different portrait surfaces. Few people today are ignorant of photographic processes. Many understand as well as you what goes on in your camera and darkroom and what is involved in the production of the several sheets of paper, each bearing a photographic image, which are what they will eventually receive for the money they pay you. Many of them know that there is no difference in cost to you between one surface of paper and another and that all are interchangeably processed. Your price list will find more believability if it mentions black and white prints instead of such terms as "Silvertones" and the like. People today are fully aware that the direct and primary result of a negative is a black and white print and they will respect you more if you do not insult their intelligence by attempting to gloss over the fact. Similarly they know that it does cost more money and requires additional processing to change that print to another color and they will therefore accept, with little argument or explanation, a higher price for a sepia or a "browntone" or a "goldtone" which latter is an entirely legitimate term if you are actually toning in a gold solution. Such higher prices, if reasonable, can readily be justified if the question is raised.

So much for the matter of surface or finish, and now to arrive at some sensible basis for pricing different styles of work in a manner which can be easily justified to the customer. Anyone in business knows that if he is to satisfy the largest possible range of customers he should offer three styles of work: good, better and best. You still face the fact that what you are going to deliver will be an image on a sheet of paper, and that even the lowest priced print must still be sufficiently good to stand up against your competition. Is it possible, then, to work out a set of three styles or qualities which, when shown as actual samples, will indicate clearly that there is a difference which warrants varying prices and still have the lowest price style sufficiently good that it will not only be satisfactory but desirable to those who for one reason or another can or will pay no more? And, in addition, is it possible to explain this to the customer in an understandable manner? Let us explain how this is done in actual practice in a reputable studio dealing with such a public as might be expected in any average community.

We are not going to mention prices at all, because it is the method of arriving at them and justifying them that you should understand and, that accomplished, the method will apply regardless of your price in actual dollars, or cost of doing business. To avoid confusion we base what follows on a 5 x 7 black and white delivered portrait, which we propose to offer in three price groups. The principle applies to any size of print, and we are speaking of each type or style as a "group" although you may well prefer to select some suitable name or designation for each group.

The 5 x 7 which is delivered in *Group One* is a projection from a split 5 x 7 film. It is a plain lighting and simple head and shoulder pose, but other than that is in every respect a well finished portrait and one which the studio need have no hesitation in displaying or having compared with the work of competitors. No three quarter poses or full lengths are included in this group except in the case of children. The print is delivered in a plain, although good, folder or easel. This is the lowest price group and it makes sense to the customer when it is explained that the low cost is possible because a smaller negative is used and the time required in the camera room is less.

In *Group Two* each 5 x 7 delivered is made from a full 5 x 7 film and may be either projection or contact, in fact it is well to show at least some proofs projected to 8 x 10. The posing and lighting are still rather simple, careful and involving a bit more time but still not elaborate as to the use of spotlights and the like. In this group the customer may have whatever is wanted, full figures, three quarter poses, even groups, in addition to head and shoulders. The prints are well finished and well mounted, but are offered only in black and white. Prints in this group are priced twenty five percent higher than those in Group One and the increase is justified because not only is the negative larger but the larger film size and resulting larger head size (or more heads in the case of a group) mean considerably more expense for retouching, all of which is quite understandable to the customer.

The 5 x 7 portrait delivered in *Group Three* is of course made from a full 5 x 7 film. The studio expends every effort to produce outstanding portraits in this group, going to whatever length is necessary in the use of spotlights, special poses, drapes, glamour effects, posing for large heads if preferred and devoting whatever time may be required in the camera room. A minimum of six proofs is shown in this group as compared to the usual four in the other two and delivery is in the finest quality mount or folder. In black and white the price of prints in this group is twenty five percent more than in Group Two and if gold toning (and it really is gold toning) is desired the price is forty percent more than Group Two. Any customer will realize that more is being given for the price and that extra processing time is required throughout.

The success of such a pricing method depends initially on your making a suitable, though not necessarily large, profit on Group One. That assured, your profit will automatically increase as your sales progress through Groups Two and Three although you will find that, on the average, most of your sales will fall in Group Two. In any event you will have a price bracket and style to appeal to every customer while, in even the lowest price bracket, you will be giving good value for the money. That last, whatever your price range or the income bracket of your customers, is the secret of success in portrait photography, and with that statement we bring this book to a close. We hope you have found it worth while.